Revolution, Revolt, and Reform in North Africa

Providing an account of the recent revolutions or reform movements that constituted part of the Arab Spring, this book focuses on these transformative processes in a North African context.

Whilst the longer term outcomes of the Arab Spring revolts are not entirely clear, the revolutionary or reform processes in North Africa are further along than the events taking place in Levant or the Arabian Peninsula, elections having now been held in the post-revolutionary/post-revolt states. Understanding and examining North African events has become critical as the countries in question are part of *Mare Nostrum*; events in North Africa inevitably have effects in Europe. Using examples from Tunisia, Egypt, Libya, Morocco, and Algeria, *Revolution, Revolt, and Reform in North Africa* provides an insider scholar's account of these recent revolutions or reform movements.

One of the first attempts at undertaking an analysis of possible transitions to democracy in the region, this book is a valuable resource for students and researchers with an interest in the Middle East, Political Science or contemporary affairs in general.

Ricardo René Larémont is Professor of Political Science and Sociology at SUNY, Binghamton. His recent publications include: *Islamic Law and Politics in Northern Nigeria*; *Islam and the Politics of Resistance in Algeria, 1783–1992*; *The Causes of War and the Consequences of Peacekeeping in Africa*; and *Borders, Nationalism, and the African State*.

Routledge Studies in Middle Eastern Democratization and Government
Edited by: Larbi Sadiki, *University of Exeter*

This series examines new ways of understanding democratization and government in the Middle East. The varied and uneven processes of change, occurring in the Middle Eastern region, can no longer be read and interpreted solely through the prism of Euro-American transitology. Seeking to frame critical parameters in light of these new horizons, this series instigates reinterpretations of democracy and propagates formerly 'subaltern,' narratives of democratization. Reinvigorating discussion on how Arab and Middle Eastern peoples and societies seek good government, *Routledge Studies in Middle Eastern Democratization and Government* provides tests and contests of old and new assumptions.

1. **Revolution, Revolt, and Reform in North Africa**
   The Arab Spring and Beyond
   Edited by Ricardo René Larémont

Revolution, Revolt, and Reform in North Africa

The Arab Spring and Beyond

Edited by
Ricardo René Larémont

LONDON AND NEW YORK

First published 2014
by Routledge
4 Park Square, Milton Park, Abingdon, Oxon OX14 4RN

Simultaneously published in the USA and Canada
by Routledge
605 Third Avenue, New York, NY 10017

Routledge is an imprint of the Taylor & Francis Group, an informa business

© 2014 Ricardo Larémont

The right of the editor to be identified as the author of the editorial material, and of the authors for their individual chapters, has been asserted in accordance with sections 77 and 78 of the Copyright, Designs and Patents Act 1988.

All rights reserved. No part of this book may be reprinted or reproduced or utilised in any form or by any electronic, mechanical, or other means, now known or hereafter invented, including photocopying and recording, or in any information storage or retrieval system, without permission in writing from the publishers.

Trademark notice: Product or corporate names may be trademarks or registered trademarks, and are used only for identification and explanation without intent to infringe.

British Library Cataloguing in Publication Data
A catalogue record for this book is available from the British Library

Library of Congress Cataloging in Publication Data
Revolution, revolt and reform in North Africa : the Arab Spring and beyond / edited by Ricardo René Larémont.
pages cm
Includes bibliographical references and index.
1. Revolutions–Arab countries–History–21st century. 2. Revolutions–Africa, North–History–21st century. 3. Arab countries–History–21st century.
4. Africa, North–History–21st century. 5. Arab Spring, 2010- I. Laremont, Ricardo René
DS39.R49 2013
320.961–dc23
2013006154

ISBN: 978-0-415-83946-4 (hbk)
ISBN: 978-0-415-83947-1 (pbk)
ISBN: 978-0-203-79739-6 (ebk)

Typeset in Times New Roman
by Taylor and Francis Books

To
Mohamed Bouazizi
In Memoriam

Contents

List of figures and tables	viii
List of contributors	ix
Acknowledgements	xi

1 Revolution, revolt, and reform in North Africa 1
 RICARDO RENÉ LARÉMONT

2 Demographics, economics, and technology: background to the North African revolutions 15
 RICARDO RENÉ LARÉMONT

3 The Tunisian revolution: the revolution of dignity 30
 AMIRA ALEYA-SGHAIER

4 The Egyptian revolution: the power of mass mobilization and the spirit of Tahrir Square 53
 EMAD EL-DIN SHAHIN

5 The February 17 *intifada* in Libya: disposing of the regime and issues of state-building 75
 YOUSSEF M. SAWANI

6 Morocco: a reformist monarchy? 105
 MOHAMMED DARIF

7 Algeria: untenable exceptionalism during the spring of upheavals 125
 AZZEDINE LAYACHI

8 Moving past revolution and revolt: transitions to democracy in North Africa 148
 RICARDO RENÉ LARÉMONT

Index 172

Figures and tables

Figures

1.1	Relative deprivation and the impetus to violence	13
2.1	Total fertility among North African women	17
2.2	Median age	19
2.3	Tunisia population pyramid	20
2.4	Egypt population pyramid	20
2.5	Libya population pyramid	21
2.6	Algeria population pyramid	22
2.7	Morocco population pyramid	23
2.8	Mobile cellular subscriptions (per 100) in North Africa	26
2.9	Internet and Facebook participation rates: North Africa (2011)	27

Tables

2.1	Total population and youth population in North Africa (2010)	17
2.2	Total fertility (children born per woman) in North Africa	17
2.3	Median age	19
2.4	GDP growth rate: North Africa (2000–2010)	24
2.5	Youth unemployment (ages 15–29) in North Africa (2008)	25
2.6	Internet and Facebook participation rates for North Africa	27
3.1	Individuals killed from Tunis and the suburbs	41
7.1	Select results of Algerian parliamentary elections from 1997 to 2012	142

Contributors

Amira Aleya-Sghaier is a research professor at the University of Tunis, specializing in the history of national movements in North Africa. He is the author of seven books, most recently *Bourguiba* (Éditions MIPE, 2011) and editor-in-chief of the academic journal *Rawafed*.

Mohammed Darif is a professor in the Faculty of Law at Hassan II University, Mohammedia, Morocco. His most recent book is *Monarchie Marocaine et Acteurs Religieux* [The Moroccan Monarchy and Religious Actors] (Afrique Orient, 2010).

Ricardo René Larémont is professor of political science and sociology at SUNY Binghamton and a Carnegie Corporation scholar on Islam. His principal books include: *Revolution, Revolt, and Reform in North Africa*; *Islam and the Politics of Resistance in Algeria, 1783–1992*; *Islamic Law and Politics in Northern Nigeria*; *Borders, Nationalism, and the African State*; and *The Causes of War and the Consequences of Peacekeeping in Africa*. His research focuses upon political Islam, Islamic law, conflict resolution, democratization, and civil/military relations, usually in the region of North Africa and the Sahel.

Azzedine Layachi is professor of political science at Saint John's University, New York and Rome. He specializes in North African politics. Among his publications on the region are the books *Economic Crisis and Political Change in North Africa*, and *The United States and North Africa: A Cognitive Approach to Foreign Policy*.

Youssef M. Sawani is the acting director general for the Centre of Arab Unity Studies in Beirut and professor of political science at the University of Tripoli, Libya. He is also editor-in-chief of *Al Mostaqbal Al Arabi* in Beirut and a member of the editorial board of *Contemporary Arab Affairs*. He is the author of numerous books and articles in English and Arabic, including: 'The "End of Pan-Arabism" Revisited: Reflections on the Arab Spring', *Contemporary Arab Affairs* 5(3), 2012; *Revolution and Democratic Transition in the Arab World: A Road Map,* co-edited with Abd Al Illah Belqaziz (Centre for Arab Unity Studies, 2012, Arabic text);

The Arab Spring: Revolt, Reform and Revolution, co-edited with Ricardo Larémont (Al Maaraef Forum, 2013), *Contemporary Libya: Issues & Challenges* (Tripoli: World Center, 2007, Arabic Text), *Democracy and Political Reform in the Arab World*, co-edited with Kamal Manoufi, Cairo University (Tripoli: World Center, 2006, Arabic Text), *Reflections of African Scholars on the African Union* (Tripoli: World Center, 2005); and, *Arab Political Thought on Arab Nationalism and Unity* (Beirut: Center for Arab Unity Studies, 2003, Arabic Text).

Emad El-Din Shahin is professor of public policy and administration at the American University in Cairo. Before rejoining AUC in 2012, Shahin was the Henry R. Luce associate professor of religion, conflict and peacebuilding at the University of Notre Dame's Kroc Institute for International Peace Studies (2009–2012). He was associate professor of political science at the American University in Cairo (1998–2006), visiting associate professor in the department of government at Harvard University (2006–2009), and visiting scholar in the Islamic Legal Studies Program at Harvard Law School (2006–2007). Shahin holds a Ph.D. (1989) from the Johns Hopkins School of Advanced International Studies, an M.A. (1983) and B.A. (1980) from the American University in Cairo. He is also the editor-in-chief of *The Oxford Encyclopedia of Islam and Politics* and co-editor (with John L.Esposito) of *The Oxford Handbook of Islam and Politics* (both forthcoming from Oxford University Press).

Acknowledgements

This work would not have been possible without the contributions of my worthy collaborators: Amira Aleya-Sghaier, Emad El-Din Shahin, Youssef Sawani, Mohammed Darif, and Azzedine Layachi. They are all *intellectuels engagés*. They have been friends and colleagues for some time now and *in cha Allah* they will be in the future. Besides these contributors I would like to thank Khalid Bekkaoui and Lotfi Zerkaoui who helped with several translations from Arabic into English and vice versa. Their translation expertise accelerated the publication of this work.

Several chapters in this volume were published in earlier versions in the *Journal of the Middle East and Africa*. Revised versions appear in this book. I thank the editor of that journal, J. Peter Pham, and the journal's outside readers for their useful critiques. Colleagues at my home university, the State University of New York at Binghamton, and elsewhere provided commentary on this work. I would like to thank them. They include: William G. Martin, Clement Henry, Gamal Soltan, Youssef Sawani, Khalid Bekkaoui, Toivo Asheeke, Beniam Awash, Huahsuan Chu, Sophia Givre, Seokmin Lee, Khagendra Prasai, and Sunghee Ru. Binghamton provost Donald Nieman, vice-president for research Baghat Sammakia, and especially my esteemed colleague at the Office for Naval Research, Harold Hawkins, provided the needed funds to undertake this research. The tireless staff at Binghamton's Research Foundation, especially Cathy Dixon, Paul Parker, Joseph Walker, Christopher Karl, Melissa Spencer, Amber Smith, and Dennis Saunders, provided the needed logistical support to assure that this work would appear in print. Thank you all.

Last, my life would not have any meaning without the presence of my wife Lisa Yun and our two daughters, Liana and Alina. While undertaking and completing this work I was often absent from home. Thank you for your patience and understanding. I promise not to wander as much in the future.

1 Revolution, revolt, and reform in North Africa

Ricardo René Larémont

It all started with a young fruit and vegetable street vendor in Tunisia. His name was Mohamed Bouazizi. On December 17, 2010, while he was quietly attempting to sell fruits and vegetables from his stand in the city of Sidi Bouzid to support his family, Mr. Bouazizi was confronted by a municipal inspector who challenged him on his right to sell his wares because he had not obtained a license from the local government authority to do so. Mr. Bouazizi protested. He thought he was being harassed. His goods were confiscated, and while his goods were being seized, he was allegedly slapped in the face by the city inspector, who was a woman. Having lost his means of economic livelihood and having suffered a public affront to his dignity and sense of masculinity, Mr. Bouazizi purchased a can of petrol, poured it over himself and self-immolated in front of the provincial governor's office police in protest. His self-immolation caused the city of Sidi Bouzid to rise in public demonstrations. Those demonstrations spread throughout rural Tunisia throughout the month of December and eventually reached the capital of Tunis during January 2011. On January 14, 2011, President Zine El Abidine Ben Ali, an authoritarian ruler who had reigned over Tunisia for 23 years, relinquished his rule and boarded an airplane for Saudi Arabia. The Tunisian revolt and Ben Ali's departure encouraged a chain of revolutions, revolts, and mass demonstrations that would lead to the ousting of President Hosni Mubarak in Egypt and President Ali Abdullah Saleh in Yemen, the assassination of Leader/Colonel Muammar Qaddafi in Libya, constitutional reform in Morocco and Jordan, economic reform in Saudi Arabia, the repression of demonstrations in Algeria and Bahrain, and an ongoing revolt in Syria that at the date of this writing has claimed more than 70,000 lives.

This edited volume examines revolution, revolt, and reform in North Africa during this tumultuous period. North Africa is the subject of this study because it is in North Africa where these processes of social change began and where they have evolved the most. While the longer-term outcomes of the Arab Spring revolts are not entirely clear, they are further along in North Africa than what can be observed elsewhere, for example in the Levant or the Arabian peninsula. In the post-revolution/post-revolt environments of North Africa, elections have been held in each North African state (Egypt,

Libya, Tunisia, Algeria, and Morocco). During these elections Islamist parties won pluralities in Tunisia and Morocco and then formed coalition governments with secular parties. In Egypt, the Islamist party decided not to share power with secular parties. In Libya and Algeria, however, the results were different. When elections were held there, secular parties won pluralities of the vote.

The Arab Spring or Arab Awakening revolts have altered the authoritarian landscape in North Africa but the transitions to democracy there are not yet complete. We have new, democratically elected regimes but important questions remain concerning the content of democracy, the role of religion in government, and the protection of dissidents.

We need to clarify what has occurred in the region. Are we witnessing revolution or revolt? To answer that question we need to ask, have the relationships of power in society, in the economy, and politics fundamentally changed or have the deck chairs in the ships of state been rearranged—without a real impact on power relations? Are we witnessing revolutions or are less significant events such as revolts or *coups d'états*?

Besides defining whether we are witnessing revolutions, revolts, or *coups d'états*, additional questions remain. First, why did these revolutions or revolts take place at this moment in time? Second, which social classes mobilized to resist or oust authoritarianism? Third, what role did the army and the police play in determining political outcomes? Fourth, what role did technology (particularly television, cell phones, and internet-based social media) play in spreading political revolution or revolt? Fifth, were these "leaderless" revolutions and, if so, what are the longer-term consequences of having either political revolutions or revolts that lacked either a clear leadership or a well-articulated ideologies or programs for political change? Sixth, how did these movements of social resistance accelerate to create a chain reaction across the region, affecting almost every state in North Africa and the Middle East? Seventh, what are the short-term, mid-term, and longer-term outcomes of the Arab Spring revolts?

Social revolutions and political revolutions

For our analysis we need to articulate the differences among the concepts of social revolution, political revolution, revolt, *coup d'état*, and mass demonstrations. In this regard, we find Theda Skocpol's distinctions between *social revolutions* and *political revolutions* to be helpful.[1] According to Skocpol, social revolutions are profound events: they involve a fundamental reordering of the relationships of power in a state and society. They are rare. They most often result from class struggle and conflict. The French, Russian, and Chinese revolutions can be counted among them. What has occurred in North Africa we define as *political revolutions* rather than as *social revolutions*. That differentiation is crucial to any analysis of recent changes in North Africa, as the key question remains: Have the fundamentals of power relations within North African states and societies changed? After defining what has occurred in North Africa during 2011 as political revolutions, we go on to describe two categories of political revolution (the *revolt* and the *coup d'état*) and then move on to describe yet another category (the *mass demonstration*). These three movements can be distinguished from social revolutions because while they may affect the operation of the state (who rules and how they rule) they do not necessarily transform power relations among classes in society.

Of the five North African cases that we examine, Tunisia and Libya fit within the category of revolts because they displaced authoritarian rulers. The Egyptian case was a hybrid, involving a revolt and *coup d'état* because Egypt's military leadership decided to join the rebels to depose President Mubarak and his apparent heir, his son Gamal. Morocco and Algeria were mass demonstrations that demanded political or economic reform; these two movements did not hinge upon the *displacement* or *replacement* of the regimes in place.

None of these North African movements, thus far, have radically transformed relationships of power in society. We argue further that none had the capacity to evolve towards social revolutions because they lacked an identifiable, sustainable political leadership prepared to implement an ideology or a set of programmatic objectives whose objective was the fundamental and long-term transformation of power relations in society.[2] These movements in North Africa were interested in ousting or decapitating the head of state (Tunisia, Egypt, Libya) or reforming the state (Morocco, Algeria). Importantly their inability to create a cohesive political leadership with a clearly articulated ideology or consistent set of programmatic objectives led to their eventual dissipation. What lies in the wake of the 2011 revolts and demonstrations are social movements and conflicts that are diffuse. The absence of programmatic objectives being driven by an identifiable, cohesive and committed political leadership explains why these North African revolts and demonstrations—despite their considerable success in displacing authoritarian leaders in some cases—seem to have lost momentum. The 2011 North African social movements were very important, legitimate, large-scale social resistance movements against leaders of authoritarian states who had created oppressive systems of chronic governmental surveillance and police abuse that frustrated their citizens' aspirations for civil liberties, personal dignity, and a better economic life. Nevertheless, viewed in their totality, these movements stopped short of becoming revolutions.

Revolts, *coup d'états*, mass demonstrations

Of our five cases, two (Tunisia and Libya) were revolts that displaced authoritarian leaders. Egypt was a hybrid, involving mixing a massive social revolt with a *coup d'état*. The role of the military in Tunisia, Egypt, and Libya helps us understand differences among these three cases. In Tunisia the military chose to return to their barracks and submitted itself to the control and direction of a civilian government. Egypt became a hybrid revolt/*coup d'état* because the Egyptian military decided to join the rebels so that it would continue to play a dispositive role in the determination of future politics. In Libya the military imploded. Our cases of Morocco and Algeria were large protest movements that demanded political and economic reform rather than displacement of the regime. The Moroccan protest movement resulted in constitutional reform that officially constrained the power of the king in a limited way. The Algerian movement quickly dissipated when the Algerian government reacted to the protests by reducing the cost of important food commodities and investing in large-scale development projects that were aimed at improving employment prospects in the country.

The Tunisian revolt, the Egyptian hybrid revolt/*coup d'état*, and the Libyan revolt undertook different paths. The Tunisian revolt started in interior Tunisia, which historically has been poorer and less economically developed than coastal Tunisia. The Tunisian revolt then moved from the interior of the country to the capital. On its way to its eventual success, the initiators of the political revolution (marginalized working class or unemployed youth from interior Tunisia) joined forces with urban-based liberal secularists who took advantage of the electronic technologies of television, cellular telephones, and internet social media, to create a larger and more diverse social movement including middle-class lawyers and judges, labor union organizers, and urban youth clubs (especially soccer clubs) to create a multi-class revolt. The Egyptian hybrid case was urban-based, being principally located in Cairo, the center of government and media. Like Tunisia it too united lumpenproletarian, proletarian, and *petit bourgeois* elements into a cross-class revolt that eventually united with the army to effect the unique hybrid: the combined revolt/*coup d'état*. The Libyan case began in the city of Benghazi in the eastern province of Cyrenaica, which initially gave the Libyan revolt a regional rather than a national expression. NATO then joined the revolt and by providing indispensable military, logistical, and advisory support, the rebels were able to expand their revolt from the eastern province to the southern and western parts of the country, causing the Qaddafi regime eventually to fall. Morocco and Algeria were categorically different. They were mass demonstrations that demanded political or economic reform rather than the displacement or replacement of the regimes in place.

Why now? Explanatory variables

The chapters in this book reveal multi-causal explanations for the suddenness and velocity of the 2011 North African revolts and mass demonstrations. In the chapters that follow five factors emerged as most relevant for our analyses: (1) the significant growth of large numbers of youth in society that clamored for greater participation in politics and economics yet were denied opportunities for participation; (2) the existence of consistent economic growth in all five North African states that raised expectations among all sectors of the population for economic benefits emerging from that growth;

(3) the disillusion of the *moyenne bourgeoisie* and the *petite bourgeoisie* with ruling elites that led them to break off with them and join with the aspirant revolutionaries and rebels; (4) decisions made by military leaders either to side with the rebels or revolutionaries or with the regime; and (5) the availability of mobilizing electronic technologies, including global television (especially Al Jazeera and Al Arabiya), texting via cellular telephones, and internet-based social media (especially the use of Facebook in the Tunisian case). These electronic technologies accelerated and facilitated the mobilization of citizens and residents in mass movements of social protest.

Chapter 2 of this volume theoretically and empirically addresses the concurrence of three of the factors mentioned above: (1) the emergence of large cohorts of youth in North Africa that created a demographic bulge within society and demanded changes in politics; (2) the constancy of economic growth in the region that enriched elites without providing redress for excessive youth unemployment; and (3) the availability of and access to global television (especially Al Jazeera and Al Arabiya), cellular telephones, and internet social media (especially Facebook) all of which intersected in 2011 to serve as catalysts to the North African protest movements.

Chapter 2's analysis demonstrates via the provision of data that population distributions in North Africa became demonstrably skewed to those in the age cohort under 30 years of age at the beginning of the twenty-first century, which led to the creation of a large group of persons that became disillusioned with the stasis of existing political and economic systems. This significantly large cohort of youth was available to be mobilized into mass movements for social change. Chapter 2 provides population pyramid data on a country-by-country basis and then ties the existence of this large youthful cohort with other macroeconomic data demonstrating consistent economic growth in each North African state for the period from 2000 through 2010. While this consistent economic growth occurred during the first decade of the twenty-first century, the problem with the type of growth that occurred was that wealth was not equitably shared with either alienated youth or disaffected elements of the *petite bourgeoisie*. The data reveal that the economies of the region were demonstrably improving. The economic quality of life and employment circumstances for most persons, however, were not. This combination of economic growth and static or declining economic quality of life created a classic case of relative deprivation, which is a condition often cited in the literature on causal factors of revolution. Put simply, humans "have basic needs, wishes, or instincts, which if frustrated give rise to feelings of aggression that sometimes take the form of revolutionary behavior or violence."[3] In all our North African cases, what was observable from field observations, public opinion research results, and macroeconomic data was that large swathes of the population believed themselves to be economically marginalized and politically repressed, and that they could observe smaller, more elite elements within their societies benefiting disproportionately from economic growth. Under these conditions of both mass perceived repression and relative deprivation, possibilities for collective political mobilization rose considerably. Political psychologist Ted Gurr in his explication of the concept of relative deprivation emphasized that relative deprivation has two important aspects: *scope* (the number of issues causing resentment) and *intensity* (the degree of resentment felt).[4] The North African revolts and mass demonstrations fit into Gurr's third paradigm of "progressive deprivation," where society's aspirations for betterment rise while the economic capacity of the state rises as well (please see Figure 1.1 on page 13).

Another theorist, the economist Mancur Olsen, offered an analysis that concurred with Gurr's observation. Olsen claimed that the concurrence of rapid economic growth with increasing numbers of the poor leads to conditions of relative deprivation, social instability, and revolt.[5] Besides these questions of relative deprivation, Chapter 2 also explains that while a considerable youth bulge exists in North Africa now, fertility rates will dramatically decline in the region during the next 20 years (with the exception of Libya). When that decline occurs and as the population becomes both more aged and smaller, the demographic pressures that presently exist will dissipate. Twenty years from now a new period of demographic stability will arrive in the region.

To Gurr's and Olsen's notions of relative deprivation and rapid economic growth we add Samuel P. Huntington's notion that the most fertile ground for revolution can be found in "societies which have experienced some social and economic development and where the processes of political modernization and political development have lagged behind the processes of social and economic change."[6] Huntington claimed that political leaders need to make adjustments and modifications to their governmental systems to make them more inclusive and participatory during periods of economic growth. The failure to do this is precisely what occurred in our two revolts (Tunisia and Libya), our hybrid case (Egypt), and our two movements of mass social protest (Morocco and Algeria). All five countries experienced economic growth from 2000 through 2010. Yet all five states and economies were unable to absorb the demands made by the demographic bulge of youth that emerged during the first decade of the twenty-first century. The poverty created and the inadequate wages that prevailed in the midst of growing economies provided prime conditions that would create mass resentment of privileged classes. Given the combination of real demographic pressures, economic growth, and a failure of political accommodation, a spark (the self-immolation of Mohamed Bouazizi) pushed the youth of Tunisia to revolt. After Tunisia was successful in ousting the dictator Ben Ali, organizers in Egypt were encouraged and they used electronic media to accelerate the pace of their demonstrations. The successes in Tunisia and Egypt in turn created a chain of revolts and demonstrations that would affect Libya, Morocco, Algeria, Bahrain, Yemen, Saudi Arabia, and Syria in varying ways.

We take the phenomenon of the concurrence of a significant youth bulge with very high youth unemployment, and an expanding economy that exacerbated the population's sense of their relative deprivation and to these we add to our analysis the mobilizational capabilities of the old technology of television and the new technologies of cell phones and internet social media. Old and new electronic technologies combined with our preceding factors to create conditions that accelerated the mechanisms and processes of protest to make them regional phenomena. These components combined with an eventual fracturing of the relationship between the ruling elites and the *moyenne* and *petite bourgeoisies* that led to very unstable conditions. Members of the middle class including intellectuals, civil servants, labor union activists, lawyers, judges, engineers, technicians, entrepreneurs, and managers joined marginalized and unemployed rural and urban youth and in some cases the military (especially in Tunisia and Egypt) to accelerate these processes of social change.

Crane Brinton, Karl Mannheim, Gaetano Mosca, and Edward Shils in their separate works emphasized that the transfer of allegiance of the middle class and especially its intellectuals from the ruling regime to rebels or revolutionaries was essential for the conversion of revolutionary situations into revolutions.[7] In North Africa the *moyenne* and *petite bourgeoisies*' shift of allegiance from either support or passivity towards the ruling regime towards support of rebellion by proletarian and lumpenproletarian youth was essential to the creation of a multi-class coalition that either toppled authoritarian regimes or forced them to reform.

The final dispositive factor that played a role in these processes of social change would be the extent to which the military as an institution chose to support either the rebels or the regime. In Tunisia and Egypt the military establishment made the essential choice of supporting the rebels or the demonstrators. Libya was qualitatively different where the military simply imploded and stopped functioning as a viable political or military actor. Consequently, when NATO provided critical support to the rebels, the regime fell. Morocco involved an effort to reform rather than depose the monarchy and the allegiance of the military was not called into question. Algeria has had a regime in which the military has been the central force or *pouvoir primordial* behind the operation of politics for decades. The demonstrators in Algeria were simply unable to muster sufficient social resources to displace the regime. Our review of the role of the military makes evident, in all of our cases, that the extent to which the military chose either to support the regime or the putative revolutionaries was essential. Whether the military coheres, fractures, or implodes and whether the military decides to support the regime or the revolutionaries becomes critical in these processes of revolution, revolt, and mass demonstrations. Viewed from an historical perspective and from different eras (for example, Charles I of England in 1640, Louis XVI of France in 1789, or Nicholas II of Russia in 1917), if rulers had had the support of a unified and cohesive military during their periods of social unrest, their *revolutionary situations* would not have been transformed into *revolutions*. For example in Russia, the Russian military cohered in 1905 (leading the failure of that first revolutionary attempt) while it fractured in 1917 (leading to the success of that revolution).[8] The cohesiveness and decisions made by the military, therefore, become essential to our analysis.

The consequences of "leaderless" revolutions and the absence of revolutionary ideology

The Arab Spring revolts were characterized not only by spontaneity and rapidity but also by the absence of an identifiable leadership and by a deficiency of ideology. These combination of forces, as philosopher Hannah Arendt has asserted, may lead to revolutionary situations. They may not necessarily lead, however, to revolutions.[9] Although there had been smaller scale labor strikes and street demonstrations throughout North Africa before 2011, these previous strikes and demonstrations never reached a magnitude that threatened or toppled the authoritarian regimes. The 2011 revolts and demonstrations were significantly larger, spontaneous, and they accelerated rapidly; some planning was involved but it was not extensive. The absence of extensive planning, a clearly defined ideology or set or programmatic objectives, and an identifiable political leadership urges us to contemplate the midterm and longer-term consequences of having social protest movements that lacked these elements.

At this point in this introduction we assert that movements of social change that have an articulated ideology or set of programmatic objectives that are steered by an identifiable and cohesive political leadership create a set of hard interests that can provide motive force to politics. The lack of a clearer set of ideological or programmatic objectives in the North African revolts has led these movements to dissipation in the near-term and mid-term. These movements—at least at this moment in time—have dissolved into considerable post-revolt or post-demonstration confusion and even apathy. These movements have temporarily lost their way. What needs to be contemplated next is whether the rebels or organizers who initiated these projects of political and social change will recognize the systemic weaknesses that have manifested and whether they will be able to pivot to articulate either a clearer ideology or set of political objectives that are led by an identifiable and cohesive set of revolutionary or reform leaders. If this does not occur it seems quite likely that these movements of political resistance will continue to lose force and that the forces of counterrevolution will have better opportunities to organize and mobilize. These two factors—a clearer ideology and an identifiable and cohesive political leadership—will be necessary for the next stage of political reform. If this were not to occur, these revolutionary situations will fizzle out.

Waves of revolution?

What was striking about the Arab Spring revolts and mass demonstrations of 2011 was their spontaneity, rapidity, and infectious quality that created a "wave" of "revolution" and "revolt" across North Africa, the Levant, and the Arabian Peninsula. What explains this rapidity and seemingly infectious quality of revolt? Have these "waves" occurred before?

We assert that three factors (the *demonstration effect* of having an initial successful revolt, *normative preparedness for change*, and *communications technology*) play roles in the creation of "waves" of revolution. Discernible waves of revolutions and revolts have occurred in the past. One wave took place between 1776 and 1798. That was arguably one rather long wave but it was nevertheless a wave. It began with the American War of Independence in 1776, which successfully established on a transoceanic level the notion that anti-monarchical and republican political revolution was possible. After the success of the War for American Independence, that particular political revolution had a demonstration effect in the European, Caribbean, and South American regions that would include the 1789 French Revolution, the 1791 Haitian Revolution, the 1798 Irish Rebellion, and the revolutionary wars in Latin America. The American War of Independence, through its republican philosophy and its military success, served as the model for this republican wave. The communications modality used in the wave was the printed political pamphlet, which was used to incite revolt and encourage the wave.

A second more rapid and arguably more relevant wave for our analysis here were the revolts and revolutions that took place in Europe during 1848. That wave began in Palermo, then spread to the Italian peninsula, then France, the Habsburg Empire, the German states, Belgium, Denmark, and Ireland. Like the 2011 Arab wave, these revolts took place within one year or two years at most. Also, like the 2011 Arab Spring wave, populations had surged in Europe just before the onset of the 1848 revolutions and revolts and these populations created demands and concessions from the political systems that were in place.[10] The specific demands being made during the 1848 revolts were mostly liberal and occasionally socialist in orientation: the establishment of constitutional monarchies, the expansion of suffrage so that more citizens could participate in the vote, the end of press and book censorship, the expansion of progressive taxation, the provision of free state-provided education for boys and girls, the abolition of serfdom, political equality for Jews, and the abolition of the nobility.[11] European populations during the 1840s were surging, relations between labor and capital were under stress, and by the 1840s two alternate political philosophies were emerging to displace the conservatism of absolute monarchism: liberalism and socialism. The 1848 revolutions and revolts ultimately had a mostly liberal expression, with the establishment of constitutional monarchies being the rebels' primary objective.[12] At the same time socialist activists (notably Karl Marx and Friedrich Engels) advocated more substantial political and economic change and the specific empowerment of workers within politics.[13] Nevertheless, in the final analysis, most of the 1848 socialists endorsed republicanism with an expanded electorate that would include the working classes rather than the dictatorship of the proletariat. These socialists also endorsed a universal voting franchise (including women), which distinguished them from their nineteenth-century liberal counterparts who favored a franchise limited to eligible male property owners.

The 1848 wave has similarities to and differences with the 2011 wave. The similarity between these waves and what caused them eventually to be less effective was that both waves were conducted by political leaderships that did not cohere after they removed the regimes in place. The leaderships within both waves had within them factions that had shared the objective of regime change but beyond that goal they did not share a common set of objectives of what was going to be constructed after the fall of the regimes. Because of the lack of cohesion within the political leadership, the initial achievements of the 1848 and 2011 waves were not adequately consolidated and, at least in the 1848 wave, this failure of cohesive leadership created time and space for the forces of counterrevolution to organize and act. The 1848 and 2011 waves can also be distinguished. In contrast to the 2011 wave the proponents of the 1848 wave had a clearer set of political demands (i.e., constitutional monarchy, the expansion of the franchise, public education, etc.) while the activists in the 2011 wave were exclusively focused on regime change while not uniting upon a common set of political objectives that would follow the destruction of the regimes that had been the focus of their attention. The communications modalities used in the 1848 wave were newspapers, pamphlets, and the emerging use of the telegraph.

The third wave of revolutions and revolts took place in the wake of the 1917 Russian Revolution and US President Woodrow Wilson's 1918 Declaration of Fourteen Points in which he argued for national self-determination in the colonial world. The socialist wave of revolts began in Russia in 1917 and then spread to proclamation of the Munich Soviet Republic in 1918, the Hungarian Revolution of 1919, the establishment of the Persian Socialist Soviet Republic in 1920, and lastly the Chinese Revolution of 1949. The Munich, Hungarian, and Persian revolts were short-lived; the Russian and Chinese revolutions were successful. A second anti-colonial wave was initially inspired by President Wilson's publication of his "Fourteen Points" in 1918. That declaration contributed to an anti-colonial revolt in Egypt in 1918 that would spread to India, Korea, and China before reaching its zenith of success during the 1960s. In these two waves (the socialist and the anti-colonial) the relevant communications modalities were the political pamphlet, the telegraph, and the radio.

The last and temporally closest wave of revolts to those experienced during the 2011 Arab Spring came in 1989. This wave began with protests against authoritarianism that were launched in Hungary and then followed by the Solidarność-led labor and political protests in Poland. These demonstrations spread to East Germany, Czechoslovakia, Romania, and Bulgaria, eventually breaking Soviet control over Eastern Europe. Two factors played important roles in the velocity of this wave. First, the electronic communications technologies of television, radio, and fax broadcast and accelerated this series of revolts. Second, Western governments (particularly West Germany and the United States) provided significant material and diplomatic support to the rebels, which materially contributed to their success. It should be parenthetically noted that outside of the region of Eastern Europe, China experienced the massive Tiananmen Square protests in Beijing during the same year.

The 2011 revolts fit into this wave pattern. Once Tunisia's rebels were successful in ousting their authoritarian leader, their accomplishment provided a model to other states and societies in the region that massive popular revolts could have favorable outcomes. The Tunisian revolt, therefore, furnished an *initial model* that had a *demonstration effect* across the region. Second, the populations in the region were *normatively prepared for change*. Public opinion polls conducted before the 2011 revolts revealed that citizens and residents in the region were eager for liberalization in government. For example, a 2010 Pew Center survey revealed that majorities within the Muslim world (with the exception of Pakistan) favored democracy to authoritarianism.[14] Last, the advent of the communications technologies of globally accessed television (principally Al Jazeera and Al Arabiya), cellular telephones, and social media (especially Facebook and Twitter) accelerated the dissemination of news and provided new electronic platforms for political organizers who were intent upon organizing popular masses to oust their authoritarian leaders.

The outline of the book

After this introduction, Ricardo René Larémont in Chapter 2 examines the interlocking roles that demographic change, economics, and internet and cellular telephone technology played in fomenting and accelerating revolutionary and reform movements in North Africa in 2011. The author provides a country-by-country demographic analysis of each state in North Africa and then ties these demographic analyses with macroeconomic data, youth unemployment data, cellular telephone use data, and Facebook usage data to explain the origins, the dissemination, and the velocity of the North African revolts. The author also predicts that, given predictable fertility declines, North African states and societies will arrive at a state of demographic stability within 20 years.

The case studies are provided in Chapters 3 through 7. Chapter 3, "The Tunisian revolution: the revolution of dignity," was written by Amira Aleya-Sghaier, a Tunisian historian who was a witness and activist in the revolution. In this chapter Aleya-Sghaier provides an analysis of the causes and the significant actors in the Tunisian uprising and attempts to put that revolt in comparative perspective with the other revolutions or revolts that followed in the North African region. To explain the Tunisian case, Aleya-Sghaier focuses on the disparities in wealth distribution between interior and coastal Tunisia;

the bleak employment prospects of Tunisian youth; general fatigue with President Zine El Abidine Ben Ali's authoritarian system; the use of email, text messaging, and Facebook to broadcast the revolution; and the special roles played by lawyers, judges, and labor union activists in organizing the later stages of the revolt. Aleya-Sghaier also provides analyses of the disparate roles played by the army and the police in the revolt.

In Chapter 4 Emad El-Din Shahin provides a chapter entitled "The Egyptian revolution: the power of mass mobilization and the spirit of Tahrir Square." This chapter examines the power of mass mobilization in Egypt and the strategies and tactics that were used to topple President Mubarak's regime in 18 days. Shahin examines the structural causes behind the revolution and the role of influential actors, including the April 6 movement, the Muslim Brotherhood, the Popular Campaign for the Support of ElBaradei, and labor unions. In his chapter Shahin argues that the January 25 revolution emerged from a cumulative process that built up over several years of political repression, economic mismanagement, social injustice, police brutality, and systematic efforts at political activism. Shahin assesses the crucial mistakes that the Mubarak regime made that contributed to its demise and he discusses the use of traditional and modern mobilization strategies and the use of non-violence as a tactic. Finally, Shahin's chapter discusses the ambiguous role of the military in the revolution and its role in the transition.

Youssef Sawani, a political scientist from Libya, contributes Chapter 5, "The February 17 *intifada* in Libya: disposing of the regime and issues of state-building." Here Sawani explains the different trajectory and more violent nature of the Libyan *intifada* against Leader Muammar Qaddafi's regime. He explains the revolt's origins in eastern Libya, its complex assemblage of disparate rebel elements, and the unique role that NATO played in the revolt, which distinguishes the Libyan case from the others discussed in this book. Sawani describes the rise and partial consolidation of the various components that would comprise the Libyan rebel movement and he explains the eventual and perhaps necessary intervention by NATO forces. He adds to his analysis the vital role played by global television media, especially Al Jazeera, in the reporting and the promotion of the revolt and he explains why violence was needed in Libya to overturn the regime. Sawani goes into considerable detail to describe the tactics undertaken by the Qaddafi regime to quell the revolt and Saif al-Islam Qaddafi's frustrated efforts to liberalize his father's economic and political policies, all of which failed in the final analysis. Finally, Sawani comments on the role of militias in Libya and their possible role in impeding the consolidation of the new Libyan state.

In Chapter 6 Mohammed Darif, a professor of political science and law from Morocco, argues that Morocco avoided revolution in 2011 because King Mohammed VI had already begun a longer-term process of liberalizing the Moroccan state. Darif claims that this process began in 2004, when the king encouraged a state-sponsored inquiry into governmental abuses of human rights. Also, in 2010, Mohammed began a process of transferring

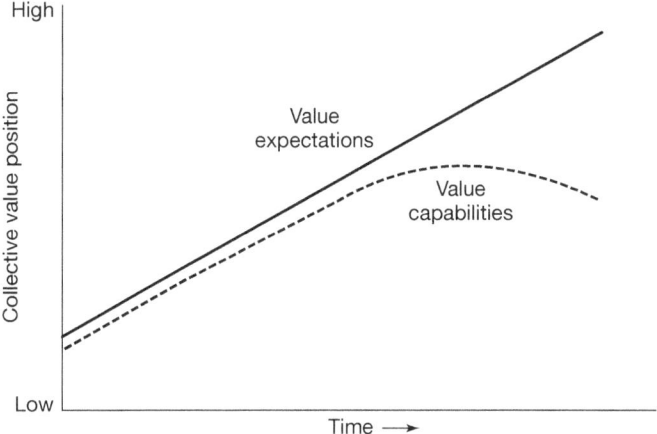

Figure 1.1 Relative deprivation and the impetus to violence

governmental decision-making authority from the central government to provincial governments. Although the mass protests that occurred in Morocco during 2011 were successful in inducing the king to accelerate constitutional reforms that devolved some of his power to the parliament, the king at the end of this process still retained his authority to appoint his preferred candidates to key ministries and he remained in control of the army. Darif contends that Mohammed VI has created a process that has liberalized the Moroccan polity and that has encouraged controlled and gradual political evolution rather than revolution.

Azzedine Layachi, in Chapter 7, explains why neither revolt nor revolution arrived in Algeria during 2011. Algeria would seem primed for revolt. Its youth suffer from underemployment and marginalization. Why no revolution in Algeria? Layachi contends that while there were underlying currents that should lead to instability in Algeria, the army as a force in politics and society continues to cohere and it can direct the politics of the nation from behind the scenes. Also, Algeria suffered from a terrible civil war during the last decade of the twentieth century that created a considerable and systemic public aversion to a new round of violence and instability. In this risk-adverse environment, the army benefits as an institution that can provide stability. Besides having a cohesive army, Algeria enjoys the additional advantage of considerable natural gas and petroleum rents that enable the regime to "buy" social compliance during periods of crisis. Last, the Algerian regime has attempted to incorporate non-violent Islamists into politics while vigorously prosecuting those Islamists who aspire to challenge the regime by force. These combined factors of mass social aversion to and fatigue from violence, a strong and cohesive army, the availability of gas and petroleum rents, and the attempted incorporation of non-violent Islamists explain why Algeria avoided revolt and revolution—at least during 2011.

In the concluding chapter, Chapter 8, the editor examines the outcome of the revolts and revolutions in North Africa. The youth who initiated these revolts were successful in dismantling old forms of authoritarianism in Tunisia, Egypt, and Libya while they obtained modest gains of constitutional reform in Morocco and very little change in Algeria. Youth stimulated and led these revolts. In the final analysis, however, they were not the victors when these processes came to an end. In three of our cases (Tunisia, Egypt, and Morocco) Islamist parties became empowered as a result of these processes of change. In our two other cases (Libya and Algeria) Islamist parties play a role but they are not dominant. The youth leaders of the revolts had insisted that their movements were "organic," "leaderless," and "party-less." They failed to organize their interests into their own effective parties and after the bodies were counted, the leaders were removed, and the constitutions were drafted, they did not reap the rewards of victory.

Notes

1 See, especially, Theda Skocpol, *States and Social Revolutions* (Cambridge: Cambridge University Press, 1979), pp. 4–5.
2 See, Jacques Ellul, *Autopsie de la révolution* (Paris: Calman-Levy, 1969), p. 50.
3 Mark M. Hagopian, *The Phenomenon of Revolution* (New York: Dodd, Mead & Co., 1974), p. 168.
4 Ted Gurr, *Why Men Rebel* (Princeton: Princeton University Press, 1971), pp. 29–30.
5 Mancur Olsen, "Rapid Growth as a Destabilizing Force," in J.C. Davies (ed.) *When Men Revolt and Why* (New York: Free Press, 1971), p. 219.
6 Samuel P. Huntington, *Political Order in Changing Societies* (New Haven: Yale University Press, 1970), p. 265.
7 Crane Brinton, *The Anatomy of a Revolution* (New York: Vintage, 1938, 1965); Karl Mannheim, *Ideology and Utopia* (London: Routledge, 1936); Gaetano Mosca, *The Ruling Class* (New York: McGraw Hill, 1939, 1960); Edward Shils, "The Intellectuals and the Powers: Some Perspectives for Comparative Analysis," *Comparative Studies in Society and History*, 1:1 (October 1958): 5–22.
8 Leon Trotsky, *History of the Russian Revolution* (New York: Pathfinder, 1932, 1961), pp. 331–347.
9 Hannah Arendt, *On Revolution* (New York: Viking, 1963), p. 263.
10 Jonathan Sperber, *The European Revolutions, 1848–1851* (Cambridge: Cambridge University Press, 2005), pp. 23–24.
11 Mike Rapport, *1848: Year of Revolution* (New York: Basic Books, 2008), p. 243; Sperber, *European Revolutions*, pp. 56–57.
12 See Benjamin Constant, *Des réactions politiques,* http://ebookbrowse.com/reactions-politiques-doc-d63091614; Benjamin Constant, *Des effets de la terreur,* http://classiques.uqac.ca/classiques/constant_benjamin/effets_de_la_terreur/effets_terreur.html; Rapport, *1848: Year of Revolution*, p. 105.
13 Karl Marx and Friedrich Engels, *The Communist Manifesto* (New York: Norton, 1988, originally published in 1848).
14 http://pewresearch.org/2011/01/31/egypt-democracy-and-islam.

2 Demographics, economics, and technology

Background to the North African revolutions

Ricardo René Larémont

Introduction

An examination of the demographics of North Africa, the Levant, and the Arabian Peninsula quickly reveals the emergence of a significant youth bulge that is both angry and unemployed. This youth cohort has access to new international media and technology—especially cell phone texting capabilities and the social media platforms of Facebook and Twitter—that have allowed it to obtain critical support from Arab-language international television outlets such as Al Jazeera and Al Arabiya. In turn, this attention has emboldened youth to use the instantaneous transmission of messages and images to mobilize locally around such issues as improved economic standards of life, freedom of expression and the press, access to high-quality education, and employment opportunities. This participatory, web-inspired social and political movement has forced youth to realize that a wide gap exists between their standards of living and those enjoyed by their peers in the rest of the world. And for these youth, that difference has become intolerable.

North African youth's consciousness of their conditions, their evolving capacity to organize, their access to cell phone texting capabilities and social media networks such as Facebook and Twitter, and the international media support provided by Al Jazeera and Al Arabiya have combined to create an electronic platform for social and political organization that governmental authorities find very difficult to control. The government's option of simply cutting off internet or cell phone service has limited utility in suppressing social protests, because cutting off these electronic services also impedes the flow of the economic transactions that are the lifeblood for the survival of all states. The doors of electronic communication need to remain open not only for those who use these tools to execute financial transactions, but also for those who organize revolutions and social protests.

The electronic, media-informed techniques of social revolution that have emerged from the allegedly moribund Arab and Muslim world reveal as a shibboleth the belief that innovation—especially political innovation—is impossible in these regions. The youth of these areas have inaugurated a new age of revolution and social protest that is arguably post-Islamist. This chapter will examine this youthful activist cohort, the conditions that propelled them to advocate for change, the tactics that they undertook to challenge authoritarianism, and the challenges that still lie before them.

The conditions for change

This first section of this chapter scrutinizes demographic change in Tunisia, Egypt, Libya, Morocco, and Algeria to reveal continuities and variations across the five countries. The second section examines youth access to cell phones and social media such as Facebook and Twitter and their use of these tools as bases for social and political organization. The final section interprets the revolutionary implications of the youth bulge and transformations in electronic communications.

The youth bulge: trends and reality

From the 1789 French Revolution to the 2011 revolutions of the Arab world, the young have played essential roles in the organization and execution of revolutions. Classical political economists such as Thomas Malthus and modern analysts such as Herbert Möller, Jack Goldstone, Gunnar Heinsohn, Christian Mesquida, and Henrik Urdal have examined how political destabilization can occur when rapid technological, economic, and political change combines with a demographic "youth bulge."[1] Are similar processes at work now in the Arab world? In North Africa and the Middle East we observe a youth bulge that simultaneously benefits and suffers from the flow of previously inaccessible information from cell phones, internet portals, and satellite televisions. The benefits emerge from the communications possibilities of these electronic media; the suffering stems from the tendency of these media sources to accentuate the disparities between Arab youth's lives and the lives enjoyed in other regions of the world, including the industrialized West and rapidly developing states in Asia and South America.

To begin our analysis, let us look at demographic trends in the five target countries and identify continuities and differences across them.

General trends: data across North Africa

The populations of Tunisia, Egypt, Libya, Algeria, and Morocco are youthful today but will notably begin aging around 2030. Table 2.1 displays population data from 2010 for our five cases. These data reveal that these populations are highly youthful. Demographers have pointed out that youth are historically more susceptible to mass mobilizations for political change. While these North African populations are currently youthful, however, they are projected to change and age during the next 20 years, especially as fertility rates among women in the region decline. Figure 2.1 and Table 2.2 document projected changes in fertility over time in the region.

Table 2.1 Total population and youth population in North Africa (2010)

Country	Total population (millions)	Youth percentage of population (ages 0–24)
Tunisia	10.48	43.5
Egypt	81.12	51.2
Libya	6.36	48.2
Algeria	35.47	47.6
Morocco	31.95	47.7

Source: United Nations, Department of Economic and Social Affairs, Population Division, www.un.org/esa/population/meetings/egm-adolescents/roudi.pdf

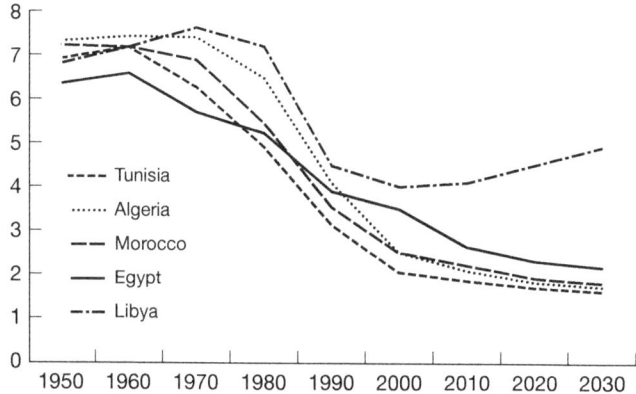

Figure 2.1 Total fertility among North African women

Table 2.2 Total fertility (children born per woman) in North Africa

Year	Tunisia	Egypt	Libya	Algeria	Morocco
1950	6.93	6.37	6.87	7.28	7.18
1960	7.25	6.55	7.18	7.38	7.15
1970	6.21	5.7	7.59	7.38	6.89
1980	4.92	5.2	7.18	6.49	5.4
1990	3.13	3.9	4.5	4.13	3.6
2000	2.04	3.5	4.0	2.53	2.52
2010	1.91	2.64	4.1	2.14	2.18
2020	1.72	2.32	4.5	1.82	1.9
2030	1.67	2.2	4.9	1.72	1.81

Source: United Nations, Department of Economic and Social Affairs, Population Division, www.un.org/esa/population/publications/wfr2009web/data/comparativetables.html.

These data reveal a revolutionary change in the demographics of North Africa in both retrospective and prospective terms. Whereas women in the five countries in our study had, on average, between 6.37 (Egypt) and 7.28 (Algeria) children in 1950, those numbers had dropped significantly by 2010 for three of our states (Tunisia, Algeria, and Morocco), with more modest decreases recorded in Egypt and even more modest decreases in Libya. At present, the fertility rate in Libya is an average 4.1 children per woman, followed by a rate of 2.64 in Egypt, 2.18 in Morocco, 2.14 in Algeria, and 1.91 in Tunisia. What is statistically significant is that by 2010 Tunisia had already lowered its fertility rate beyond the replacement rate of two births per woman, which means that Tunisia's population will decline in the near term and political, economic, and social pressures for change will probably relent during the next 20 years. Furthermore, United Nations Populations Division forecasts indicate that by 2030, fertility rates for both Algeria and Morocco will also fall below the replacement fertility rate (with projected rates of 1.72 births per woman for Algeria and 1.81 births per woman for Morocco), which means that social and economic pressures in Algeria and Morocco will also likely diminish within 20 years, provided that their economies continue to expand and their political leaders move toward more inclusionary policies. By contrast, the somewhat higher projected fertility rates for Egypt (2.2 in 2030) and Libya (4.9 in 2030) still lie above the rate needed to produce a decline in population size, which means that their economies will need to expand in both the mid- and long-term to relieve the social and economic demands of their growing populations. Libya's demographic trends are particularly worrying, because the rates of fertility there are expected to remain comparatively high through 2030 (with a projected 4.5 to 4.9 births per woman).

Using these data on declining fertility in North Africa, we can then graph how the region has and will become older (and eventually more stable) over time. Figure 2.2 and Table 2.3 track the median age of the five states in our region from 1950 to the 2030 projections.

Given these data trends, by about 2030, the median age in all five of our countries will rise above the age of 30, which is usually the threshold age for individuals most inclined to participate in mass movements of political resistance. By the age of 30, most youth—especially young men who have engaged in political action—have moved into more static relationships involving career and family that inhibit them from participating in more risky forms of behavior, including movements or acts of political resistance, that may put their lives at risk. This proposition is not universally applicable, but it generally holds true. From our data, it is therefore generally foreseeable that although the North African region is prone to dramatic political upheaval now, it will be less likely to manifest these conditions in the future, especially given predictable fertility declines and the aging of the population.

Given these general trends and projections, let us look at the population pyramids for each country as of 2011. Figures 2.3 through 2.7 provide a visual picture of the youth percentage data that were provided earlier.

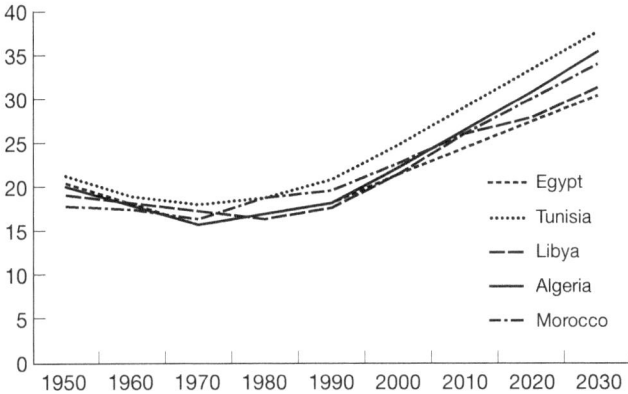

Figure 2.2 Median age

Table 2.3 Median age

	Tunisia	Egypt	Libya	Algeria	Morocco
1950	20.9	20.4	19	19.9	17.7
1960	18.9	18.5	18.4	18.2	17.5
1970	16.8	18	17.4	15.8	16.3
1980	18.5	18.5	16.5	16.9	18.5
1990	20.8	19.4	17.7	18.1	19.7
2000	24.7	21.4	21.9	21.7	22.6
2010	28.9	24.4	25.9	26.2	26.3
2020	33.3	27.5	27.9	30.7	30.1
2030	37.8	30.5	31.4	35.3	34

Source: United Nations Population Department.

According to the US Census Bureau and the United Nations Population Division, Tunisia had an estimated population of 10.48 million in July 2010. Figure 2.3 reveals that the largest group within this population comprised individuals aged 25 to 29 years, followed by individuals aged 20 to 24 years and individuals aged 15 to 19 years. The group aged 15 to 29 years—or, to slightly enlarge the group, aged 15 to 34 years—were the most demographically preponderant group in a society that had been relatively deprived of the riches enjoyed by the Ben Ali regime, and they were also the group that was most inclined to participate in the political actions that led to the revolution. These cohorts were also the most exposed to mobile media and most likely to participate in the electronic communications via cell phones, Facebook, and Twitter that helped mobilize the revolution. Although Tunisia's youth population made up 43.55 percent of the population, its distribution differed from that of Egypt (see Figure 2.4). If we look at Tunisia's population

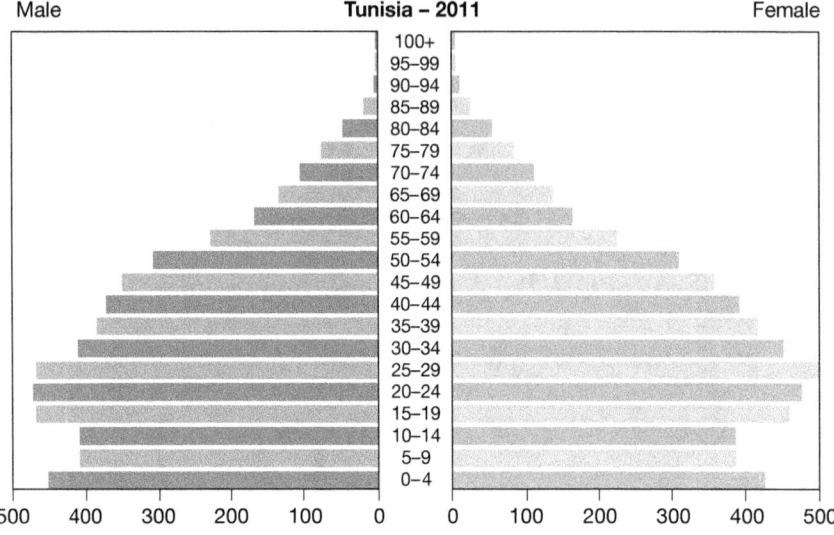

Figure 2.3 Tunisia population pyramid

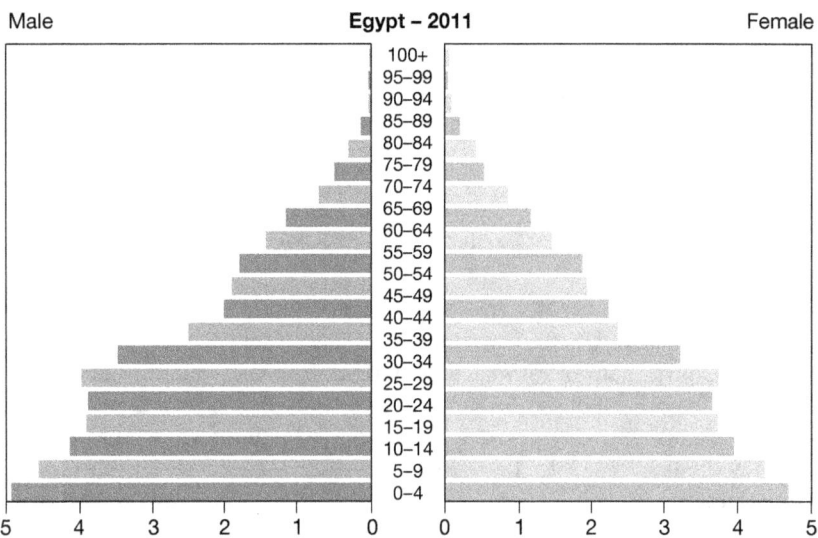

Figure 2.4 Egypt population pyramid

period carefully, we can predict future population declines among the youth cohort as a result of observable declines in the 0–4 and 5–9 categories.

In contrast, if we look at Egypt's 0–4 and 5–9 categories (Figure 2.4), we can see that the youth population is continuing to expand. These combined

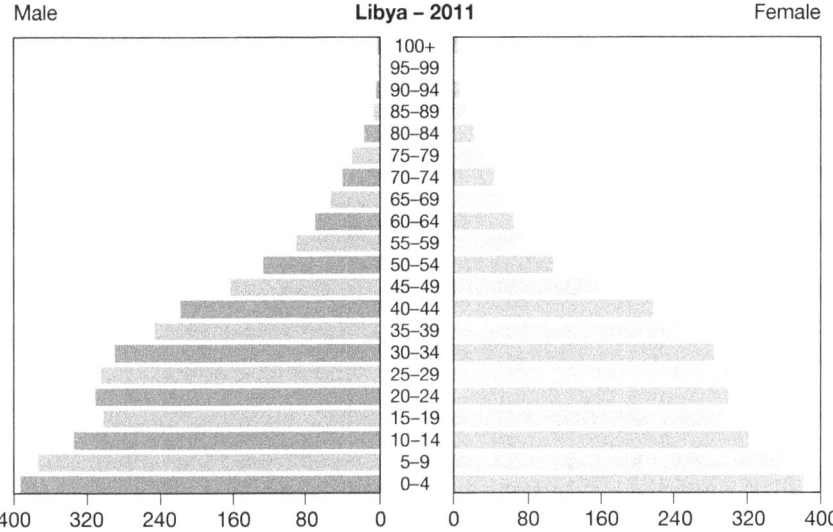

Figure 2.5 Libya population pyramid

data confirm that Tunisia will undergo a more rapid decline in fertility, leading to a more quickly aging population than either Egypt (Figure 2.4) or Libya (Figure 2.5). Given this aging population, we can infer that Tunisia should become more stable over the long run, at least from a demographic point of view, provided that it can form a political leadership to guide the country's politics and economics.

Like Tunisia, Egypt's population distribution is skewed toward youth, with the largest groups being, in order, ages 0–4, 5–9, 10–14, 25–29, 15–19, 20–24, and 30–34. This distribution is clearly skewed toward youth but is distinctly different from Tunisia's distribution, which indicates a tapering off of the 0–14 categories. Close observation of Egypt's population pyramid reveals that Egypt's population will likely decline, but not as rapidly as the populations of Tunisia, Algeria, and Morocco. From the viewpoint of political stability, this higher rate of fertility in Egypt will pose a challenge to leaders of the post-Mubarak regime, because the Egyptian economy will have to expand faster than historical rates to satisfy the demands of a growing population. Egypt enjoys a large economy, recording a total GDP of $82.4 billion for 2010, but it also has the largest population in the region (82.9 million). Consequently, its per capita GDP is only $1,150. This continually growing population will continue to exert pressure on the state, especially if the economy continues to decline as it has since the onset of the Egyptian revolution in February 2011. To establish and maintain demographic, economic, and political stability, the leaders of the new regime will have to simultaneously grow the economy and provide incentives to slow the rate of population growth.

Of our five cases, Libya's population pyramid produces the most long-term concern. Libya's population is dramatically skewed toward youth. Although the nation has the smallest population in the region (6.3 million people), its fertility rate is the highest in the region (4.1 children per woman). Furthermore, the United Nations Population Division forecasts that Libya's fertility rate will increase to 4.9 births per woman by 2030. The installation of a new post-Qaddafi regime in September 2011 provides Libya with an opportunity to contemplate new population and economic policies, such as a redistribution of the country's considerable wealth (Libya's 2009 GDP was $62.36 billion and its per capita GDP was $9,714) to benefit its people. Despite this wealth, which is generated by petroleum and natural gas revenues, it would be in the country's long-term interests to begin crafting a population policy that would eventually moderate its fertility rate. Unfortunately, because of the continuing profitability of the petroleum and natural gas industries and Libya's short- and medium-term demands for labor, the development of a population and fertility program does not stand out as an immediate concern. This goal will become more important, however, when petroleum reserves decline, as they inevitably will.

Demographic change in Algeria since 1950 has been dramatic, which can clearly be seen by examining the population pyramid of Figure 2.6 and comparing it with the pyramids of Libya, Egypt, and Tunisia (see Figures 2.3–2.5). The population contraction is particularly startling in the 0–4, 5–9, and 10–14 age cohorts. With a 2010 fertility rate of 2.14 per woman, Algeria has the second lowest fertility rate in the region (after Tunisia's 1.91)—a rate that comes close to the replacement rate of two children per woman. Furthermore, the UN

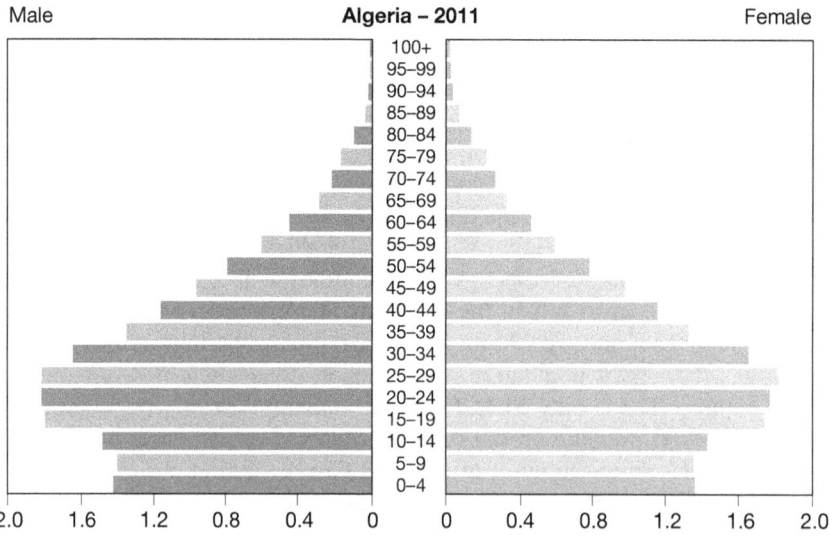

Figure 2.6 Algeria population pyramid

Population Division projects that Algeria's fertility rate will drop to 1.82 children per woman by 2020, which means that Algeria's population will begin to decline within 15 to 20 years, barring considerable immigration into the country. These demographic changes will have considerable economic, political, and social implications. Like Libya, Algeria's economy relies heavily on petroleum and natural gas sales. Algeria's population, however, is considerably larger than Libya's (34.8 million in Algeria in contrast to Libya's 6.4 million). Because of its larger population, Algeria's 2009 per capita GDP was $4,029 compared to Libya's $9,714 per person. The Algerian government has experienced ongoing political challenges, starting with the Islamist-led insurrection of the late 1990s and continuing through today's protests of youth who feel marginalized from the country's politics and economics. The Islamist insurrection, which has been led by various groups since its inception, continues but is now contained to the northern Kabylie mountain regions and the southern Saharan provinces because of a successful government counterinsurgency program. The youth-led demonstrations, some of which have been substantial in size, accelerated in Algeria after the success of the Tunisian and Egyptian revolutions. To this date, however, these demonstrations have not led to revolution.

Morocco joins Tunisia and Algeria in trending toward decreased fertility and an aging population, which is projected to have a median age of 34 by 2030, in contrast to the current median age of 26.3. The population pyramid for Morocco (Figure 2.7) is most similar to Tunisia's pyramid, especially in the 0–4, 5–9, and 10–14 age cohorts, and less dramatic (in terms of contraction at the lower end of the age spectrum) than Algeria's. All three

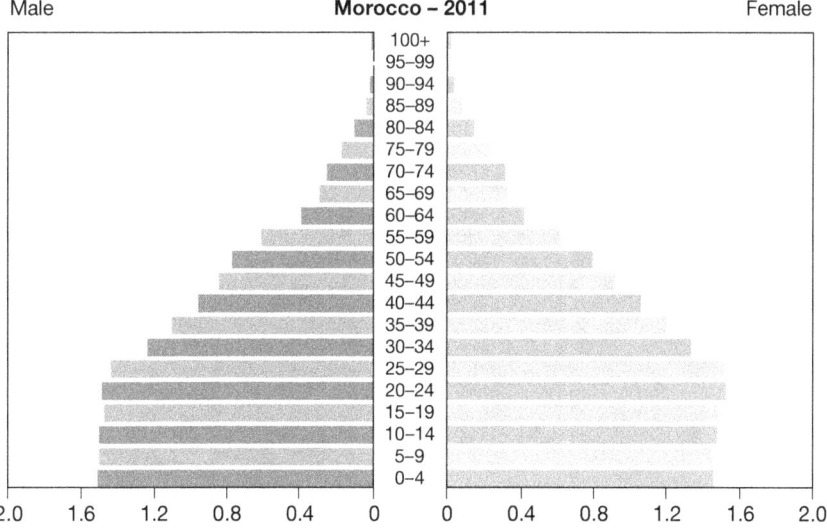

Figure 2.7 Morocco population pyramid

countries—Morocco, Algeria, and Tunisia—are trending older, which means that they will be demographically less prone to political volatility as the population ages. The bulk of Morocco's population lies in the 15–39 age range, which may create a more active community interested in more immediate political change. Unlike the revolutionary movements in Tunisia, Egypt, and Libya, the youth movement in Morocco has demonstrated in favor of placing constitutional constraints upon the monarchy, rather than demanding a revolution that would displace the existing regime.

Politics and economics

Iranian analyst Richard Javan Heydarian has observed:

> Revolutions rarely happen in stagnant, destitute countries. Recent history shows that revolutions are most likely to occur in countries that experience a long period of unprecedented economic growth not accompanied by political reform or that undergo a sudden economic crisis followed by a sustained period of economic expansion. In the context of rising expectations and relative deprivation, the masses—mobilized by opposition forces—gradually withdraw their support of the regime, step outside of their comfort zones, and increasingly embrace the opportunities and challenges of revolutionary upheavals.[2]

This observation is applicable to a number of revolutions, including the Iranian Revolution of 1979, the fall of the Suharto regime during the Asian financial crisis of 1997, and the present revolutions and mass protests in North Africa. Within this section, we will provide two sets of data that will document how many of the North African economies grew substantially during the first decade of the twentieth century without producing an increase in youth employment opportunities in real terms. Table 2.4 documents

Table 2.4 GDP growth rate: North Africa (2000–2010)

	Tunisia	*Egypt*	*Libya*	*Algeria*	*Morocco*
2000	4.3	5.38	3.7	2.15	1.6
2001	4.85	3.52	–4.33	2.7	7.6
2002	1.7	3.19	–1.25	4.7	3.3
2003	5.47	3.19	13	6.9	6.32
2004	5.99	4.09	4.4	5.2	4.8
2005	4	4.47	10.29	5.1	2.98
2006	5.65	6.8	6.71	2	7.76
2007	6.26	7.08	7.5	3	2.7
2008	4.52	7.16	2.35	2.4	5.59
2009	3.1	4.67	–2.31	2.38	4.94
2010	3.69	5.14	4.16	3.33	3.15

Source: International Monetary Fund, www.imf.org/external/data.htm.

Table 2.5 Youth unemployment (ages 15–29) in North Africa (2008)

Tunisia	27.3%
Egypt	21.7%
Libya	27.4%
Algeria	45.6%
Morocco	18.3%

Note: Figures for Algeria are for 2006, the last date for which data are available.

economic growth rates in our five cases from 2000 until 2010. Table 2.5 documents rates of youth unemployment in our five countries.

As these data demonstrate, with the exception of Libya (whose data volatility makes it an outlier within the dataset), economic growth accelerated rapidly in three countries—Tunisia, Egypt, and Morocco—and to a much lesser extent in Algeria. All these countries grew substantially in economic terms without liberalizing their politics or expanding employment opportunities for youth, which may have created "perfect storm" conditions for a revolution. The data for Libya are so volatile that they do not establish any trend. It is also important to sound several notes of warning regarding the data. First, Algeria's growth rates are considerably less robust than those of Tunisia, Egypt, and Morocco. Second, the growth rates for Morocco are quite high, like Tunisia and Egypt, but in contrast to these two states, Morocco's period of robust growth begins in 2006 rather than 2003. Finally, Morocco's reversals in 2007 can be explained at least partially by the incidence of a considerable drought in the country that year. All things being equal, the data indicate that Morocco should be the second most vulnerable state in the region after Libya. It remains to be seen whether King Mohammed VI's constitutional reforms of June 2011 will be extensive enough or sufficiently well timed to reverse the general trends of revolution and rebellion in the region.

While these regional economies were expanding, the opportunities for youth employment were contracting. In August 2010, just before the 2011 revolutions and rebellions, the International Labour Organization published a report called Global Trends for Youth that stated: "More than 20 per cent of the youth labour force in the Middle East and North Africa in 2008 was unable to find jobs."[3] Raw data obtained from the ILO website[4] enabled us to recalculate youth employment rates for our five cases. These calculations were then confirmed by alternate data analyses available at the Wolfensohn Center for Development at the Brookings Institution.[5]

The combination of rapid economic growth, declining job prospects for youth, and the lack of political liberalization throughout the region created close to ideal conditions for either revolution or rebellion—provided first that a spark could be furnished (ultimately supplied by the self-immolation of Mohamed Bouazizi in Tunisia) and provided that youth had methods of organization that could elude government control. Cell phone text messages, Facebook, and Twitter provided youth with these means of resistance.

Youth mobilization via cell phones, Facebook, and Twitter

Many have asserted that the availability of internet communication via Facebook and Twitter and cell phone text capabilities played an important role in the organization of the revolutions in Tunisia and Egypt and the large demonstrations in Algeria and Morocco. Cell phone accessibility was very wide in Libya, but internet accessibility and Facebook participation in that country were quite small. One important issue that needs analysis is the comparative utility of cell phone usage, internet usage, and face-to-face communication in the organization of social protests. Technology has played important roles in contemporary revolutions—particularly the telegraph in the 1917 Russian Revolution, audio cassette tapes in the 1979 Iranian Revolution, and fax machines in the 1989 Eastern European revolutions—and so it is important to determine these new technologies' comparative utility in the context of the protests in the Arab world. Analysis of our data and on-the-ground investigations lead us to conclude that while Facebook did play a role in these various social movements, cell phone text messages, use of Twitter on cell phones, and face-to-face communications were more important factors. Figure 2.8 displays data on cell phone usage across our five cases.

These data reveal that mobile cellular telephone subscriptions sky-rocketed in North Africa between 2002 and 2007. Subscriptions jumped from 5.9 percent to 75.9 percent of the population in Tunisia, from 6.4 percent to 39.8 percent in Egypt, from 1.3 percent to 73.1 percent in Libya, from 1.4 percent to 81.4 percent in Algeria, and from 20.6 percent to 64.1 percent in Morocco. These percentages (except for the case of Egypt) reveal the widespread availability of cell phones in these countries, which, along with face-to-face

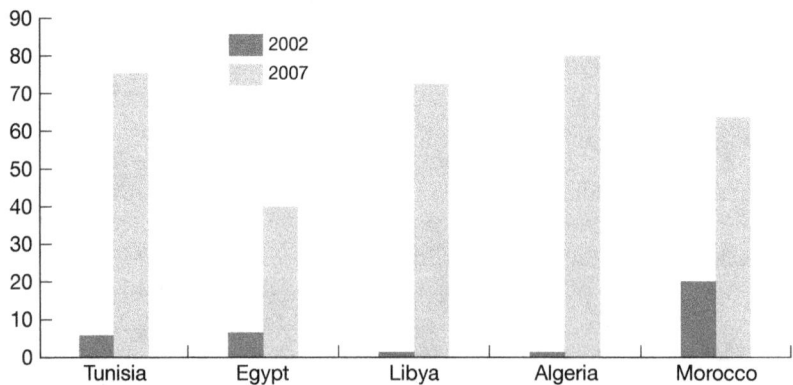

Figure 2.8 Mobile cellular subscriptions (per 100) in North Africa

communications, became the primary means of information dissemination for protest organizers.

By contrast, despite claims that the Tunisian[6] and Egyptian revolutions were "Facebook revolutions," the data reveal a different story, in which internet participation was comparatively high in Tunisia and Morocco (and only significant in Tunisia) and less prevalent elsewhere. Our data and on-the-ground interviews support the contention that of all of these North African revolts, only the revolt in Tunisia was facilitated by Facebook. Our data and interviews do not support the contention that Facebook played a large role in the other revolts (Egypt and Libya) or large protests (Algeria and Morocco) in the region. Figure 2.9 displays information on internet and Facebook usage in these five countries in 2011.

These data reveal that Tunisia's internet usage rate was the second highest in the region at 33.9 percent (only exceeded by Morocco, at 41.3 percent), and its Facebook usage rate was the highest in the region, at 24.5 percent. This level of Facebook usage explains why Tunisians resorted to Facebook, tweeting, and texting on cell phones to organize their demonstrations.

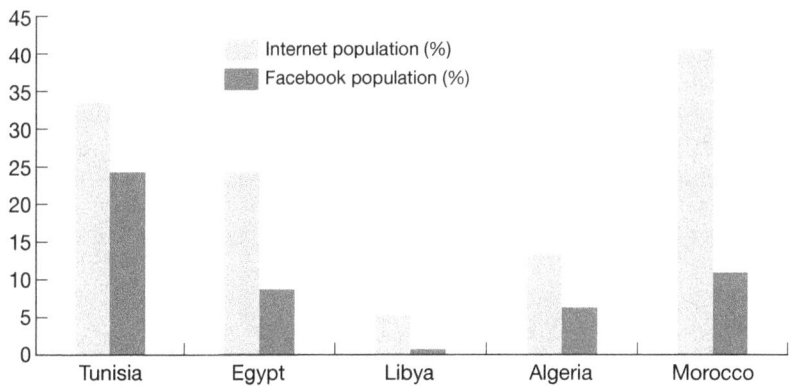

Figure 2.9 Internet and Facebook participation rates: North Africa (2011)

Table 2.6 Internet and Facebook participation rates for North Africa

	Total population (2011)	Internet population	Facebook population
Tunisia	10,629,186	3,600,000 (33.9%)	2,602,640 (24.5%)
Egypt	82,079,636	20,136,000 (24.5%)	7,295,240 (8.9%)
Libya	6,97,960	353,900 (5.4%)	52,860 (0.8%)
Algeria	34,994,937	4,700,000 (13.4%)	2,293,560 (6.6%)
Morocco	31,968,361	13,213,000 (41.3%)	3,596,320 (11.2%)

Source: Internet World Stats, Usage and Population Statistics, www.internetworldstats.com/africa.htm#tn.

Access to these various technologies also explains the rapidity with which the revolutionaries in Tunisia were able to organize and mobilize their forces for protest and then revolt. These data and the accounts given by participants in the Tunisian revolt reveal that only in Tunisia was Facebook comparatively important. In all the remaining cases of revolt and protest, cell phone text messages, Twitter, and face-to-face communication were more important.

Conclusion

Revolution, rebellion, and liberation seem to have finally arrived in North Africa, the Levant, and the Arabian Peninsula. A region that once seemed immune to change—and whose authoritarian regimes had been sustained by the United States and the European Community in the interests of security and geopolitical stability—has crumbled in a twinkling of an eye. Ben Ali—gone! Mubarak—gone! Qaddafi—gone! Other authoritarian regimes in the region worry about whether they can withstand the demands of youth who yearn for meaningful employment, freedom of expression, and meaningful inclusion in participatory politics. Given their numbers, the youth of North Africa, the Levant, and the Arabian Peninsula constitute a demographic force that will be difficult to deny. Their numbers are plentiful, they are impatient, and the success of the models of revolt used in Tunisia, Egypt, and Libya are urging them on. Lacking fear; desirous of the restoration of dignity; and armed with faith, hope, cell phones, and laptops, they have made the old authoritarian guard quiver. A regional revolution has begun. The end is not yet in sight.

Notes

1 See Thomas Malthus, *Essay on the Principle of Populations* (London: J. Johnson, 1798); Jack Goldstone, *Revolution and Rebellion in the Early Modern World* (Berkeley: University of California Press, 1993); Gunnar Heinsohn, *Söhne und Weltmacht: Terror in Aufsteg und Fall der Nationen* [Brotherhood and World Power: Terror in the Rise and Fall of Nations] (Munich: Piper, 2008); Christian Mesquida and Neil I. Wiener, "Male Age Composition and Severity of Conflicts," *Politics and the Life Sciences*, 18 (September 1999): 181–189; Herbert Möller, "Youth as a Social Force in the Modern World," *Comparative Studies in Society and History*, 10:3 (1968): 237–260; Henrik Urdal and Kristian Hoelscher, "Urban Youth Bulges and Social Disorder: An Empirical Study of Asian and Sub-Saharan African Cities," World Bank Policy Research Working Paper 5110, November 2009; Henrik Urdal, "The Devil in the Demographics: The Effect of Youth Bulges on Domestic Armed Conflict, 1950–2000," paper presented at the Peace Research Institute Oslo conference, New Orleans, March 24–27, 2002.
2 Richard Javad Heydarian, "The Economics of the Arab Spring," *Foreign Policy in Focus*, April 21, 2011, www.fpif.org/articles/the_economics_of_the_arab_spring.
3 International Labour Organization, *Global Trends for Youth*, August 2010, p. 4, www.ilo.org/wcmsp5/groups/public/—ed_emp/—emp_elm/—trends/documents/publication/wcms_143349.pdf.

4 International Labour Organization, www.ilo.org/global/research/global-reports/global-employment-trends/lang–en/index.htm.
5 Brookings Institution, "Understanding the Generation in Waiting in the Middle East," www.brookings.edu/research/books/2009/agenerationinwaiting.
6 See the account of the Tunisian revolution elsewhere in this book.

3 The Tunisian revolution
The revolution of dignity
Amira Aleya-Sghaier

Introduction

Writing the history of a revolution in progress is a difficult task. It is even more difficult when the author was himself involved in this revolution. I do not claim a prominent role in its leadership—I simply meant to participate humbly in my people's march for freedom. And while I reject any claim to neutrality, I deemed it a duty to maintain objectivity in writing the chapter that follows. However, the task to which I am devoted faces an additional difficulty regarding the availability of sources. The opacity of the police state of Tunisia's former dictator and president Zine El Abidine Ben Ali has not facilitated the task. The sources for this article are diverse, including both written materials and events that were personally experienced. The testimony provided here is corroborated by a wide array of information gleaned from various media outlets, as well as the testimony of militants.

The first miracle of this revolution was that it toppled a police dictatorship. In less than a month of struggle, the people deposed their despot. Ben Ali fled the country on January 14, 2011. The second miracle was that the revolution did not plunge the country into terror. Rather, the peaceful nature of the revolutionary process convinced Tunisians that their nation would succeed in establishing democracy and restoring dignity to its people.

The Tunisian revolution is particular to Tunisia. It was not a classical revolution like the French Revolution, with a transition from a feudal to a *bourgeois* regime. It was not a communist class-driven revolution like the 1917 Bolshevik Revolution in Russia. Nor was it a national liberation revolution like those of Vietnam and Algeria, or a revolution for human rights like the Eastern European revolutions of the 1990s. The Tunisian revolution was unique. It was neither red nor orange nor jasmine; it was a "revolution of dignity." It was special because it was spontaneous, lacking a centralized leadership, a clear ideology, or any pre-established political program. It was a revolution of all the Tunisian people. It was also the first revolution of this century that employed the internet and television on a large scale.

I have divided this historical survey of the "revolution of dignity" into six parts: the causes of the revolution, the process and slogans of the revolution, the actors of the revolution, the army and the police in the revolution, the Tunisian revolution in the world, and the achievements and perspectives of the revolution.

The causes of the revolution

The explosion of anger that grew into a revolutionary whirlwind that spread beyond the borders of Tunisia to other Arab countries began on December 17, 2010. The trigger for this explosion was the dramatic suicide of Mohamed Bouazizi, a 26-year-old fruit and vegetable street vendor. On December 17, Bouazizi was selling his wares without official authorization from governmental authorities when agents of the municipality of Sidi Bouzid, where he was residing, confiscated his scales and goods. One official slapped Bouazizi, which affronted his dignity and resulted in his desperate cry for justice. In response to this physical and psychological attack, he immolated himself in the street outside of the provincial governor's headquarters. On January 4, 2011, he died in the trauma and burns unit of a hospital in Ben Arous.

His suicide provided a spark to a social situation in Tunisia that was ready to explode. The first protest began the same day that Bouazizi immolated himself—December 17, 2010—in Sidi Bouzid, a city in Tunisia's midwestern region, and eventually engulfed the rest of the country.

The revolution that began in Sidi Bouzid can be seen as part of a longer process of popular uprisings that originated in the Gafsa mining region of Tunisia in 2008 that was brutally crushed by the government. The Gafsa uprising was followed by a revolt in Ben Gardane, on the southern border with Libya, in August 2010. These regions provided the first indications that Tunisia was ripe for revolution or revolt. The midwest (including Sidi Bouzid and Kasserine) and the south (including Gafsa, Kebili, and Medenine) were also the most disadvantaged regions of Tunisia.

In contrast, the coastal areas of Tunisia, as a result of both historical reasons and unjust regional policies, had grown economically at the expense of other regions. For example, although the coastal region (the provinces of Sousse, Monastir, and Mahdia) comprised less than 14.4 percent of the Tunisian population in 2010, it had more infrastructure, social facilities, factories, hotels, and universities than all the provinces of the midwest and south (Sidi Bouzid, Kasserine, Gafsa, Kebili, Tozeur, Medenine, Tataouine). These disadvantaged regions comprised more than 70 percent of the landmass of Tunisia and were home to 19.3 percent of its population in 2010, but they always suffered from a lack of investment. By 2010, the sense of injustice and marginalization in the midwest and south had become unbearable.

Although poverty in Tunisia greatly declined between 1990 and 2003, a large percentage of the country's poor continued to reside in the rural midwest and south and in smaller pockets in the north. The contrast between rich and poor areas is clearly evident when one examines per capita governmental annual expenditures. In 1990, the average annual expenditure per person for the whole of Tunisia was 716 dinars per person, but in Sidi Bouzid, this number did not exceed 437 dinars.[1] In Kasserine in 2002, 11.12 percent of families did not have a steady income. In 2004, Kasserine's illiteracy rate was 33 percent (and 56.7 percent in the case of women), whereas the national level of illiteracy was 20 percent.[2] The consequence of this unequal development has been that these disadvantaged areas have sent their inhabitants outwards—either to the coastal cities or overseas. Furthermore, high fertility rates in the midwest and the south had worsened these regions' levels of unemployment.

Besides factors of regional and social imbalance, another major factor leading to the ignition of the Tunisian revolution involved the "youth bulge." In 2010, 42 percent of Tunisians were under 25 years of age. Even the educated youth were left without any future. Youth from poor or affluent backgrounds faced despair. Studying and earning higher degrees did not guarantee the improvement of living conditions. According to a March 2008 World Bank report, unemployment was on the rise even among university graduates; in 2006–2007, 336,000 graduates of a higher education institution were unemployed, compared to 121,800 in 1996–1997.[3] A 2005 survey of about 4,800 graduates revealed that almost half of the master's degree holders and technicians interviewed were unemployed. Despite the routine falsification of figures by Ben Ali's government, unemployment was worsening in the years leading up to the revolution. According to official figures, the unemployment rate was 13.2 percent in 2010,[4] but the actual number was much higher, with youth unemployment being estimated at between 40 and 60 percent for 2009 graduates. "This means that for this category, the misery index was close to 70 percent. We can, therefore, understand how the frustration of youth led to massive participation in the revolution, especially in the deprived areas of the country."[5]

The global economic crisis and the closure of all forms of legal emigration to Europe accentuated the confusion of Tunisian youth and compelled them to struggle against Ben Ali's regime. The revelations that the internet provided about the degree of luxury in which the privileged members of the regime lived (villas, private jets, palaces, luxury cars, private clubs, bank accounts in Tunisia and abroad) deepened feelings of hatred among Tunisian youth toward their rulers.

In reality, after 23 years of absolute power and plunder, the regime of Ben Ali ended up uniting the whole society it governed against it, except for those individuals it had privileged. The victims of the regime were not only the youth or Tunisians living in the inland areas. All social and professional categories were more or less harmed by the mafia system that Ben Ali created.

The US ambassador to Tunisia regarded the Ali regime as a "quasi-mafia" and, in a top-secret report uncovered by Wikileaks, noted:

> Tunisia has big problems. President Ben Ali is aging, his regime is sclerotic and there is no clear successor. Many Tunisians are frustrated by the lack of political freedom and angered by First Family corruption, high unemployment and regional inequities. Extremism poses a continuing threat. Tunisia is a police state, with little freedom of expression or

association, and serious human rights problems. For every step forward there has been another back, for example the recent takeover of important private media outlets by individuals close to President Ben Ali.

[Ben Ali] and his regime have lost touch with the Tunisian people. They tolerate no advice or criticism, whether domestic or international. Increasingly, they rely on the police for control and focus on preserving power. And, corruption in the inner circle is growing. Even average Tunisians are now keenly aware of it, and the chorus of complaints is rising. Tunisians intensely dislike, even hate, First Lady Leila Trabelsi and her family. In private, regime opponents mock her; even those close to the government express dismay at her reported behavior. Meanwhile, anger is growing at Tunisia's high unemployment and regional inequities. As a consequence, the risks to the regime's long-term stability are increasing.[6]

The US diplomat's description of the Ben Ali regime as a police state was no exaggeration. With the complicity of Western countries and under the pretext of combating fundamentalism, Ben Ali had turned his country into a large prison. Between 120,000 and 150,000 police officers regularly crisscrossed the country, far exceeding the number of police officers in France, whose population is five times larger than Tunisia's. The party in power, the Rally for Constitutional Democracy (RCD), used its 2 million members to supplement and support the Ministry of the Interior by spying on people and hunting down party opponents. In many neighborhoods, Ben Ali's agents spied on the population using what the regime called "neighborhood committees." Ben Ali used the justice system for his own purposes, prosecuting political opponents, trade unionists, students, journalists, and human rights defenders.

To create a democratic façade, Ben Ali created political parties that participated in so-called legislative assemblies. The regime managed to corrupt some of the political elite by providing bonuses and privileges that were not available to the general populace. It also tried to control the working class by bribing the leaders of the Tunisian General Labour Union (UGTT), the only trade union in the country. Nevertheless, other social, professional, and civic organizations continued to resist the regime, particularly the Tunisian League for Human Rights (the oldest such association in Africa, founded in 1976), the Association of Lawyers, and the Association of Judges.

In the economic sphere, Ben Ali and his allies created a minority mafia of families who privatized national companies, especially businesses in the telecommunications, transport, and cement industries, for their own enrichment. State financial services were made available to these families to promote their businesses. The president's wife, in complicity with the governor of the Central Bank, allegedly stole one-and-a-half tons of gold from the bank's reserves. This mafia clan extorted money from business owners in several ways, including threats of prosecution by the government's tax department.

Ben Ali and his accomplices among the Trabelsi, Chiboub, Matri, and Mabrouk families constituted a mafia that ruled Tunisia until January 14,

2011. To some extent they are still in control, especially in the sectors of banking, commerce, transportation, food, petroleum, cement, construction, and agriculture.

The progress of the revolution

The Tunisian revolt began on December 17, 2010, when the self-immolation of Bouazizi evolved into a revolution that toppled the dictator Ben Ali and led to his flight to Saudi Arabia on January 14, 2011. The details of the events of the revolution are developed in the timeline that accompanies this section. The evolution of the revolution can be summarized in three stages.

Stage one: the beginning of the revolution

The insurrection began in Sidi Bouzid with demonstrations, strikes, the closure of stores, and clashes with the police. The discord then spread to neighboring areas, including Menzel Bouzaiane, Ben Aoun, Jelma, and Meknassi Regueb. The rebellion spread first to the west, especially to the city of Kasserine, and then to the southern cities of Gafsa and Kebili. Unlike the revolt of Redeyef in 2008, the regime failed to contain the rebellion or impose a media or internet blackout. Young people used mobile phones, the internet, social networks, and satellite channels to keep the uprising in the public eye and succeeded especially in exposing the repressive measures of the police, including the deliberate killing of young demonstrators, mass arrests, and collective punishment. The regime was powerless to contain the rebellion, despite its mobilization of the police forces, RCD Party militias, and the army. The obvious failure of the regime to handle the situation on either the ground or on the political and media levels led to the spread of the revolution throughout the country. The protests spread to the northern cities of Jendouba, Béja, and Bizerte and the southern cities of Kebili, Degueche, Tozeur, El Hamma, Medenine, and Zarzis before proceeding to Sfax, Tunisia's second largest city, and cities of the coast (Sousse, Monastir, and Chebba) before finally arriving at the capital, Tunis.

The massive Tunis demonstration of January 14, 2011, was a historic and decisive moment in the history of the Tunisian revolution. This demonstration started in Mohammad Ali Square near the headquarters of the UGTT trade union and grew to occupy all of Habib Bourguiba Avenue in the center of Tunis, where tens of thousands of Tunisians, young and old, unemployed and employed, and from all social and professional groups, including teachers, students, pupils, lawyers, merchants, employees, and civil servants, cried in unison in front of the Ministry of the Interior: "Step down! Step down!" On the evening of Friday, January 14, the national Tunisian television station TVM announced that President Ben Ali had been temporarily deposed, and that Prime Minister Mohamed Ghannouchi had replaced him, pursuant to Article 56 of the Tunisian Constitution. The following day, a dramatic turn of events took place. The Constitutional Council declared that Article 57 of the Constitution had been invoked, making Fouad Mebazaa, the president of the Chamber of Deputies, the acting president. That evening, Ben Ali arrived in Jeddah, Saudi Arabia, where he has since been living in exile.

Stage two: January 14–March 4, 2011

Initially, Ben Ali's political allies (the police, the Ministry of the Interior, the RCD, and some elements of the army) continued to operate as though nothing had happened. They believed that the revolution was nothing more than a popular uprising that had ousted the president but had not displaced the political system. The Ghannouchi government and its RCD ministers promised to elect a new president within 60 days, ignoring the aspirations of the people who led the revolution. The popular insurrection then became radicalized. Demonstrations, strikes, and sit-ins in Tunis and the interior of the country were organized and coordinated by people's committees called "Revolutionary Safeguard Committees." These committees were elected by the revolutionaries on the spot to ensure the safety of citizens, especially during the first 60 days after the ousting of Ben Ali, when armed and uncontrolled militias engaged in looting, arson, robbery, and murder around the nation, sowing terror among the population. These crimes were generally attributed to members of the Presidential Guard, who were eager to seek revenge for the arrest of their leader, General Seriate, on January 14, 2011. These security professionals intended to create chaos and disorder in an effort to bring Ben Ali and his wife back into power. Although the revolutionary forces asked the government to account for these counterrevolutionary activities and demanded the trial of those responsible, the government did nothing.

This second phase of the revolution was marked by two important acts. First, young people from the interior of the country came to Tunis in "caravans of freedom." These young people, in coordination with the revolutionary committees, occupied the prime minister's offices in a large sit-in that lasted from January 23 to January 28, 2011. This sit-in disrupted the operation of the government, which consequently arrested and expelled the protesters from the prime minister's offices. A second sit-in, which was better organized and better represented by various political and professional organizations, including the Union Générale Tunisienne des Travailleurs (UGTT) and the Association of Lawyers, occupied the Kasbah from February 20 to March 4, 2011, and managed to bring down the Ghannouchi government, which the revolutionaries considered a mere extension of the deposed dictator.

Stage three

After the deposition of the Ghannouchi government, the third stage of the revolution began with the appointment of former Bourguiba Minister, Beji Caid Essebsi, as prime minister. Essebsi's government was composed of technocrats and did not include ministers affiliated with the previously dominant RCD Party, which was held in contempt by the forces of the revolution.

The transitional government's duty was to manage the state's daily affairs and prepare for National Assembly elections, which the sit-ins and popular forces had succeeded in imposing on the government on March 3. To meet the people's demands and prevent the further radicalization of the revolution, three transitional management commissions were established, chaired by persons close to the government: the Commission on Law Reform, chaired by Yadh Ben Achour, an independent jurist; the Commission of Inquiry on Corruption, chaired by Abdelfattah Amor, an RCD lawyer close to Ben Ali; and the Independent Commission of Inquiry chaired by lawyer Taoufik Bouderbala, which was charged with investigation of the role that security forces played in the bloody suppression of protests. This last commission was later disbanded.

On February 11, leftist groups (Marxists and Arab nationalists in particular), the Islamist movement al-Nahda, and representatives of the UGTT, the Association of Lawyers, and the Association of Judges of the Tunisian League of Human Rights united to set up the National Council for the Protection of the Revolution. To weaken this revolutionary body, Essebsi created the High Committee for the Achievement of the Objectives of the Revolution on March 14, 2011. This committee, which incorporated Ben Achour's Commission on Law Reform under its umbrella, was at first composed of 71 persons representing political parties, civil society organizations, and national associations. The number of members was later doubled after criticism was leveled at the committee's lack of representativeness. Because it did not have decision-making power, the sole task of the High Committee was to assist the government and suggest legislation. Committee legislation was submitted to the interim government, which then had the right to refuse or accept it. Opponents, however, considered the Committee essentially to be a move by Essebsi's government to sabotage the National Council for the Protection of the Revolution, and it was therefore never recognized as representative of the people who had participated in the revolution.

The Committee drafted a law for the election of the next Constituent Assembly, which was adopted by the government and published on May 7, 2011. These elections, initially scheduled for July 24, 2011, were postponed until October 23, because the High Committee for Elections, chaired by Kamel Jendoubi, declared that it was unable to guarantee a "transparent and pluralistic democratic election" on the scheduled date of July 24.

Violence and nonviolence in the Tunisian revolution

Frederick Engels has observed that "violence is the midwife of history."[7] The American Revolution (1776–1783), the French Revolution of 1789, the Bolshevik Revolution of 1917, and the national liberation revolutions of the colonized countries were all violent. The Tunisian revolution was different because peaceful resistance brought down the regime.

The Tunisian revolution was peaceful for the most part. However, the regime consistently practiced violence while the violence of the masses was epiphenomenal. The revolution had recourse to neither armed revolutionaries nor partisan guerrillas. After its success, the nation did not experience a vengeful wave of terror with accompanying revolutionary courts and public executions. Not all Tunisians participated in the revolution; it was a revolution of youth and the popular classes.

During the first months of the revolution, the revolutionary masses acted peacefully through demonstrations, marches, sit-ins, strikes, building occupations, roadblocks, and the establishment of camps in front of the ministries. Their weapons were their voices, which shouted their slogans; their banners, which made their claims known; and their graffiti, which marked their existence.

The regime's counterrevolutionary violence

Violence has been an integral part of the expression of political power in Tunisia since the nation gained independence in 1956. The new state of Tunisia was established through violence. Bourguiba's regime was preserved by the repression and exclusion of its opponents. Established in an atmosphere of fear, executions, trials, and torture, the so-called "modern" state created by Bourguiba and his successor Ben Ali was modern in nothing but its façade. All the government's ministries, meetings, and legislation concealed a medieval despotism. The use of violence to counter popular demands was systemic.

After the outbreak of the revolution on December 17, 2010, the regime's violence gradually increased. The use of gas and batons as a means of repression gave way to the use of live bullets against demonstrators. The massacre of the protesters was deliberately ordered by the ousted president and his advisors, and judicial investigations have since revealed that Ben Ali also planned to bomb the rebellious town of Kasserine.[8] Special police units and snipers aimed at protestors' chests and heads when shooting.

The police forces were the first group involved in the perpetration of violence. The army was then asked to join the police in quelling the revolution but initially refused; this issue will be discussed in more detail later. The RCD militia was a significant third actor involved in the violence. This party, which had ruled the country since independence in 1956, always had its own militia. Members were recruited from the lower classes and criminal gangs and, working upon the direction of party leaders, were mobilized to smash, spy on, and terrorize opponents.

As crowds besieged the Ministry of the Interior in Tunis on January 14, 2011, the RCD leaders had at their disposal more than 600 militiamen in the party headquarters on the adjacent Mohammed V Avenue.[9] The militiamen were there to offer help to the Minister of the Interior in cracking down on the protesters. These militias raged throughout the country in coordination with the leaders of the RCD, who patrolled the country and were responsible for much of the revolution's violence. In the days that followed Ben Ali's flight on January 14, police forces were unable to secure civil order, leading to an atmosphere of anarchy and insecurity. The situation would have become catastrophic without the intervention of the army.

Between December 17, 2010, and January 14, 2011, more than 330 people were killed and 700 injured as a result of counterrevolutionary violence.[10] The majority of victims were shot dead at the site of protest, and a minority (72) were either asphyxiated or shot dead while attempting to escape from prisons such as Monastir, Mahdia, Kasserine, Bizerte, and Gafsa. Other acts of violence perpetrated by the police and the militias included the kidnapping of opponents and the torture and rape of women. Some cases of rape were recorded at Kasserine and Regueb.[11]

Counterrevolutionary violence continued for five months after the fall of Ben Ali. Fires and their depredations affected both public establishments—such as schools, administrative buildings, and police stations—and private property such as factories and farms. However, compared with other Arab revolutions in progress at the time, the Tunisian revolution produced fewer victims. In Egypt, at least 840 were killed and 6,000 wounded during the 15 demonstrations that led to the fall of Hosni Mubarak.[12] In Yemen, Libya, and Syria, hundreds and perhaps thousands have been killed.

The violence of the masses: a revolutionary violence

Frantz Fanon argues in *The Wretched of the Earth* that the oppressed are liberated by the exercise of violence, and the infliction of pain on their oppressors is a step on the path toward healing the suffering of their bodies and souls.[13] The youth of the Tunisian revolution never used formal weapons, and no victims died at their hands. In extreme cases, some participants threw stones or used batons to defend themselves in clashes with security forces or to punish individuals deemed dangerous to their cause. Two types of violence were committed by the Tunisian masses during the revolution: violence as an instrument of vengeance in pursuit of dignity and violence as an instrument of vengeance against social injustice.

Offended by long years of dictatorship, the masses set fire to and pillaged buildings that symbolized the regime, particularly in January 2011. RCD Party premises were burned or damaged. Some headquarters were renamed "People's House" or "House of the Revolution." Government buildings, especially police and *gendarmerie* stations, were damaged, with several stations being burned and their documents pillaged by jubilant rebels.

This violence, which sought to restore dignity to the people, targeted the regime's henchmen and never degenerated into bloodshed. Police officers, leaders of RCD cells, delegates, governors, members of parliament, and ministers were directly or indirectly humiliated and condemned as torturers, thieves, and traitors. Some governors were driven out of their offices by angry mobs. Entrepreneurs and other officials were similarly expelled by their employees, who chanted, "Step down! Step down!" Some individuals who were known to be members of militias or police informers were beaten severely, although no murders were recorded. However, such acts of violence were not frequent. They expressed a deep hatred of the dictatorship and a real desire to overthrow the dictatorial regime.

Violence was also employed to avenge the unfair distribution of wealth in Tunisia. Throughout the entire country, angry masses pillaged goods that were considered to have been acquired illicitly. Almost all the palaces of the ruling families (including those of the Trabelsi, Ben Ali, Materi, and Chiboub families) were looted and burned in Tunis, Hammamet, Sousse, and elsewhere. Shops, warehouses, and luxury cars that belonged to the ruling elite were burned as symbolic acts. Large department stores in Tunis and elsewhere were looted or burned. According to the perpetrators, looting consumer goods was not stealing; rather, it was a way of taking the law into their own hands and regaining those things of which they had been unjustly deprived.

The protagonists of the Tunisian revolution

The Tunisian revolution started as a geographically specific social movement and developed into a revolution that encompassed the whole country. From Sidi Bouzid, the revolution spread out across the country, rallying angry, mostly unemployed youth. It inflamed children and disadvantaged youth and then spread to the middle class. Social, professional, and political groups such as unionists, lawyers, students, judges, doctors, and political parties all eventually contributed to the revolution. At its inception, however, the youth were the key protagonists.

Youth as the spearhead of the revolution

The phrase "youth revolution" is a correct description of this revolution. Young Tunisians were and still are the most fervent group carrying the flag of the revolution. They were its initiators, propagandists, and primary protagonists. Who were they?

They were mostly young, unemployed, or informal workers; students; civil servants; itinerant peddlers; and marginalized and excluded individuals. They were not all from the same social background, although the poorer young people of the housing estates of Kasserine, Sfax, Sousse, and Tunis were the most numerous in the theater of operations of protests. Indeed, it was in these cities that the major confrontations with the police took place. Even before the outbreak of the revolution, young people had organized themselves into networks that were based on residence in the same neighborhood; support for the same sports team; or, for those who had recently moved to the city, origin in the same region. These networks created relationships of solidarity and self-defense. Participating in or supporting sports teams were often the only outlets available to young people to express themselves and let off steam; as a result of these activities, urban youth were experienced in chanting martial songs and fighting in groups.

The police had never been welcomed in these neighborhoods, where young people combated boredom by sitting in cafés, hoping to cross to the other shore of the Mediterranean. These youth were determined to fight with the police and the Ben Ali regime. Because of their background, they were more sensitive to the social inequalities perpetuated by the Ben Ali regime. They involved themselves in the revolution as if it were a matter of life or death, but they acted without an ideology or a pre-established political program.

The youth of the *bourgeois* areas were also actively involved in the revolution, albeit to a lesser degree. In Tunis, the youth of the Manzah, Manar, Ariana, La Marsa, and Carthage neighborhoods in particular contributed to the revolution. The children of the wealthy were uncomfortable with the regime too. Their future in Ben Ali's Tunisia was insecure despite their higher education. Although these youth were connected to what was happening in the Western world, they nevertheless lived badly. These youths rejected a political system that appeared far removed from what they saw on their television screens.

Social networks were the way out for these young people. They were a useful means for establishing friendships and encountering other ideas. Despite the fact that these young people were indifferent to ideology and a politically engaged life, they aspired to greater freedom and emancipation. These wealthy young people became active participants in the revolution through the internet and Facebook in particular, attempting to bring the revolution to the web and keep themselves and others informed so that they could engage in collective action. Comparatively well-off youth were also present during the January 2011 demonstrations that took place on Avenue Bourguiba. Sometimes they organized rallies in their respective cities, but they never entered into direct confrontation with the police. None of the victims of the Tunisian revolution came from the nation's well-off areas. Nevertheless, whether rich or poor, unemployed or employed, from the capital or from cities in the interior of Tunisia, these young revolutionaries were sympathetic to each other and united in one aim: the deposition of the dictator.

It is important to note the high percentage of youth among those killed in the revolution, demonstrating the youth's role as its predominant protagonists. A definitive and comprehensive set of death statistics is still lacking, but the figure of 300 killed provided by UN special adviser Juan Méndez seems plausible.[14] A survey conducted during the revolution shows that the individuals killed came from areas distributed across the country, with a high percentage from the towns of the midwest and the metropolitan Tunis region. For example, six came from Sidi Bouzid, 20 from Kasserine, three from Degueche, four from Kebili (southwest region), three from Zarzis, one from Djerba (southeast region), two from El Hamma (south region), one from Sfax, and two from Sahline (Sahel region). The highest number of

Table 3.1 Individuals killed from Tunis and the suburbs

Age	Number of deaths
19	1
20	2
21	3
23	2
24	4
25	5
26	2
30	1
31	1
32	1
34	3
35	1
36	2
38	1
44	1
45	1
46	1
63	1

deaths was registered in Tunis, where 33 people were shot dead. These figures exclude people killed in prison which constitute about a quarter of the total number of recorded deaths. A sample study of deaths of individuals from the city and the suburbs of Tunis confirms the young profile of the revolution's actors. Table 3.1 shows the range of ages of the 33 individuals killed, as published by *Echchourouk* newspaper on January 25, 2011.

The majority of individuals killed were between 19 and 35 years of age, with an average age of 29.6 years. Our study also found that the majority of individuals killed came from the poor suburbs of Tunis (Douar Hicher, Mnihla, Ettadhamen, Ezzouhour, Sijoumi, and El Karam), which is to say that they were among the excluded and marginalized of the country. By contrast, no individuals killed were recorded as coming from the rich neighborhoods of Tunis. The most dangerous clashes of the revolution involved children of the poor neighborhoods, who were revolting against the state's repressive apparatus.

Was the Tunisian revolution a masculine revolution?

The Tunisian "revolution of dignity" was a mass movement that also involved women.[15] Generally, in Muslim countries, the public sphere and political action are restricted to men. In Tunisia, however, the presence of women in the workforce, their level of social advancement, and their wide participation in education (more than 60 percent of students are female) led to a high level of female participation in the revolution. Female lawyers, civil servants, jobless individuals, and university and high school students were all present. I witnessed women at demonstrations, rallies, strikes, and sit-ins, shouting slogans, discussing relevant issues, throwing stones, cooking, and sweeping. In night clashes with the police in Kasserine and Thala, women stood in solidarity with men—a reality made clear by the 12 women recorded among the dead.[16]

The organized forces of the revolution

The young people who participated in the revolution were not guided by ideology. But were they really without leadership and influence? We can assert that the revolution was spontaneous and leaderless at first. As time passed, more organized forces seized the revolution and gave it a more political meaning. These organized forces included trade unionists, lawyers, teachers, and judges. Let us examine these forces, beginning with the most important segment: the trade unions, led by the UGTT.

The UGTT in the revolution

The UGTT and the RCD were influential actors in Ben Ali's regime. The trade union federation, which was founded in 1946, had a presence across the country and in all areas of professional life, with 350,000 registered members. The UGTT was behind the explosions of social unrest that shook the country during the 1970s and 1980s. Because of its numbers and the solidarity among its members, the UGTT was able to guarantee social benefits to its members despite the effects of a nationwide liberal economic policy. The Ben Ali regime, like any antidemocratic regime, ensured its survival through repression and corruption. As a result, all mass organizations, including the largest labor union, had to gain the approval of both the RCD and the president. In return, labor leaders were granted certain privileges. As a result, labor leaders collaborated with and supported Ben Ali and his regime and subsequently enjoyed extra income and privileges (e.g., gifts of money, land grants, employment of their children in conspicuous positions).

When the revolution broke out, the secretary-general of the UGTT, Abdessalem Jrad, went to see Ben Ali in his palace in Carthage on January 13, 2011, to guarantee the UGTT's support without taking into account his union members' opposition to the regime. Compounding this divergence, militants within the union, often on the left, had been challenging the union leadership even before the revolution began.

During the beginning of the revolution, the position of the UGTT's leadership remained uncertain. When snipers killed demonstrators in Kasserine on January 8, 2011, the union's leadership began turning from Ben Ali and expressed its opposition to the use of force against protesters.

In the centers of protest in the interior of the country, such as Sidi Bouzid, Kasserine, Gafsa, and Kebili, trade unionists mentored young people during the revolt and gave the burgeoning social movement more political direction. Politicized elements of the union's left wing (including Marxists and Arab nationalists) also provided guidance to residents and students.

Because of either opportunism or fear of being overrun by the masses, the UGTT's leadership little by little joined the general revolt against Ben Ali and even began authorizing strikes at the local level. The union's local and regional offices eventually became centers of organization for the revolutionaries. Activists gathered there and demonstrations left from their premises. In Tunis, the UGTT's headquarters on Mohamed Ali Square became the rallying point for the rebels. The UGTT assumed a more prominent role in the major demonstrations of January 12–14, especially in the cities of Tunis, Sfax, Gabes, and Kairouan.

The flight of Ben Ali to Saudi Arabia on January 14 positioned the UGTT as an important interlocutor between the revolutionaries and the new transitional government, but the union was unable to exert full control over the revolutionaries, who were disillusioned by its previous collaboration with the regime. As a result, the union leadership shifted its own political position, aligning itself with the revolutionaries. It declared the formation of the Front of January 14 to "achieve the objectives of the revolution, political reform and the transition to democracy."

Lawyers in the revolution

Besides the UGTT, another key organizing force in the revolution was lawyers. By continuing to defend the oppressed, this profession belonged to a protest culture. The Bar Association of Tunisian lawyers numbered 1,000 members. Its council, which was democratically elected, included individuals of various ideologies, from secularists and Islamists to members of the ruling party and Marxists, and Arab nationalists. Some lawyers campaigned against repression, defending the victims of political trials or individuals active in organizations defending human rights. These lawyers created the Tunisian League for Human Rights, the Association Fighting against Torture in Tunisia, the International Association Supporting Political Prisoners, and other groups. The most active of these lawyers attracted the wrath of Ben Ali and suffered reprisals in the form of office fires, police surveillance, physical assaults, travel bans, and even imprisonment.

From marches in sympathy with the rebels at Kasserine, Sidi Bouzid, Gafsa, and Tunis, to work stoppages in courts around the country, Tunisian demonstration, suppressed by the police, led to their decision to stage a general strike on January 6, 2011.

From that day onwards, the "black robes" were present at all demonstrations. On January 14, 2011, they wore their black gowns to line up outside the door of the Ministry of the Interior on Avenue Bourguiba. Given their high profile, the lawyers galvanized the crowd and deterred the police from taking violent action.

At the official level, the Bar Association of Tunisia not only expressed solidarity with the people, but also supported the revolution with its legal skills. Lawyers joined the High Council of the Revolution and became active members beginning January 14, 2011. A legal arm of the revolution called the Lawyers' Group of 25 initiated legal cases against Ben Ali and associated ministers and security officials.

To a lesser extent, judges too were involved in the revolutionary process. The Tunisian judiciary had lost its apolitical identity during the Bourguiba and Ben Ali regimes. The executive dominated the judiciary, and the judiciary served the interests of the politicians. On Ben Ali's orders, the judicial machinery condemned any opponent of the regime. Judges who resisted the regime were forcibly transferred away from their families and denied promotion.[17]

At the outbreak of the revolution, these blackballed judges were the first to express their solidarity with the people. The Association of Tunisian Judges (AMT), which boasted 1,400 members, expressed its full support for the revolution and its right to operate as an independent judiciary. Among the major actions led by the lawyers was the large February 12, 2011, sit-in at the Tunis law courts, which was later branded "the day of the liberation of the judiciary." Ahmed Rahmouni, spokesman for the judges of the revolution, called for respect for the judiciary's independence while condemning the executive's stranglehold on the various wheels of justice.

Parties, political groups, and the revolution

A notable aspect of the Tunisian revolution is that the people were more radical than their elites. The people wanted to both overthrow Ben Ali and destroy his system, whereas the elites only wanted to reform the system. The political elite itself was divided. Some parties were close to Ben Ali, with members assuming minor roles in the parliament and receiving wages and other benefits. Three other legal parties—the Democratic Progressive Party (DPP), the former communist party Ettajdid, and the Forum for Democracy and Labour—were openly critical of the regime. At the outbreak of the revolution, these parties denounced the repression but failed to join the revolution. They accepted Ben Ali's proposal to form a national unity government on January 13, 2011, and initiated some reforms. Eventually, the DPP and Ettajdid joined the government of Ben Ali's prime minister, Mohamed Ghannouchi, in an effort to deflect the revolution.

Besides these legally recognized parties, a conglomeration of groups organized to oppose the government. The most active was the Marxist-oriented Communist Labour Party of Tunisia. Another group, Al Watad (the Movement of Democratic Patriots), claimed to represent Maoism. Arab nationalists were represented by a group called Kawmiyyine. This group included several branches: Nasserites, Baathists, and Arab Marxists. Islamist parties were hardly present before the events of January 14, 2011, because they had been severely repressed by the Bourguiba and Ben Ali regimes.

These groups acted secretly to undermine the regime of Ben Ali. They were particularly active among students and unions, but failed to effectively supervise or dominate the mass of young people who were the leading force of the revolution.

The Islamists began to appear on the political scene after January 14, 2011. The release of their prisoners after a general amnesty and the return of their exiles from abroad encouraged the Islamists to act. The Islamists are now an important player in the new political landscape of Tunisia. The Islamist Ennahdha Party presents itself as a democratic, reform-oriented party patterned on the Turkish AKP (Justice and Development) Party.

The role of the internet and television in the revolution

Tunisia has one of the highest rates of internet connectivity in Africa. In 2001, the number of subscribers rose to 547,763, with 618,621 email accounts and 11,913 websites. In the same year, the number of internet users reached almost 4 million, out of a population of 10.5 million.[18] The estimated number of Tunisian subscribers to Facebook was 2.5 million and included high school students, university students, academics, journalists, lawyers, and ordinary people.

However, Ben Ali opposed free use of the internet, monitoring its usage and censoring most communications. In addition, internet users were required to show their identity cards before connecting, regardless of whether they were at home or in cybercafés. The estimated number of cyber-officers appointed to control access to the internet in Tunisia was more than 600.[19]

To avoid this censorship, many Tunisians changed their internet proxy addresses. Despite this effort, many administrators' accounts were disabled and users were often prosecuted and subjected to police harassment.

What role did the internet play in the Tunisian revolution? Certainly, it contributed to the formation of an enlightened and politicized citizenry, even before the revolution. In the midst of the revolution, the web became a significant organizational tool, a transmitter of information, and an instrument of mobilization and media attention. But different web platforms played different roles: Facebook in particular was important while Twitter and Wikileaks were less so.

Activists' use of mobile phones fueled the web and television channels with both images and real-time video. Two Arab satellite channels were particularly important: El Hiwar, broadcasting from London, and Al Jazeera, broadcasting from Qatar. Al Jazeera played a critical role during the revolution by transmitting videos, images, comments, live broadcasts, and discussions on what was happening in Tunisia, expressing a clear sympathy for the revolution's goals. The main French channel, France 24, was less involved. Its coverage of the revolution became more important after January 14, 2011, in clear symbiosis with the policy positions taken by the French government. Other television stations were half-hearted, if not hostile, in their coverage of the revolution.

In short, television and the internet were indeed invaluable guides and supporters of the revolution, but they did not play any role in launching the revolution or determining its outcome. Furthermore, the youths of Sidi Bouzid, Kasserine, or Thala—who constituted a quasi-majority of the revolutionaries—were not continuously connected to the web nor guided by instructions posted on Facebook. The outburst of social unrest in working-class communities and other major cities was initially spontaneous and later facilitated by laptops and friendship networks. After the lifting of censorship and surveillance on January 14, 2011, information transmitted via the internet and social media rose in importance, leading to the creation of a free space for political discussion for Tunisians, both young and old.

The army and the police in the revolution

The Tunisian army was established on June 30, 1956. Formed in a republican environment, its purpose was to protect the borders of the country and assist civilians in need. Unlike neighboring countries such as Morocco and Algeria, the Tunisian army was not founded by resistance fighters for independence. Rather, it was formed from the Ottoman bey's old army and a detachment of Tunisians who had served in the French army. At its birth, the Tunisian army was substantially apolitical. Nevertheless, Bourguiba, the first president of modern Tunisia, was always suspicious of the army, fearing that they would stage a *coup d'état*—and indeed, the army did intervene on several occasions, especially when the police apparatus was unable to maintain order, notably in 1978, 1980, 1984, and 2008.

However, the Tunisian army always tried to remain distant from politics. When Ben Ali initiated his *coup d'état* in 1987, he was serving as a general in the police force—not the army. After his ascent to power, Ben Ali remained suspicious of the army and maintained his power base within the police. His regime was based on a large police force that exceeded 120,000 officers, in contrast to the armed forces' 35,000 men (with 27,000 of them serving in the army).[20] The army was poorly equipped, and most of its budget was drawn from American and French military aid. As a sign of disillusionment with Ben Ali, the United States cut the amount of military aid it provided to the Tunisian army from $15 million in 2010 to $4.9 million in 2011.[21]

Within Tunisia, the army was viewed as a professional organization that was worthy of respect and enjoyed a good reputation among the people. Because it never became involved in the mafia-like practices of the ruling clans, it remained close to the people. The army's role in the 2011 revolution has only enhanced that reputation.

On January 12, 2011, General Rachid Ammar,[22] joint chief of staff of the army, decided to not comply with President Ben Ali's order to shoot at demonstrators in Tunis. Dismissed on the spot and placed under house arrest, he was reinstated on January 14 by Prime Minister Ghannouchi. After being abandoned by the army, Ben Ali fled Tunisia. A new chapter in the history of the country was begun, and it was being co-written by the army.

This army did not make the revolution—it simply allowed it to occur. Did the army have a choice in the matter? Yes. If the army had followed the president's orders, Tunisia would have followed the same pattern of revolution that occurred in Yemen or Libya. Undoubtedly, carnage would have taken place, and no one would have been able to predict the outcome.

In the days after January 14, 2011, the army rose in popularity as it deployed throughout the country to ensure the safety of citizens, fight armed militias loyal to the deposed president, and arrest looters.

In this process, General Ammar became a hero of the revolution. Even before the flight of Ben Ali, his soldiers had fraternized with the demonstrators, exchanging hugs, flowers, and kisses. Frequently, soldiers prevented the police from attacking youths.

On January 24, the army explicitly allied itself with the revolution and became committed to defending it when General Ammar stated before hundreds of young revolutionaries in the sit-in of the Kasbah:

> We are faithful to the constitution and we will not get out of this framework. We are the guarantors of the youth revolution and will ensure its safe arrival. We do not repress peaceful demonstrations, but these should not lead to a vacuum because the vacuum would lead to a return to dictatorship.[23]

The army saved the country from disorder. In conjunction with the Tunisian people, the army foiled the plot of General Sériati, head of the Presidential Guard, who sought to bring the country into chaos. General Ammar and his forces also guaranteed security on the Libyan border, where real dangers arose after the eruption of civil war in that country in June 2011.

Some doubted that the army was truly committed to the revolution. Some accused it of permitting Ben Ali and his family to flee when they should have been arrested, or of being complicit with the former regime when the police violently dispersed young campers at their first sit-in in the Kasbah on January 28, 2011, or of lacking professionalism in the prosecution of individuals implicated of crimes, or of violently opposing certain demonstrations.

In fact, the army may not have been as committed to the revolution as some have claimed; nevertheless, at the decisive moment, it did decide to secure the advances of the revolution and act as a counterbalance to the counterrevolutionary forces. As a result, it wound up becoming a leading player in the revolution.

In contrast to the army's place of honor, the Tunisian police came out of the revolution with a tarnished image. Hated both before and after the revolution, the police symbolized repression, injustice, and corruption for violence, murder, torture, theft, and rape.

Aware of the poor regard in which they were held, many police officers demonstrated during the month of January 2011 in Tunis, and in other cities they proclaimed their innocence and adherence to the revolution. They even formed the first police union in the Arab world. Despite the police forces' clear wish to disconnect themselves from the past, these actions have not remedied the damage inflicted before the revolution. Reconciliation between the Tunisian population and the police forces will surely take time.

The Tunisian revolution in the world

Because it managed to bring down—so quickly and with so little violence—one of the strongest police dictatorships in the world, the Tunisian revolution has brought the Tunisian people respect and esteem from many peoples and countries. Its shock waves were felt across the world, even in China. Young people in Russia, Spain, and elsewhere were inspired by young Tunisians to oppose their own countries' regimes.

Because Tunisia is a small country in an important geostrategic position, its revolution provoked a significant response in the West, especially in the United States and France. Ben Ali's regime, which was seen as a bulwark against Muslim fundamentalism and a strong supporter of the fight against terrorism, was viewed favorably by these nations almost up to his last day.

In France, both former President Jacques Chirac and President Nicolas Sarkozy supported Ben Ali to the last moment. France continued to support Ben Ali and his regime during the first months of revolution. Foreign Minister Michèle Alliot-Marie even suggested to Ben Ali that France could send experts to "settle the crisis of law and order." The French planned to send supplies of tear gas and batons to the dictator, but they could not be delivered on time. After Ben Ali's flight to Saudi Arabia on January 14, 2011, the French government made a policy u-turn, giving "its full support to the revolution in Tunisia." Nevertheless, France's deportation of young migrants who escaped from Tunisia to France cast doubt on the sincerity of this support.

Calls for good sense, calm, and self-control constituted the official stance of the countries of the European Union. After January 14, the high representative for foreign policy, Catherine Ashton, expressed on behalf of the EU "support and recognition to the Tunisian people and their democratic aspirations."[24] In the Deauville summit held on May 28, 2011, Tunisia received from the G8 "the assurance of assistance within the scope favoring the Arab Spring." At that summit, the Tunisian revolutionary forces rejected the transitional government's request for financial assistance from the G8 and called for the nullification of questionable loans incurred by Ben Ali and his government. Furthermore, the revolutionary forces requested financial assistance to help sustain the fledgling democracy.

The US position was not much better than that of France. Ben Ali came to power on November 7, 1987, with the support of the United States. The deposed dictator's regime was a cornerstone in the American strategy for fighting terrorism. Moreover, the United States Africa Command (AFRICOM) has long enjoyed access to military facilities in Tunisia.

What position did the United States take regarding the Tunisian revolution? French political analyst and founding president of the Voltaire Network Thierry Meyssane has written: "On 13 January, refusing to obey the order to fire, General Rashid Ammar announced to President Ben Ali that Washington, through AFRICOM's commander, General William Ward, commanded him to flee."[25] Officials within the American administration have contested this claim.[26] For example, in his visit to Tunis on May 8, 2011, William Burns, the under-secretary of state for political affairs, denied any US involvement in the events and affirmed that "this revolution is 100% Tunisian."[27]

The US Congress applauded the Tunisian revolution and President Barack Obama paid tribute to the revolution of dignity in a May 19, 2011, speech devoted to the Arab revolution. He compared Mohamed Bouazizi to Rosa Parks, a heroine of the struggle against racial segregation in the United States. Other US officials who visited Tunisia, including Jeffrey Feltman, the under-secretary of state for Near Eastern affairs, and Senators John McCain and Joseph Lieberman expressed their country's commitment to support of the people of Tunisia both in their transition to democracy and in the country's economic recovery.

The image of the United States held by Tunisians is deeply negative. US policy toward the Arab world, its war in Iraq, and its unconditional support of Israel against the Palestinians makes confidence in America difficult.

Whatever the positions of Western governments may have been, people around the world approved and welcomed the revolution of dignity and expressed their support for the Tunisian people. The shock waves of this revolution are still being felt in the Arab world in particular. Although the Tunisian revolutionaries never thought of exporting their revolution, their achievement of bringing down a dictator through peaceful protest became an example to follow. Arab youth in other countries have imitated the Tunisians by using the internet for organizing, occupying public places, and chanting slogans, of which "the people want to overthrow the regime" and "go away" (in Arabic, *irhal*) have become famous throughout the region. Some persons have even immolated themselves like Bouazizi in Algeria, Morocco, and Yemen.

However, if other Arab countries exhibit similarities with Tunisia, they also display differences adequate enough to prevent a domino effect. Even if these countries are governed by despotic regimes and their peoples have suffered from the same troubles, injustices, unemployment problems, social disparities, corruption, nepotism, and disaffection, they differ in terms of their history, their wealth, and the room for freedom given to their citizens.

Youth demonstrations in Algeria, Morocco, and Jordan seem to have run out of steam. The revolt in Bahrain was quelled with both bloodshed and US complicity. On the other hand, the Egyptians carried out a month of demonstrations and sit-ins in Tahrir Square before deposing Hosni Mubarak on February 11, 2011. The Libyan revolution was eventually successful after the assassination of Muammar Qaddafi on October 20, 2011. The regime of

Bashar al-Assad in Syria has faced a revolution since March 15, 2011, which has produced the deaths of more than 70,000 insurgents. The Syrian president has been subjected to greater pressure from the United States and European nations as a result of geopolitical reasons related to the Palestinian issue and Lebanon. The Tunisian revolution has indeed inaugurated an "Arab spring."

Achievements and perspectives of the revolution

To assess a revolution in progress seems risky. However, since its inception, many things have changed in Tunisia. The first achievement of the revolution was the psychological liberation of its people. Since the attainment of independence in 1956, Tunisians had lived under a regime of political and police surveillance. Now, however, they have recovered their freedom. Since the flight of Ben Ali on January 14, 2011, fear, which had lasted for decades among the people, has disappeared. Tongues have become untied; public spaces have become fora for political discussion. Tunisians are reclaiming their homeland. Their prisons have been emptied of political opponents, and a general amnesty has restored civil and political rights to thousands of Tunisians.

The RCD, the symbol of dictatorship and the pillar of despotism, has been banned. Dozens of new political parties have emerged since then.[28]

These are the first steps toward democracy. Civil society has awakened, and a multitude of civic associations have been formed. Political change has also been demonstrated at the level of free speech. Newspapers, radios, televisions, and the internet are publishing more freely than ever before. The revolution has given confidence to Tunisians who increasingly claim their right to examine the political choices of government, the appointment of executive officers of the state, and other issues.

The revolution's major political achievement thus far has been the abrogation of the 1959 Constitution. The former legislature and the Constitutional Council have been dissolved, and free elections for a new National Constituent Assembly were held on October 23, 2011. A new political system is being born.

A plural society in political, social, and doctrinal terms is clearly beginning to take shape in Tunisia. The societal effort to coexist and reconcile differences and oppositions is the next great challenge for Tunisians.

These great achievements are only the prelude to future profound changes. Ben Ali may no longer be in power, but his system remains influential. The winds of revolution have not blown sufficient change into the Ministry of the Interior or the Department of Justice, which are still regarded as bastions of repression and deprivation of freedom. Judges and torturers who worked for the old regime are still working in many of their positions. The judicial framework constructed to support despotism still stands. The beneficiaries of the corrupted regime who engaged in nepotism, robbery, and the pillage of both property and public funds have not been prosecuted. In short, the mafia accomplices of Ben Ali are still roaming freely. Much remains to be done.

Acknowledgment

This article was translated from Arabic into English by Khalid Bekkaoui.

Notes

1. Ali Abaab, "Modernisation agricole et développement régional en Tunisie Centrale (cas de la région de Sidi Bouzid)," in A.-M. Jouve (ed.) *La modernisation des agricultures méditerranéennes (à la mémoire de Pierre Coulomb)* (Montpellier: CIHEAM, 1997) pp. 249–254, http://om.ciheam.org/om/pdf/a29/CI971520.pdf.
2. Mouldi Gassoumi, "Kasserine: Du Colonialiste Capitaliste á l'Inteémoire et Histoire [Kasserine, Memory and History] (Tunis: Mil, 2009), p. 190.
3. www.mediaterranee.com/Tunisie/Economie/Tunisie-le-chomage-des-jeunes-une-bombe-a-retardement.html, accessed May 18, 2011.
4. Moncef Guen, "La crise économique mondiale, un déclic dans la révolution tunisienne," ["The International Economic Crisis, the Tiger of Tunisian Revolution"] *Jeune Afrique*, February 9, 2011, www.jeuneafrique.com/Article/ARTJAWEB 20110209103052.
5. Guen, "La crise économique mondiale."
6. "US Embassy Cables: Tunisia—a US Foreign Policy Conundrum," *Guardian*, December 7, 2010, www.guardian.co.uk/world/us-embassy-cables-documents/217138.
7. Frederick Engels, *Théorie de la Violence* [Theory of Violence] (Paris: Gilbert Mury, 1972), p. 42.
8. See the website www.gnet.tn/temps-fort/tunisie-ben-ali-a-donne-lordre-de-bombarder-kasserine/id-menu-325.html.
9. See the website www.scribd.com/doc/52995479/Journal-LE-MONDE-14042011.
10. Declaration by Juan Meéndez, special UN reporter on torture, citing the governmental official figures in May 20, 2011.
11. According to evidence provided by local youths, security agents committed at least three cases of rape on January 24, 2011 (personal interview).
12. Zach Zagger, "Egypt Revolution Resulted in at Least 840 Deaths: Amnesty Report," *Jurist*, May 19, 2011, http://jurist.org/paperchase/2011/05/eqypt-revolution-resulted-in-at-least-840-deaths-amnesty-report.php.
13. Frantz Fanon, *The Wretched of the Earth* (Paris: Petite Collection Maspero, 1974), pp. 44–45.
14. Lazher Merjri, *The Tunisian Revolution: 17 December* (Tunisia: MIP, 2011), pp. 68–86.
15. www.youtube.com/watch?v=SkPVSZIVzXk.
16. Zoghlami Naget, "Women at Tunisian Revolution," communication á la journée sur la révolution organisée par L'Association des sociologues tunisiens, Tunis, February 10, 2011, unpublished.
17. This was the case for the president of the Bar Association, Ahmed Rahmouni, and the judges Khathoum Kennou, Wassila Kaaba, Raoudha Karafi, Leyla Abid, and Leyla Bahria.
18. Figures of the Tunisian Agency of the Internet, December 2011, www.ati.tn/fr/index.php?id=90& rub = 27.
19. According to the website of the Tunisian opposition, September 25, 2009, http://nawaat.org/portail/2009/09/25/Tunisie-les-cyberflics-doublent-leur-effectif-et-se-lachent-sur-facebook.
20. Samy Ghorhal, "Rachid Ammar, home fort de la Tunisie: 'L'armée ne tire pas'," *Rue 89*, January 16, 2011, www.rue89.com/2011/01/16/larmee-ne-tire-pas-lhomme-fort-de-la-tunisie-est-general-185923. Compare to the 147,000 active duty troops in

the Algerian army as of 2008 (see http://en.wikipedia.org/wiki/Algeria#Foreign_relations_and_military) and the 7,600 troops in Qaddafi's army in 2008.
21 Youssef Ben Ismaïl, "Révolution tunisienne: la rationalité de l'armée," *El Mouwaten*, March 9, 2011, www.elmouwaten.com/modules.php?name=News&file=article&sid=67.
22 Rachid Ammar was born in Sayada, in the Tunisian Sahel in 1947 or 1948. An artillery officer, he pursued his studies in the military academy in Fondek Jédid and then at French military schools in Turkey. In 2001, he became joint chief of staff, and in 2010, he was appointed lieutenant general. He became commander of Joint Task Forces in April 2011.
23 Abdelaziz Barrouhi, "Le général Ammar, l'homme qui a dit non," *Jeune Afrique*, February 7, 2011, www.jeuneafrique.com/Article/ARTJAJA2612p044-049.xml1.
24 European Union Press Office, "Joint Statement by EU High Representative Catherine Ashton and Commissioner Štefan Füle on the Events on Tunisia," January 14, 2011, www.consilium.europa.eu/uedocs/cms_data/docs/pressdata/EN/foraff/118865.pdf.
25 Thierry Meyssane, "Tunisie: Comment les Américains ont vouler canaliser la révolte," *Les Echos du Maghreb*, January 30, 2011, http://jamalhafsi.unblog.fr/2011/01/30/tunisie-comment-les-americains-ont-voulu-canaliser-le-revolte.
26 Valeérie Segond, "Les révolutions arabes ne sont que des coups d'Etat militaires masqués," *La Tribune*, January 6, 2011, www.latribune.fr/actualites/economie/international/20110601trib000626151/les-revolutions-arabes-ne-sont-que-des-coups-d-etat-militaires-masques.html.
27 Raouf Seddik, "L'intérêt américain dans la révolution tunisienne: que ce soit un 'modèle de réussite'," *La Press de Tunisie*, February 25, 2011, www.turess.com/fr/lapresse/23362.
28 As of May 2012, about 100 parties had been already recognized.

4 The Egyptian revolution
The power of mass mobilization and the spirit of Tahrir Square

Emad El-Din Shahin

The fall of Mubarak's three-decade-long regime in just 18 days revealed the fragility of authoritarianism and the power of mass movements. Despite early warnings from neighboring Tunisia, Mubarak and his top associates thought that Egypt was different, and that the regime was strong enough to survive popular pressures for change. Even Mubarak's external allies initially believed that "the Egyptian government [was] stable and [was] looking for ways to respond to the legitimate needs and interests of the Egyptian people."[1] This apparent stability concealed deep-rooted crises and structural problems that had piled up for decades. Mubarak's long period of rule had generated profound feelings among Egyptians concerning their repression, poverty, and lack of social justice.

The January 25 revolution was not a spontaneous act, but rather a cumulative process that involved numerous figures, groups, and movements over the years. Likewise, it was not merely a youth or Facebook revolution, but a people's revolution that skilfully used traditional as well as modern means of mobilization. The youth ignited this revolution, the people supported and defended it, and the military managed it. Several key factors ensured the success of the January 25 revolution, but the most fundamental factor was mass mobilization, expressed as the outpouring of millions of Egyptians who battled security forces and articulated clear demands for change. One protester summarized the impact of mass force:

> From the very first day we felt we could win because of the huge numbers of people involved, the masses. When you're at a protest and you see small numbers, you panic and you are afraid. This was different. We could see right away that we might win. We felt more confident.[2]

The predominantly nonviolent strategy that the protesters adopted accentuated the regime's brutal repressive measures and fostered domestic and international support for the revolution. This chapter analyzes the particular features of the Egyptian revolution and examines the deep-rooted crises that lie behind it. It discusses the role of different forces: the youth, political parties, the Muslim Brothers, and the military. Finally, it attempts to answer the question of why this revolution was successful and explains the traditional and modern means of mobilization that benefited the organizers.

"A unique revolution!"

Egyptians have revolted several times in recent history—in 1882, 1919, 1952, 1977, and 2011. Several characteristics, however, distinguish the January 25 revolution from the rest. The most distinct feature was the incredibly large number of protesters who participated throughout the 18 days of this revolution. According to a member of the Supreme Council of the Armed Forces (SCAF), the number of demonstrators who participated in the revolution throughout the country reached 15 million. David Cortright, a renowned expert on nonviolent social movements, considers this revolution to be "one of the largest outpourings of mass civil resistance in human history."[3] On February 11, the day that Mubarak resigned, Tahrir Square and its surrounding areas hosted more than 4 million protesters. The next closest revolution in terms of size was the 1989 Polish revolution, in which 10 million people participated.

The second significant feature of the January 25 revolution was its predominantly peaceful nature. The organizers of the January 25 protests expected a harsh and repressive response from the regime. They avoided clashes with the security forces in order to not alienate potential participants and to raise sympathy for their cause. Their main slogan, particularly when confronting the brutal crackdowns of the security police, was "Peaceful. Peaceful."

A third feature of the revolution was its classless nature. In other words, this uprising was a true people's revolution that was not limited to or instigated by only one class, but rather drew support from various social classes. The youth of the middle and upper-middle classes called for and led the revolution and were then joined by the poor and marginalized, the upper classes, workers, peasants, women, Copts, Muslims, young people, old people, urban residents, and rural residents.

A fourth remarkable feature was the "leaderless" nature of the revolution. The revolution had no leading figure, group, vanguard, or movement. It did not follow the traditional pattern of leadership that relies on hierarchical structures. Instead, it was the work of various groups and organizations, with no one claiming a principal role. Nevertheless, the revolution was highly organized, remaining united on one main demand: "The people want to change the regime." This demands-oriented nature of the revolution kept the movement together and helped it to progress.

Organization was the fifth unique characteristic of the Egyptian revolution. Different actors coordinated and interacted throughout the revolution. They organized protests, articulated demands, and turned Tahrir Square into a "mini-state" that provided food and supplies, health services, defense and security, media and communications, and entertainment for the millions of participating protesters. Modern technologies such as the internet and social media were key factors in the mobilization and organization of this revolution. Explaining the particular nature of the revolution, David Rothkopf writes:

> We are accustomed to political movements requiring charismatic leaders and political infrastructure. But what happened in Egypt was, thanks to social networks and a new information culture, a revolution led by networked clusters of individuals in which all the grassroots capabilities of old infrastructures were instantly available via the application of new technologies."[4]

Finally, the January 25 revolution engendered an extraordinary aura of tolerance, acceptance, and pluralism, values that were absent for long periods of Mubarak's rule. The protesters came from different ideological backgrounds, religions, political orientations, and geographical areas, but they were tolerant and accepting of each other and were able to transcend their differences. Faith and religion played a remarkable role in the revolution. The importance of these factors could be seen in the repeated incidences of collective prayers, Friday and Sunday sermons, and men and women praying and bowing on the ground to confront police brutality. Prayer was used to break fear and promote a feeling of security and mutual support. Scenes of thousands of protesters kneeling on the ground while forces besieged and fired at them generated immense sympathy for the demonstrators. Photos of Copts protecting Muslims during their Friday prayers and then being protected by Muslims during their own Sunday services became iconic. An extraordinary atmosphere of civility quickly emerged and was clearly noticeable to any observer.[5] Throughout the 18 days, not a single incident of theft or sexual harassment was reported.[6] It is this atmosphere of tolerance and civility that Egyptians later called the "Spirit of Tahrir." Activists are now trying to infuse this new spirit into the entire Egyptian society.

Structural crises

Despite its sudden outburst, the January 25 revolution was neither spontaneous nor planned. Rather, it was a cumulative process that evolved over the decade between 2000 and 2011, emerging from structural failure, growing political discontent, sporadic protests, and a strong desire for reform. The January 25 revolution revealed deep structural problems that affected the majority of Egyptians, particularly the educated middle classes, the youth, and the poor.

The most important of these problems were the economic crisis, political stagnation, and the regime's astonishing disregard for rising popular discontent.

Economic grievances

Since the early 1990s, Mubarak's regime had adopted neoliberal economic policies and embarked on a major structural adjustment process. While this program produced some success, it also hurt large numbers of the population. After long years of economic stagnation, however, the country's economic performance improved. Egypt's gross domestic product grew an average of 6 percent annually between 2007 and 2011. In 2007, foreign direct investment (FDI) increased to $11 billion (a remarkable jump from $400 million in 2004), and Egypt's exports increased by 20 percent. At that time, the Egyptian economy ranked as the fourth largest among the Arab countries ($128 billion in 2007), exceeded only by oil-rich Saudi Arabia ($381 billion), Algeria ($135.2 billion), and the United Arab Emirates ($129.7 billion).[7] The economy seemed to be doing well, but the majority of Egyptians were not. Only a few state cronies benefited from this growth.

Mismanagement, cronyism, mal-distribution, massive corruption, a substandard educational system, and rising unemployment undermined these achievements and inflamed the anger of the majority of the population. Most of this growth was achieved by rent-seeking operations—increases in the sale of natural gas, workers' remittances, revenues from the Suez Canal, sale of public enterprises, and real estate—and not through the creation of a competitive industrial base or other productive economic sectors. The economy suffered from soaring inflation (17.1 percent in 2008), high unemployment (20 percent at the end of 2006), a large public debt that reached 100 percent of GDP in 2007, and a trade deficit that amounted to $60.8 billion in imports, compared to $34.5 billion in exports, in 2008.[8] During the last years of Mubarak's rule, corruption became massive and institutionalized, with Transparency International's 2006 Corruption Perceptions Index ranking Egypt 70th out of 163 countries. The regime failed to provide the 600,000 new jobs that were needed annually to absorb the country's new entrants to the job market. The deteriorating educational system failed to meet the expectations of university graduates who lacked the necessary competitive skills and were forced to join an army of unemployed youth. Unemployment among university graduates averaged 40 percent for men and 50 percent for women.[9]

The government's neoliberal policies produced many losers and few winners. Chief among the losers were the poor, workers, the middle class, and people from rural areas. All of these groups struggled to survive on a fixed income that could not keep up with the rising prices of food and basic necessities. Poverty levels became phenomenal, engulfing about 40 percent of the population. Disparities in lifestyle and incomes became increasingly alarming. Whole gated communities mushroomed on the outskirts of Cairo and other major urban areas, provoking the anger of the deprived. The number of shantytowns increased exponentially. According to the Cabinet's Information and Decision-Making Support Centre and other government-sponsored institutes, there were more than 1,000 shantytowns in Egypt spread among 20 governorates, with a population of 17.7 million.[10]

Starting in 2002, the state-business nexus grew particularly strong with the grooming of Mubarak's son Gamal as a possible heir. Gamal relied on the state party, the National Democratic Party (NDP), and business and state cronies to build his own power base and in return helped them infiltrate the government and the party. These partners in economic crimes accumulated wealth through the privatization of state-owned enterprises, real estate, doubtful business dealings, and financial breaks (e.g., tax exemptions, bank loans, and price incentives). As these newly rising businessmen became richer, the poor, middle, and working classes were increasingly crushed by inflation, job shortages, and hopelessness. It is important to note that these segments of the population have historically constituted the backbone of Egyptian society. They were now marginalized, unable to satisfy their basic needs, and exposed to the pressures of social disintegration. Statistics demonstrating economic improvement and the many economic and political opportunities that were available to elites blinded the regime to the mounting wrath of large segments of the population.

Political stagnation

Egyptians associate Mubarak's reign with political stagnation. Astonishingly stubborn and unyielding when faced with pressures for change, Mubarak kept the political life of the country under tight control and prevented both true political contestation for power and any change to the basic structures of the political system. The state party, the NDP, wielded complete hegemony over the state institutions and parliament and monopolized the political process. With the potential ascendance of Gamal Mubarak in 2002 as an heir, the NDP became even more dominant and vicious in suppressing opposition to this plan for Egypt's political future.

Mubarak tolerated political parties as long as they did not pose a serious threat to his authority. Weak, fragmented, and divided, the legalized opposition was resigned to its subsidiary role and was seemingly incapable of posing a serious challenge to the regime. Effective movements and parties, including the Muslim Brotherhood, the Nasserite Karama (Dignity) Party, the Islamic centrist al-Wasat (Center) Party, and al-Ghad (Tomorrow) Party, were either banned or harassed. The legalized political parties were constrained by regime-imposed legal restrictions, and their aging leadership, lack of innovation, and lack of internal democratic practices added to their ineffectiveness. Many of these parties were easily coopted into the service of the regime, creating the illusion of pluralism and political dynamism. Because they always failed to gain people's trust and mobilize an adequate following, this legal opposition performed poorly in elections and became discredited. By 2004, activists, including the youth, were looking for other channels to articulate their protest and aggregate their demands. Alternative protest movements such as the Egyptian Movement for Change (Kifaya) emerged as a response to activists' need to transcend the obsolete style of political parties and their ineffectiveness.

The emergence of a large number of protest and pro-change movements greatly altered Egypt's political landscape. These movements energized the political arena and ended the decades-long stagnation that Mubarak's regime had forced on Egyptian politics. Reform movements, advocacy groups, public figures, critical journalists, independent judges, and activists mushroomed in a relatively short time. In 2004 and 2005, more than a dozen groups surfaced in opposition to the renewal of Mubarak's presidency for a fifth term and his attempts to groom his son Gamal as a successor. "Change" became the buzzword and driving force behind all these movements, which adopted such names as Kifaya, the National Rally for Democratic Change, Journalists for Change, Doctors for Change, Intellectuals for Change, Writers for Change, and Youth for Change. All of these movements took to the streets to protest against government policies, breaking the barriers of fear, laying the foundations of grassroots activism, and challenging the regime's security measures. The growth of the pro-change movements reflected a wide dissatisfaction with the existing political parties and the need to come up with alternative structures and tactics to pressure the regime for reforms.

Obviously, some of these movements were more influential than others. Kifaya was the most well-known and one of the most popular. This group formed in August 2004 and included members of different political parties and activists. To build a broad base of support, Kifaya embraced basic reform demands that called for an end to the state of emergency, an end of the regime's monopoly over power, the amendment of the constitution, and the creation of a system that would allow for the transfer of power. Its slogan, "No extension for Mubarak, no hereditary succession," became a mantra for the change movement. Gradually, the movement began to take to the streets to express its demands and, more significantly, to achieve mobilization and end the culture of fear that was so prevalent among Egyptians. Indeed, Kifaya succeeded in organizing dozens of demonstrations in a few years and gradually managed to articulate a list of reform demands that many began to share and advocate. However, the group was never able to mobilize large numbers of the population. Kifaya's narrow ideological platform, sporadic activities, and internal disputes limited its ability to achieve mass mobilization, and by 2008, the movement had lost some of its appeal, prompting many youth to look for alternative avenues for protest.

The November 2010 parliamentary elections

Fraudulent elections have been a common trigger factor in many prodemocracy revolutions, and Egypt was no exception. The regime was blind to all mounting domestic pressures. Its political and economic elites had grown completely isolated from society and were even more determined to push for the succession of Gamal Mubarak, despite growing popular opposition to this plan. Ahmad Ezz, a business tycoon, top NDP official, and close associate of Gamal, wanted to make sure that his friend's path to the presidency was secure and smooth, and as a result, he oversaw one of the most tainted parliamentary elections in the country's recent history.

The parliamentary election of November 2010 was another major turning point that contributed to the downfall of Mubarak's regime. The NDP used massive vote rigging, intimidation, and repression to secure an overwhelming 97 percent majority in the parliament. Fraud was widespread, obvious, and provocative. Activists captured numerous incidents of ballot stuffing in photographs and videos and posted them on the web. Because opposition parties were almost completely excluded from the parliament, the regime alienated and delegitimized itself even further. Thomas Demmelhuber concluded in December 2010:

> Such obvious election manipulation should not be seen as reflecting the strength of the regime or as a sign of efficient government action. On the contrary, it is an expression of weakness, as stable authoritarian regimes can nowadays put up with a numerically strong opposition.[11]

The fraudulent November elections also confirmed the belief that the next presidential election, scheduled for September 2011, would certainly be rigged. Mubarak added insult to injury when he publicly mocked the opposition, which had formed a parallel parliament in protest of the sham elections, during the joint session of the newly "elected" parliament. He insulted and antagonized the Egyptians, blocked any possibility for reform, and highlighted the urgency for rapid change.

Main actors

The youth factor

The Egyptian youth led the January 25 revolution, the people embraced it, and the military managed it. Various youth movements played a central role in calling for protests and organizing the mass mobilization that turned the January 25 protests into a people's revolution. Many of these new movements benefited from the political and organizational experience that they had gained from their past involvement with protest groups that had emerged a few years previously, as well as from the adoption of new strategies and tactics of confrontation with the regime.

While these groups drew on past experiences, they also improvised new techniques for challenging Mubarak's regime. As we will see later, they were also successful at moving with ease between the virtual reality of social media, such as SMS, blogs, YouTube, Facebook, and Twitter, and the real world on the ground. This new dynamism produced a critical mass that was necessary for making this revolution successful. Ahmad Eid, a young activist, shared his experience:

> I consider myself and the main groups that participated in the January 25 Revolution, the children of the context created by the emergence of

Kifaya. I, therefore, see January 25 as a coronation of the state of political and social activism that began in 2004 with the establishment of Kifaya.[12]

The youth groups that called for and participated in the revolution shared certain common features that helped in their success. Many of these movements had been recently formed. The oldest was the April 6 Movement, which was formed in 2008, only three years before the revolution. Other newly formed groups included the Campaign for the Support of ElBaradei, the We Are All Khaled Said group, Youth for Justice and Freedom, the Youth of the Muslim Brotherhood, the Youth of Kifaya, young people of the Tomorrow Party, and young people of the Democratic Front Party. These groups were later joined by young people from the Leftist Tagammu Party, the Nasserite Party, the Popular Movement for Democratic Change (HASHD), young people of the Labor Party, young people of the Wafd Party, and the Front of Coptic Youth. The recent formation of these groups ensured that many of their members were unknown to the regime and its security forces. As a result, the regime underestimated the ability of these groups to pose a threat to the stability of the regime, exercise influence, and have the capacity to move large masses. In a YouTube clip that was widely circulated a few months before the revolution, Gamal Mubarak publicly made fun of the April 6 Movement and its members and refused even to consider the possibility of talking to the Egyptian youth.

Unlike the preceding generation of protest movements and political parties that cohabitated with Mubarak's regime for long decades, these youth movements had a strong desire for change and were eventually successful in ridding the country of Mubarak's regime.[13] For them, the possibility of Gamal ascending to power after his father was entirely unacceptable. Unlike the political parties, the youth movements were also characterized by their resourcefulness, practicality, and ability to coordinate with other political forces and among themselves, despite their different ideological orientations and intellectual backgrounds. This flexibility was a great asset that helped these movements enlist various political and social forces, form a loose yet coordinated front, and push the revolution forward. The movements were able to maintain this high level of flexibility and move across parties and organizations, which increased their network of activities, organizational skills, and mobilization capacity. Both the leaders of these movements and a large part of their constituencies were drawn from the educated youth of the middle and upper-middle classes. In addition to advocating for better socioeconomic conditions, they also aspired to institutionalize the democratic values of rule of law, transfer of power, and popular sovereignty. Finally, these movements used social media extensively and skilfully for several years to raise public awareness, expose the repressive policies of the regime, and build and organize a wide virtual constituency of people from different sectors of society.

The April 6 Movement

Five groups—the April 6 Movement, the Campaign for the Support of ElBaradei, the young people of the Muslim Brotherhood, the Youth of the Tomorrow Party, and the youth of Justice and Freedom—were key players in calling for and organizing protests during the first days of the revolution. The April 6 Movement represented the first cyber protest movement in Egypt. This group was formed in 2008 in support of the workers' strike in al-Mahalla al-Kubra, a major industrial city in the Nile Delta, and against the harsh measures adopted by the regime to suppress the striking workers. The movement used its Facebook page, which then had 70,000 members, to call for the organization of a general strike. Activists picked April 6 both as the starting day of the strike and as a name for the group, to commemorate the date on which Mahatma Gandhi ended his peaceful Salt March of 1930. The symbolic messages that lay behind the choice of name cannot be ignored. One clear message is that this strike was intended to mark the beginning of a long struggle against Mubarak's regime in emulation of Gandhi's practices. The second was the movement's intention to draw a clear inspiration from Gandhi in adopting a peaceful and nonviolent strategy of resistance. Some members of the movement reportedly received training in Serbia on nonviolent protest techniques.[14]

The April 6 Movement did not create a tight organizational structure. Describing itself on its webpage as "a group of Egyptian youth that do not belong to a specific political orientation and seek political change," the movement included youth from different political parties, movements, and organizations, as well as independent individuals. The movement was active on the internet and among the youth in different circles. It worked to improve its protest techniques in preparation for a major mass mobilization. However, its second general strike of 2009 was not successful, and its ability to mobilize a large segment of the population remained limited. According to Ahmad Salah, a cofounder of the movement: "We have been trying for a long time to build up sentiment, to choose the right moments, and come out for demonstrations, but the maximum number of people that would attend was only a few thousand."[15] The movement played a crucial role in amassing people for the January 25 protests: distributing more than 50,000 leaflets, explaining to people why they should join the protests, and organizing awareness campaigns in poor areas to educate people about their social and legal rights.[16]

The Popular Campaign for the Support of ElBaradei

In 2010, a new development energized Egyptian politics and indirectly but significantly contributed to the January 25 revolution. A group of young Egyptians wanted to create popular support for a consensual presidential candidate who could challenge Mubarak in the 2011 elections and end the chances of Gamal's succession. They wanted to raise awareness of the need for change and provide a new avenue for popular democratic change. Consequently, they rallied behind Mohamed ElBaradei as a possible candidate and formed the Popular Campaign for the Support of ElBaradei as President in 2011. Seeking to build a large constituency, this group became active in several provinces and mobilized the public in support of their campaign. These young activists were able to collect more than 1 million signatures; raise hopes of the possibility of a bottom-up, peaceful democratic change; and, more importantly, learn valuable skills in outmaneuvering the regime's repressive measures. These achievements became great assets in the January 25 revolution. The Popular Campaign urged people through its webpage to join the protests on January 25, and its members were among the youth leaders of the revolution.

The youth of other movements and parties also took part in the early days of the protests. The youth of the Muslim Brotherhood group have had a long history of activism on university campuses, as well as confrontation with the regime. This group was particularly well-known for its great discipline and organizational ability. According to many accounts, the role that the youth of the Muslim Brotherhood played during the first days of the revolution and the early confrontations with the regime's security forces was crucial in saving the revolution. These individuals courageously battled the security forces and the state-sponsored thugs. The youth of the Tomorrow Party, the youth of Justice and Freedom, and the youth of the Democratic Front Party were also all instrumental in calling for protests and mobilizing thousands of people from various neighborhoods.

The role of the Muslim Brothers

Mubarak's regime viewed and treated the Muslim Brotherhood group as the main challenger to its stability and systematically cracked down on its members. Unlike the legalized political parties, the Muslim Brotherhood challenged the regime's harassment, continued their activities, and periodically paid the price for their defiance. The period from 1995 to 2000 became known as the "bone-crushing" phase of repression, during which the regime intensified its crackdown and sent several leaders and members of the movement before six military tribunals, which awarded them harsh jail sentences. The Muslim Brothers adopted an assertive strategy in challenging the regime and a pragmatic orientation in the reform agenda they proposed. This approach became quite noticeable in early 2005, when the movement reasserted its presence in the political process, defied the regime's ban on its demonstrations, and even threatened to adopt a program of civil disobedience. The Brotherhood also cooperated with other political forces that did not share its ideological perspectives and jointly launched reform-oriented fronts. Subsequent arrests and crackdowns continued to prevent the movement from growing into an uncontrollable threat to the regime's hegemony. During Mubarak's last years, the confrontations with and repression of the group became even harsher.

The Muslim Brotherhood did not directly instigate the January 25 revolution, but it did actively participate in it. The group received strong warnings from state security not to support or join the planned protests. Concerned that the regime might use the group's participation to portray the protests as Islamist-led and thus provide an excuse for further crackdowns, the leadership of the Brotherhood announced that the group would not formally participate in the demonstrations, although its members would be free to take part on an individual basis. To defuse the situation, the group presented specific demands to the regime and urged it to introduce immediate reforms. The proposed reforms included ending the state of emergency, dissolving the fraudulent parliament, conducting new elections, and introducing constitutional amendments. The youth branch of the Muslim Brotherhood took a different position from the main group and participated fully in the revolution from its beginnings. Some prominent members of the Muslim Brotherhood also joined the protests early on and even played leading roles. Full involvement of the Brotherhood occurred on January 28, known as the Friday of Rage. Being both highly organized and popular, the Muslim Brotherhood managed to mobilize large numbers of their followers and were instrumental in confronting the brutality of security forces and the state-sponsored thugs. According to many accounts, members of the Muslim Brotherhood were at the frontlines during the violent clashes between anti-riot police and the protesters. Throughout the revolution, the Brotherhood adopted a conciliatory and pragmatic position. It agreed to not raise any of its religious slogans and gave assurances that after Mubarak's ousting, it would not field a candidate nor would it run for more than 35 percent of the seats of the parliament.

The role of labor unions

The last few years of Mubarak's reign witnessed an increase in the number of workers' strikes. The working class had been one of the main losers of the neoliberal economic policies that the government had adopted since the mid-1990s. These people were disproportionately affected by the process of privatization, repeated layoffs, depreciating wages, and job insecurity. Businessmen hired workers on temporary contracts and refused to offer them permanent appointments. Workers were also crushed by high inflation rates and increased costs of living. Starting in 2007, workers' protests and strikes began to spread throughout Egypt. In that year, workers organized close to 1,000 strikes and sit-ins in both the public and the private sectors. In 2008, the April 6 Movement was founded in support of workers' demands and strikes. In 2009, the number of workers' strikes and protests reached 800.[17]

The role of the workers was important throughout the revolution, particularly during the last days of Mubarak's reign. The leadership of the workers' unions had for a long time been intimidated by the regime and was opposed to taking part in the protests. The labor unions sometimes even forced workers to protest in support of Mubarak. However, thousands of workers joined the protesters in Tahrir Square and organized demonstrations to protest their deteriorating conditions and demand improvement of their wages and work conditions. On February 9, two days before Mubarak abdicated, workers intensified their protests and strikes in several provinces, which threatened to shut down the country. Protests were reported in major industrial cities, hospitals, steel factories, telecommunication centers, the Cairo airport, and two companies at the strategically important Suez Canal. For many Egyptians, the workers' involvement in the revolution sent a strong signal that the downfall of the regime was imminent.

The role of the military

The Egyptian military has been the main power base of all regimes in power since 1952. Since the military *coup* of the Free Officers in July 1952, the military, as an institution, has fostered a strong sense of ownership of the country. This feeling of ownership is based on a legacy of revolutionary legitimacy and the people's view that the military is a patriotic institution. For the past 60 years, all Egyptian presidents have come from the military establishment. Therefore, the military's approval of the succession of Gamal Mubarak, a civilian, to power was questionable, although it never publicly articulated its stance on that issue. In fact, Mubarak's grooming of Gamal and his increasing reliance on the Ministry of the Interior and a small circle of associates (Omar Suleiman and Safwat al-Sharif, among others) to advance this scenario created factionalism within the state institutions. One significant civilian faction was headed by Gamal and comprised the state NDP Party, the Minister of the Interior Habib al-Adli, certain business cronies, several cabinet members, and other civilians (newspapers editors, directors of state-owned media, and many intellectuals and university professors in the NDP Policies Committee). Gamal enlisted these elements to build an alternative power base, amplify his role, and promote his possible accession to power. Since 2002, this civilian faction started to exercise influence and assume control over the country's institutions, policies, and economy. In some instances, some of these policies, particularly the continued privatization of the economy and the spread of corruption, clashed with the military establishment's interests. The army, of course, represented another faction within the state and apparently disapproved of both this succession scenario and the direction the country was taking. The underlying conflict between these two factions may explain the role that the military adopted during the revolution.

Explanations for the success of the January 25 revolution

Mass mobilization

As discussed previously, several factors contributed to the success of the massive uprising of January 25. The key factor behind this success, however, was the ability of the protest organizers to achieve mass mobilization and adopt a nonviolent strategy that generated wide support for the protesters and defeated the regime's violent strategies. To be clear, this revolution could not have succeeded had it not been for the support of regular people and the role that various actors played in it. The number of Egyptians who actively took part in the 18-day protests has been estimated at around 15 million. To mobilize such a large number, regime opponents used both traditional and modern techniques of mass mobilization.

Not by Facebook alone!

Social media, particularly Facebook, has been considered the main tool behind the mass mobilizations of the revolution. However, traditional means of resistance have also been instrumental over the years in increasing people's awareness, underscoring the regime's weaknesses and vulnerabilities, and breaking the fear barrier. The Arab and Egyptian satellite stations that started to mushroom in the 1990s broke the regime's monopoly over the media and exposed its inefficiencies, corruption, and incompetence to millions of viewers. In the last few years before the revolution, talk shows provided space for critics of the regime and members of opposition parties and movements to air their opinions. These shows also raised issues that the regime considered untouchable and mounted harsh criticisms to specific policies and public figures. To project some sense of credibility and attract viewers, the state-run television stations had to emulate other talk shows and allow some criticism of state officials on its programs.

In the early 1990s, some newspapers managed to get licenses through court orders and begin publishing independently. These papers were able to attract fine journalists who had been critical of the government for years and who began to open wide cracks in the system. Many of their investigative reports revealed wide-ranging corruption in the country and provoked anti-regime sentiments. They also broadened the net of criticism to include Mubarak and his family and went as far as to publicly call for his removal from power. Mubarak's attempts to muffle these papers through a restrictive new press law did not dissuade these independent journalists from continuing their scathing criticism of the regime. Accordingly, some engaged in legal battles with the government and were given to prison sentences, particularly in the last years of Mubarak's regime. The independent papers played a remarkable role in raising the level of awareness and, more importantly, emboldening the people against the regime. Prior to January 25, young protesters also used other traditional means for mobilization such as SMS, sit-ins, night vigils, silent stands, demonstrations, strikes, leaflets, and word of mouth.

Social media

The spark behind the January 25 revolution came from the virtual world. Social networking played a critical role in Mubarak's downfall.[18] The first calls for the protests came through the Facebook page of the We Are All Khaled Said group, which had 400,000 members and had participated in the organization of several protest activities in 2010. The April 6 Movement, another major organizer, had 70,000 members, and the ElBaradie Group had 300,000 members. A few years before Mubarak's overthrow, tens of thousands of blogs reporting on the corruption and atrocities of the regime mushroomed.[19] These sites covered the efforts and protests that the different movements organized to challenge the regime, and they extensively used YouTube to document police brutality, acts of torture, and human rights violations. Video clips of police violations against ordinary citizens inside police stations and photos of Khaled Said, who was tortured to death by police, had a profound impact, provoking people's hatred against the security police and the regime as a whole. Until the regime cut off the internet on January 26, social media groups were instrumental in calling for protests and mobilizing the population on their pages. Full guidelines and detailed information for the January 25 protests were made public on the internet a few days before the revolution, and direct instructions were given to potential participants. Esam Al-Amin has noted that the January 25 revolution "was probably the only revolution in history that determined its commencement and announced its date to the world online."[20] In brief, virtual media and social networking leveraged mounting socioeconomic and political discontent through the skilful use of the internet, blogs, YouTube, Facebook, and Twitter and succeeded in mobilizing thousands of protesters on January 25. These protesters were immediately joined by hundreds of thousands of angry Egyptians, who spontaneously embraced the young organizers and their calls for economic and social justice, freedom, and dignity.

The organizers framed their demands in a way that ensured wide support for their uprising. Initially, they outlined four main economic and political demands: (1) address the problem of poverty by increasing minimum wages, improving education and health services, and providing unemployment benefits to the youth; (2) end the state of emergency, put an end to torture, and respect court sentences; (3) dismiss the Minster of the Interior; and (4) limit the president to only two terms. Taking these demands from cyberspace to the streets, the revolution began to unfold.

Protesters' strategy and tactics

Protests and demonstrations alone were not enough to change a regime. The movement needed a vision and a strategy. Organizers adopted a strategy of linking political and socioeconomic demands, achieving mass mobilization, and adopting nonviolence resistance. They also used clear tactics that aimed at wearing down the security forces and causing their collapse.

The instruction guidelines for the protests that the organizers posted online a few days before January 25 stressed the peaceful nature of the demonstrations. The protesters described themselves as peace advocates and did not call for any violence. They urged the participants to protect the rights of others while demanding their own. They warned participants not to respond to any provocation from the security forces or provide the state police with the opportunity to portray the protesters as saboteurs aiming to destroy the country. The instructions asked that participants exercise self-restraint and refrain from any illegal action that might jeopardize the safety of other participants, cause damage to private or public property, or unnecessarily disrupt the traffic. Protestors called for the extensive use of the Egyptian flag, requested that no particular banners be raised, and urged parties and movements not to use any ideological or religious slogans. The instructions described January 25 as a day for all Egyptians to call for basic rights of equality, social justice, and unity. Therefore, the unified slogans focused on common and popular demands such as employment, higher income, freedom, dignity, and social justice.

The adoption of a nonviolent strategy and the combination of political and socioeconomic demands secured a wide base of support from millions of Egyptians who joined the young and unarmed protesters and embraced the revolution. One protester explained the rationale behind the adoption of a nonviolent approach:

> We wanted to project a positive image to the people at home, to maintain a positive spirit. If the people saw us clashing with the police they would be scared. But when we did not attack the police, we conveyed a sense of calm, and sent a message that we were not afraid.[21]

Past experiences with strikes and demonstrations helped the organizers devise new tactics that proved decisive in confronting the security forces and ultimately bringing down the regime. The main objective was to wear down these forces and outlast them. In the past, protesters had gathered in main streets, grouped together in one location, and allowed themselves to be cordoned off by the security forces, who eventually forced them to disperse, usually after harsh confrontations and brutal crackdowns. This time, the protesters adopted different tactics. In response to calls for mass demonstrations on January 25, the Ministry of the Interior placed its antiriot forces on full alert 48 hours prior to that day. Taking no chances, it also deployed all its forces to control and decisively crack down on the demonstrations, leaving no back-ups available. Aware of this tactical error, the protesters managed to keep the antiriot police engaged and deployed for relatively long periods of time. Demonstrators started from mosques and side streets in poor neighborhoods. They also sought the help of major soccer fan groups, known as the "Ultras," that have hundreds of thousands of followers and long experience in dealing with security forces. These usually apolitical groups helped increase the number of protesters and instructed protesters in self-protection techniques and ways to avoid direct clashes with the antiriot police.[22] Finally, protesters also organized demonstrations in other major cities such as Alexandria, Suez, and

Ismailiya, using almost the same tactics: starting from poor areas, inviting people to join, and then pouring into main squares in massive numbers through various channels. This approach made it difficult for the anti-riot police to contain the demonstrators. By the time the protesters reached the main squares, their numbers had soared to hundreds of thousands and, in some cases, millions. As a result, the protesters were able to outnumber the antiriot police, and this huge number eventually defeated the regime's violent and repressive measures. Completely unarmed, the peaceful demonstrators braved the security forces for days, and on January 28—the third day of the demonstrations—the security forces ran out of ammunition, succumbed to exhaustion, and collapsed. They withdrew in a disorderly fashion, and, according to many participants, it was clear that the revolution had been won.

The regime's strategy: five mistakes that made a revolution

Mubarak's regime rested on three main pillars: the security forces, the NDP and its business cronies, and the military. All of these groups were defeated or neutralized in the first days of the revolution. The security forces were defeated on January 28, the NDP was defeated on February 2, and the military was neutralized on February 9. January 25 could have passed as a regular day had it not been for five major mistakes that Mubarak's regime made that contributed to the success of the revolution.[23]

Slow response

Mubarak did not want to repeat Tunisian President Ben Ali's "mistake" of cutting short and fleeing. A former fighter pilot, he thought he could dodge, outmaneuver, and land his plane safely. His advisors, led by his son and the Minister of the Interior, convinced him that the protesters were just a bunch of internet kids, and that the situation was completely under control. The regime was confident that these protests would be suppressed and dispersed in a few days. The key was to buy as much time as possible and use repressive force to crush the demonstrators. It took Mubarak four days, from January 25 to after midnight on January 28, to appear in public to address the nation and discuss the political measures he proposed to handle the situation. In the meantime, everyone who had access to a television screen—senior US and EU officials, human rights organizations, pundits, and many others— appealed to the Egyptian regime to make the right decision and respond meaningfully and quickly to the crisis. The slow political response enraged the protesters and made them more determined to continue challenging the regime and adding more pressure. The protests started by articulating limited socioeconomic and political demands that included dismissing the interior minister, ending torture and the state of emergency, and increasing minimum wages. Many protesters asserted that Mubarak missed several opportunities to defuse the situation by refusing to give concessions early and respond positively to some of the demands. For example, had Mubarak dismissed the Minister of the Interior or changed the government, he might still be in power today.

Excessive violence

From January 25 through February 2, Egyptians were able to see a clash between entirely two opposite sides: peaceful and unarmed protesters and vicious anti-riot police who used excessive and lethal force. Adopting a strategy of massive repression, the regime applied diverse violent techniques ranging from the use of "expired" tear gas and rubber and live bullets to mowing down demonstrators with police trucks and unleashing thousands of thugs armed with swords, knives, and machetes against the peaceful, unarmed protesters. The protesters were able in the end to defeat the security forces on January 28 and the thugs on February 2 in what became known as the Battle of the Camel, thus scoring a major victory over the second pillar of the state, the NDP. As was revealed later, the Battle of the Camel was masterminded by some top NDP officials and NDP-affiliated businessmen.[24] The excessive use of force and the medieval scenes of thugs attacking protesters on camels and horses sealed the fate of Mubarak's regime and any chance for him to continue in power. With every death of a demonstrator, popular sympathy mounted and more people rushed to support the protesters. Some participants even informed me that "good thugs" from surrounding neighborhoods came to their rescue and helped overpower the "bad thugs." All in all, the regime's strategy of continued and excessive violence backfired, leaving its repressive machine completely broken by February 2. As a result, what started as a popular uprising with limited reform demands ended as a mass revolution that overthrew the regime.

Digital Iron Curtain

In preparation for a major crackdown against the demonstrators, Mubarak's regime cut off the internet and cell phone services in Egypt on January 27 for several days. This measure was another fatal mistake that benefited the demonstrators because it affected the flow of communication between the security forces on the ground and their commanding officers in the headquarters of the Ministry of the Interior. According to security officers, many lost their walkie-talkies in the violent clashes and were unable to use their disconnected cell phones, which forced them into full withdrawal and eventually led to their retreat on the afternoon of Friday, January 28. Unable to use cell phones to check on demonstrating relatives in Tahrir Square, families flocked in thousands to the square and stayed by their kin throughout the clashes with the security forces. Finally, the lack of cell phone and internet communication forced protest organizers to plan events ahead of time and devise an advance schedule. All Egypt took notice of the early invitation to participate in the planned massive demonstrations on Sunday, Tuesday, and Friday.

Targeting foreign media

The systematic targeting of foreign correspondents and some TV stations exposed the regime's ugly face and turned Western public opinion against Mubarak. The regime's strategy started with shutting down Al Jazeera and arresting its correspondents in Cairo. Because it is almost impossible to block out the media, Al Jazeera continued its direct and live coverage of the events and aired news through other satellite stations. Its coverage was broadcast live on big screens in the square, and the protesters gave Al Jazeera the name of "The Voice of the Revolution." Scenes of well-known correspondents being harassed and hit in the square by Mubarak's thugs were incredibly repulsive and were widely viewed as unprecedented cruelty against professional media crews who were simply trying to report the facts to the rest of the world. These scenes highlighted the true nature of Mubarak's regime and stressed the need for his departure.

Stubbornness

The regime's slow political response to the crisis and its excessive violence were exacerbated by its offer of too few concessions to the protesters. This refusal to take the protesters seriously created an incentive for the protesters to keep raising their ceiling of demands. Recall that the demonstrators started on 25 January by demanding freedom and ending police brutality. As days passed, the ceiling of demands started to gradually rise as the regime's disappointing responses continued to fall short of the protesters' expectations. The list of demands began to escalate from "Bread, Freedom, and Social Justice" to "The People Want to Change the Regime" to "The People Want to Try the Butcher" to "The People Want to Clean up the State Institutions."

Mubarak had at least three opportunities to offer an adequate political solution to the crisis and defuse the situation. He could have expressed understanding of the people's demands early on and shuffled the entire cabinet to bring new, more credible faces to the government. Instead, he changed the cabinet while retaining 15 of his old, corrupt ministers. He also could have assured the people that he was not running for a sixth term of office or planning to transfer power to his son. Instead, he was ambiguous on both points, which led many Egyptians to question his credibility. And when he finally did admit that he understood the demonstrators' grievances and was willing to change, the very next day he unleashed his thugs to attack and brutalize peaceful protesters. His intransigence shattered any hope that could cling to power.

On February 11, 2011, Mubarak abdicated and transferred his authority to the Supreme Council of the Armed Forces (SCAF). The SCAF moved quickly to dismiss the parliament, suspend the constitution, and promise elections within six months, but its position throughout the revolution quickly raised questions. In a few days, the SCAF moved from a pivotal supporter of Mubarak's regime to a self-proclaimed "defender of the revolution." The military waited for some time before it finally decided which side to take. Many Egyptians believe that the SCAF took the side of the people in this confrontation and sided with the revolution, while others believe that it simply took a position that served its own interests as a military establishment. In choosing not to fire at the unarmed protesters and instead letting Mubarak go, the military took control of the revolution and managed the transition process, thus ensuring its continued influence over the country's politics.

As the security forces broke down and withdrew on January 28, Mubarak called in the military to suppress the protesters and maintain order. Reportedly, instructions were already given to suppress the demonstrators, but the military officers refused to shoot and remained neutral. In fact, because the protesters had faced the brutality of the security police for several days, they cheered at the sight of military forces stepping into Tahrir Square and other parts of the country to fill the vacuum left by the disappearance of the police. Protesters greeted the military with flowers, hugs, and slogans, chanting with enthusiasm: "The army and the people are one hand!" Some protesters even slept between the tracks of the tanks to prevent the army from leaving the square. A few days later, on January 31, the army issued several statements and communiqués in which it asserted its support for the legitimate demands of the people, assured the nation that it would not use violence against the peaceful protesters, and gave guarantees to protect the freedom of expression through peaceful means.

The army's position during the Battle of the Camel raised serious questions, however. On February 2, thousands of Mubarak's supporters charged into Tahrir Square. On the backs of camels and horses and carrying swords, clubs, and machetes, these supporters began attacking the unarmed protesters in an attempt to intimidate and disperse them. For 18 hours, the unarmed protesters were subject to these attacks, which quickly escalated with the use of rocks and Molotov cocktail bombs. Snipers equipped with laser-guided rifles (only available to state security forces) shot at the demonstrators, killing dozens and injuring hundreds. Throughout these violent clashes, the army refrained from intervening and refused to protect the unarmed protesters, despite their repeated pleas for intervention. Additionally, the day after Mubarak's departure, the SCAF gave firm instructions to the protesters to disperse from Tahrir Square and go home. Military police removed the tents and blankets from the square and engaged in scuffles with the protesters, beating them with sticks. Scores of protesters were detained and allegedly tortured in the area around the Egyptian museum where army units were stationed. Despite the protesters' success in removing Mubarak, the SCAF announced that it would keep and work with the cabinet that Mubarak had appointed on January 31 to run the country until the transition process was completed. However, massive demonstrations forced the SCAF to dismiss this cabinet on February 24.

After the removal of Mubarak, tension grew between the SCAF and the protesters, who were dismayed by the slow pace of change and who felt that they may have overthrown Mubarak, but not his regime. There are serious doubts that the military will introduce true democratic reform by withdrawing from politics and handing over power to civilians.

Conclusion

The success of the January 25 revolution in overthrowing a strongly entrenched and sclerotic regime surprised many, including the organizers of the protests themselves. This revolution had built up over several years of political repression, economic mismanagement, social injustice, police brutality, and mounting political activism. The movement ultimately toppled a regime that had monopolized power for three decades, controlled the political process, and suppressed individual and collective initiatives. Despite years of government-imposed political stagnation, grassroots protest movements, public figures, and independent journals articulated a well-defined reform agenda and gradually mobilized support for it. These movements succeeded in raising the level of opposition to and criticism of the regime, breaking the fear barrier, and inciting people to take their dissent to the streets, thus defying the regime's repressive machine.

The January 25 revolution was a true people's revolution that developed some unique features. It was inclusive of various social classes, groups, and movements. It transcended ideological differences and focused on a shared list of demands that united the protesters during the 18 days of the revolution and kept the protest momentum alive and strong. The revolution exhibited remarkable levels of pluralism and tolerance that had been missing in Egyptian society for decades. These values were reified in a new national spirit, which Egyptians called the "Spirit of Tahrir."

The youth played a key role in setting the stage for this popular revolution. From 2004 onwards, they were major participants in many of the protest movements, which provided them with important political and organizational experience. The youth then built on those experiences and combined them with modern organizational skills to achieve a mobilization of the masses that led to a successful revolution. During this decade, many of the youth grew dissatisfied with the traditional style of the old political parties and the inability of many of the emerging pro-change movements to achieve any real breakthroughs.

The revolution succeeded in highlighting and aggregating the political, economic, and social grievances of the Egyptian people. The combination of the political and socioeconomic dimensions was instrumental to the formation of this mass uprising. In this regard, the revolution in Tunisia was extremely important in raising hopes and showing the way to successfully overthrow an autocratic regime through nonviolent means. The peaceful strategy that the organizers of the protests used certainly contributed to the success of the revolution. Generally committed to nonviolence, the peaceful protests generated the support of millions of Egyptians, as well as the respect of the outside world. The unarmed and peaceful response of the demonstrators accentuated the repressive measures of a desperate regime and exposed its brutality, thus delegitimizing Mubarak and generating domestic and international pressures for his departure.

Acknowledgment

The author thanks Christina Buchhold for her invaluable assistance with this article.

Notes

1 Reuters, "US Urges Restraint in Egypt, Says Government Stable," January 25, 2011, http://af.reuters.com/article/topNews/idAFJOE70O0KF20110125.
2 Youth leader, interview with the author and David Cortright, June 8, 2011.
3 David Cortright, "Glimpses of the Revolution in Egypt," *Peace Policy*, July 6, 2011, http://peacepolicy.nd.edu/2011/07/06/glimpses-of-the-revolution.
4 David Rothkopf, "Foreign Policy: Overthrowing the Old Egypt Experts," *National Public Radio*, February 15, 2011, www.npr.org/2011/02/15/133771699/foreign-policy-handling-egypt-with-little-experience.
5 In my own experience, the minute that I stepped into the square, I was always greeted with breadsticks and cheese and tomato sandwiches. I was also a witness to this encounter: Shortly before the Friday prayers of February 10, an organizer tried to persuade some women to move in a certain direction to avoid crowds of men. The women refused to change their path, asserting that the men in the square always lowered their gaze and never bothered them.
6 On the day of the celebrations of Mubarak's ousting, an incident of sexual assault against an American journalist was reported. The perpetrators were unidentified mobs, allegedly pro-Mubarak thugs that tried to intimidate American journalists to prevent them from covering the events in Tahrir Square. For the civilized aspects of the revolution, see Nadia Mostafa, *Al-Thawra al-Masriya: A Civilizational Model* (Cairo: Civilization Center for Political Studies, 2011).
7 Nathan Brown and Emad El-Din Shahin, "Egypt," in Michele Penner Angrist (ed.) *Politics and Society in the Contemporary Middle East* (New York: Rienner, 2010), p. 213.
8 Economist Intelligence Unit, *Egypt Country Report* (London: Economist Intelligence Unit, 2008), p. 8.
9 Economist Intelligence Unit, *Egypt Country Report*, p. 32.
10 Alastair Sharp, "Cairo's Poorest Live Life on the Edge," *Reuters*, September 27, 2008, www.reuters.com/article/2008/09/28/us-egypt-shanty-idUSTRE48R00320080 928. See also Egypt.com News, "Shanty Towns Are Ideal Places for Criminals," *Egypt.com News*, October 22, 2007, http://news.egypt.com/en/20071022649/news/-egypt-news/shanty-towns-are-ideal-places-for-criminals.html.
11 Thomas Demmelhuber, "Parliamentary Elections and the Mubarak Regime: Long Live the Pharaoh!" *Qantara.de*, December 15, 2010, http://en.qantara.de/Long-live-the-Pharaoh/7116c154/index.html.

12 AmrHashim Rabi', *Thawrat 25 Yanayr: Qira'a Auwaliya wa Ru'ya Mustaqbaliya* [The January 25 Revolution: Preliminary Reading and Futuristic Vision] (Cairo: Markaz al-Dirasat al-Siyasiyawa al-Istratijiya, 2011), p. 437.
13 For in-depth analysis of the role of political parties and alternative political forces under Mubarak's regime, see Emad El-Din Shahin, "Political Parties in Egypt: Alive, but Not Kicking," in Kay Lawson and Jorge Lanzaro (eds) *Political Parties and Democracy* (Santa Barbara, CA: Praeger, 2010), pp. 3–26.
14 Esam Al-Amin reports that Muhammad Adel, a leader of the April 6 Youth Movement, "was dispatched to Serbia to meet with Srdja Popovic, a proponent of non-violent resistance and leader of Otpor (Resistance) Movement, a group of young activists who helped depose Slobodan Milosevic in 2000. He came back to Cairo with DVDs and other educational and training materials that demonstrated in detail some of the non-violent means and civil disobedience techniques used to induce political change." See Esam Al-Amin, "Conditions and Consequences: Anatomy of Egypt's Revolution," *CounterPunch*, February 17, 2011, www.counterpunch.org/2011/02/17/anatomy-of-egypt-s-revolution.
15 Ahmad Salah, "Co-Founder of April 6 Movement," International Center on Non-Violent Conflict, www.nonviolent-conflict.org/index.php/learning-and-resources/on-the-ground/1547-ahmed-salah.
16 Ahmad Tuhami Abd al-Hay, "Kharitat al-Harakat al-Shababiya al-Tahawriya fi Misr," Markazal-Jazeera li al-Dirasat [The Youth of January 25], February 10, 2011, www.al-jazeera.net/NR/exeres/5898A077-3AAE-4319-BE5D-E89972395162.htm. Iman Abd al-Munim, "Shabab January 25th," OnIslam.com, February 6, 2011, www.asharqalarabi.org.uk/ruiah/b-?taqarir-53?2.htm.
17 Ikhwanweb.net, "Escalating Strikes: A New Fad in Egypt," April 23, 2010, www.ikhwanweb.com/article.php?id=24439. See also Omayma Abd al-Latif, "Al-Thawra al-Sha'biya fi Misr" ["The People's Revolution in Egypt"], Arab Center for Research and Policy Studies, February 2011.
18 For more information on the role of digital media in Egypt and Tunisia, see Philip N. Howard and Muzammil M. Hussain, "The Role of Digital Media," *Journal of Democracy*, 22 (2011): 35–48. See also Sallie Pisch, "Social Networking, Political Action and Its Real Impact in Egypt," *Bikya Masr*, March 21, 2010, www.ikhwanweb.com/article.php?id=23809.
19 For more information on the impact of blogs on Egyptian politics before the January 25 revolution, see Ikhwanweb, "Effect of Egyptian Blogs on Politics, Society," July 7, 2007, www.ikhwanweb.com/article.php?id=1221.
20 Al-Amin, "Conditions and Consequences."
21 Youth leader, interview with the author and David Cortright, Cairo, June 8, 2011.
22 On the role of the Ultras, see Muhammad Yahya and Amr Izzat, "Al-Ultras: Sira' fi Mudarrajat al-Kura waWihda fi Midan al-Tahrir" ["The Ultras: The Biography of the Football Clubs and Their Unity in Tahrir Square"], *Al-Masry al-Youm*, February 28, 2011, www.almasry-alyoum.com/printerfriendly.aspx?ArticleID=289158.
23 The following discussion has been adapted from an article by the author that was published in *The Atlantic*. See Emad Shahin, "Mubarak's 5 Fatal Mistakes," *The Atlantic*, February 24, 2011, www.theatlantic.com/international/archive/2011/02/mubaraks-5-fatal-mistakes/71661.
24 Sherif Tarek, "Bosses, Enforcers and Thugs in Egypt's Battle of the Camel to See Harsh Retribution," *AhramOnline*, April 19, 2011, http://english.ahram.org.eg/News/10293.aspx).

5 The February 17 *intifada* in Libya

Disposing of the regime and issues of state-building

Youssef M. Sawani

Introduction

In February 2011 Libya joined other countries of the Arab Spring, including Tunisia, Egypt, and Yemen when popular protests broke out against Qaddafi's decades' old authoritarian rule, which Libyans categorized as "systemless," which implies a regime that was highly eccentric and that avoided building state institutions. Widespread protests called for the overthrow of the regime and for the establishment of democracy and respect for human rights and freedom. The protests that began in early January 2011 first had origins in popular dismay over the government's failure to resolve longstanding housing shortages. However, the issue of housing was not the essential cause behind the protests. People initiated the demonstrations concerning housing to convey indirectly deeper political feelings. These protests eventually escalated into an uprising that called for Qaddafi to step down.[1]

Unlike Tunisia or Egypt, which were examples of peaceful protests that led to the deposition of long reigning despots, Qaddafi would not cede power peacefully: violence was required to change the regime. The shift from peaceful protest to violence was triggered by the regime's repressive reaction to protests following the arrest of Fathi Terbil, a young lawyer who represented an association of families representing victims who died during the Abu Salim Prison Massacre. For those who are unfamiliar with the Abu Salim Prison Massacre, in 1996 security forces opened fire on inmates at the prison that was located in Tripoli, killing 1,200 inmates in cold blood. The only crime they had committed was to ask for basic rights and the implementation of courts' decisions that dictated the release of most of them. Most of the Abu Salim victims were from the eastern part of the country. Their families had regularly organized weekly gatherings and sit-ins in Benghazi. At the beginning the government tolerated these protests. However, when calls for nationwide protests were launched via social media websites to protest yet again on February 17, 2011, security forces opened fire and gunned down peaceful demonstrators in front of Security Headquarters in Benghazi. Libyan authorities detained Terbil on the mistaken presumption that he was linked to the call for demonstrations. His arrest triggered a spontaneous protest and the authorities were obliged to succumb to popular pressures and, in order to avoid further confrontations, they released the young lawyer.

The incident was widely reported and, despite Terbil's release, it proved sufficient cause to spark wider protests. These protests began very peacefully but escalated rapidly into an armed uprising that led to a full-scale war that later not only engulfed the country but also eventually involved intervention by external international military forces. The United Nations' Security Council invoked the Responsibility to Protect (R2P) principle and issued Resolution 1973, which imposed a no-fly zone across Libya. The resolution was intended to protect civilians in Libya and effectively created a regime for its enforcement that permitted the use of NATO aircraft to enforce the no-fly zone. For this reason, the Libyan case represents an exception among the cases being examined in this book and it requires an exceptional analysis of the role and consequences of having foreign powers, as represented by NATO, who had the internationally sanctioned right to intervene in a situation that was tantamount to a civil war in a sovereign state. At the same time the Libyan case can be distinguished from Iraq because from the standpoint of the Libyan rebels, their decision to resist the regime had the support of the Arab League and it was the League that requested Western military intervention to protect civilians and to disable the regime, which was eventually overthrown.

The Libyan case will also raise problematic questions regarding whether the future Libyan state's legitimacy has been somewhat compromised because of the military assistance it received from NATO. Another issue that needs analysis is the extent to which the R2P principle may be interpreted and applied.[2] The events occurring in Libya will have far reaching repercussions not only for the future of the country but also for the legitimacy of the R2P principle.

A narrative of the uprising: the escalation of regime violence and the making of a popular uprising

On February 15, 2011 when security forces arrested young lawyer Fathi Terbil and subjected him to interrogation, a spontaneous gathering of people from all walks of life took place in front of the security headquarters in Benghazi. Among those who participated were human rights activists, lawyers, judges, academics, journalists, doctors, educated citizens, and students. News about the protest spread swiftly throughout the country when a Libyan journalist (Idris Al-Mesmari) broke the story in a telephone conversation with the Al Jazeera news channel. The protests led the authorities to release the lawyer in an unprecedented move, which effectively indicated that protests of this sort could possibly force the regime to capitulate to public pressure. People sensed that the regime was in a state of fear and could possibly be compelled to compromise more than ever before. For the first time in more than 40 years of rule, Qaddafi's regime bent and wavered. This development raised the morale of the protesters and was a powerful incentive for those who had been planning the February 17 protests.³

In the beginning the regime attempted to placate protesters and hinted at greater appeasement by releasing more than 100 political prisoners belonging to Islamist movements. This, however, proved inadequate. The measure failed to quiet the protests and those released were likely to participate in future demonstrations. The regime then employed the tactic of detaining large numbers of activists suspected of being linked to the call for demonstrations that were held on February 17, and news of these arrests spread in Benghazi and elsewhere as security forces widened the circle of arrests to include Tripoli and other cities. The move backfired and precipitated even more protests, hence providing a rationale for accelerating the pace of events.

Just before the demonstrations of February 17, on February 16, demonstrations took place among groups scattered throughout the streets of Benghazi. The heavy hand of the security apparatus came down and increased casualties galvanized the determination of more people to respond to the call for the protests planned for the next day. The demonstrations were peaceful in nature and directed towards demands for human rights; political freedom; political and constitutional reforms; and the fight against corruption. The regime insisted on its policy of ignoring legitimate demands and turned a blind eye to reform. Instead the regime elected to characterize such demands as "echoes of foreign interest" or more ominously as "treason." Qaddafi and his media machine persisted, accusing protesters of all matter of imaginable sins and utilizing denigrating epithets and base language to describe them. Qaddafi's tactic of "naming and shaming" suggested that the protesters—and later the rebels—were mere "puppets of foreign powers," "elements of Al-Qaeda," "salafists," "jihadists," "drug addicts," "heretics," and "separatists" who might best be described as "rats."⁴ Such a position left no room for any accommodation and was clearly a rejection of dialogue, indicating lack of willingness to take any substantive steps in the direction of change or reform, and it had the effect of convincing the protesters to raise the ceiling on their demands and call for the ouster of Qaddafi. On February 17 protesters burned police stations as well as security and revolutionary committees' buildings. The arson of the regime's architectural representations of power was highly symbolic, and such buildings were set ablaze across the country from Derna in the east to Tripoli and other towns and villages in the west. These actions hardened Qaddafi, leading to his intransigence and refusal to concede to demands for change. He grew stubborn and more dogmatic than ever, withdrawing from reality to his view that the protesters turned rebels were merely "rats" and "gangsters" who used drugs to dominate the minds of young people and exploit them for evil purposes.⁵

The start of protests in the east of the country and the failure of Qaddafi's apparatuses of repression to resist their spread caused Qaddafi to panic. Regime propaganda attempted to brand the movements as "separatist," thereby tapping into the traditional division in Libya between the east and the west and attempting to mobilize the west against the east. However, when the inhabitants of the western mountain town of Zintan and coastal towns such as Misurata and Zawiya joined the protests, this markedly weakened the regime's rationale for such claims or for use of this stratagem.

At noon on February 17, 2011, people gathered outside the Court of North Benghazi (which would later become the headquarters of the revolution), and then proceeded to walk in a demonstration that came into confrontation with the elements of the regime who were wearing yellow construction helmets (publically referred to as "men of yellow helmets"). The clash resulted in the killing of a number of demonstrators and the injury of many. Angered by the violent response of the security forces and the casualties they suffered, the protesters burned police stations and shouted slogans demanding the overthrow of the regime and the establishment of a democratic system.

By February 18, protests swept through all districts of Benghazi. Buildings associated with the regime such as those of the police, the People's Congresses, and the Revolutionary Committees were set on fire. Similar actions were reported in cities and towns such as Derna, Bayda, and Ajdabiya. Further to the east enraged protesters carried out similar acts and in Tobruk a concrete monument in the form of Qaddafi's *Green Book* was demolished. The angry protests and the burning of buildings engulfed the entire eastern sector of the country while elements of the regime and security forces either withdrew or opted to join the uprising. It was not long before many cities, towns, and villages in both east and west joined the protests. The uprising then spread to more desolate locations such as the western mountain towns of Jadu, Rujban, Yefren, and coastal towns such as Zawiya and Sabratha and the Tripoli districts of Souk Al-Gomaa, Fashloum, and Tajoura.

This situation continued on February 19, in eastern Libya with significant numbers from the Libyan armed forces joining the demonstrators. On February 19 and 20 the youth attacked the headquarters of Fadeel Bou Omar Special Battalion in Benghazi, which resulted in many deaths. This particular incident, led by unarmed youth, was a milestone in the revolt and a decisive step towards the final break between the people and Qaddafi's regime. The incident aroused popular sentiments in favor of the revolt and had the direct effect of increasing its momentum. The spirit of revolt became deeply rooted and spread widely. Zawiya and Misurata joined the revolt and on February 20 Tripoli witnessed its first "day of rage." The regime responded with brute force and, as repression mounted, the revolt accelerated.[6]

Dissidents and the institutionalization of the *intifada*

The widening scale and intensity of the protests pushed the regime to tighten its grip on security to prevent the secession of other areas. Massacres became frequent and the horror of the situation led a number of officials, including politicians and diplomats at home and abroad, to defect from the regime and pledge their support for the protesters. At this moment in time, the uprising started to benefit from the services of many experts who were qualified to deal with the crisis and who understood the ways and means of obtaining global support for the revolution.[7]

Also at this moment in time, the rebels and their incipient leadership began the creation of institutions that would express and implement their interests. The liberation of the east and some of the towns and villages of the western mountains underscored the need for the creations of mechanisms to administer these areas. Therefore, a number of personalities representing a cross-section of the Libyan political spectrum set up a National Transitional Council (NTC) to speak on behalf of the rebels and to perform the task of soliciting support from the international community. The NTC was formally announced on March 5, 2011, while local councils were formed in areas that had been liberated.[8] Local councils and coalitions were entrusted with the tasks of augmenting the revolution, safeguarding its achievements, administering local affairs, and representing regions at the NTC.

Given these innovative solutions, the Libyan uprising provided an extraordinary organizational model that compensated for the absence of a unified political leadership at the beginning of the uprising. This development initiated work on the *institutionalization* of the revolution and the establishment of a transitional government before the fall of the regime.[9] Later, in Syria, the Libyan model would be emulated by the Syrian opposition. Once set up, local councils and coalitions and the NTC succeeded in gaining world recognition first as the legitimate interlocutor and representative of the Libyans and later as the *sole* legitimate representative of the Libyan people.

After several weeks of watching Qaddafi mete out violence and repression against unarmed demonstrators, with his indiscriminate killing of not less than 6,000 people in the first few weeks, the West became convinced that Qaddafi was set on a war of relentless liquidation of the opposition. For the world community it appeared obvious that Qaddafi's regime was bound to commit further atrocities, and that failure to act would permit him to carry out a war of extermination in Benghazi. There was a realization that if his forces remained unchecked, they would quite possibly commit a barbaric massacre of the sort that transpired in Srebrenica. Mass slaughter in Benghazi seemed a likely and horrific reality.[10]

While Qaddafi's ground and air forces were engaged in his war against the people and the number of victims was increasing, voices of the Libyan opposition were demanding the imposition of a no-fly zone over Libya to protect Benghazi and the lives of civilians who did not have the means to substantially resist Qaddafi's fanatical elite brigades. Those participating in the Libyan resistance requested the creation of a no-fly zone but they did not request the presence of foreign military troops on Libyan soil. History shows that their efforts succeeded and the world responded. The coordinated efforts of Western, Arab, and Muslim leaders that involved the Arab League and the Organization of Islamic Cooperation resulted in the adoption of United Nations' Security Council Resolutions 1970 and 1973, which applied wide sanctions against Qaddafi's regime and imposed a no-fly zone.[11]

The salvation of Benghazi and an irreversible tide

For Benghazi, March 19, 2011, was a historically crucial day. While troops of Qaddafi's killing machine were massing and approaching the entrances to the city, Western warplanes (mainly French) participating in Operation Odyssey Dawn, attacked Qaddafi's forces, preventing them from launching an attack on Benghazi and thus saving the city from potential annihilation.[12]

Qaddafi rejected all calls for dialogue, being convinced that this *intifada* would fail. Qaddafi had always scorned and mocked Libyans, claiming they were apathetic *vis-à-vis* politics or by maintaining that the leaders of the resistance were "agents of foreign powers" or "Al-Qaeda terrorists." He called the revolt a separatist mutiny and he refused to listen to advice coming from different sources including his friends in Europe and Turkey.[13] He continued to believe erroneously that his closer ties to the West, especially after his diplomatic "rehabilitation" following his decision to give up on a program of weapons of mass destruction in 2003, would give him a free hand to deal with this revolt in Libya.[14]

Qaddafi wagered that because his regime posed no threat to the West, he would be given a free hand to repress this *intifada*. Qaddafi underestimated the importance of international pressure and the role of public opinion in the formulation of Western foreign policy. He was not prepared for dialogue, compromise, or elections; and, instead, he provoked even more ire by insulting the Libyan people by asking the degrading question: "Who are you?"[15] Even ideas that had been voiced by his son, Saif al-Islam, on the question of the constitution, the rule of law, freedom of the press, and other reforms remained devoid of substance. In any event, nothing tangible was to materialize of such ill-fated and largely *pro forma* reforms. For more than seven years no real reform policies and initiatives had been implemented. Reform-minded Libyans and youth who had attached some hope to Saif al-Islam's ideas and initiatives were disillusioned and this led to widespread frustration.[16]

In the midst of this revolt Qaddafi allegedly changed course and tried to win over young people and reformists by announcing that his regime would consider drafting a constitution and other reform measures. Such promises were designed to weaken the uprising by satisfying some of its demands but they were at least three years too late, especially after Saif al-Islam's 2007 speech in which he appeared bent on extending the life of the regime rather than serious reform.[17] Worse still was Qaddafi's insistence on the continued denigration of the uprising at large and the youth in particular as "rats," "traitors" and "hallucinating stray groups affected by drugs and Viagra sexual enhancement pills." Such belligerence plainly undermined any show of goodwill that Qaddafi might have put forward to avoid full-scale civil war.

The noxious televised speech that Saif al-Islam made on the evening of February 20, 2011, did nothing to assuage the volatile situation but rather proved to be the straw that broke the camel's back. In his address he did not give the *intifada* or Libyans in general any option other than to back down and submit to the regime, promising an amnesty, which could hardly have been deemed credible in view of the carnage being created by the regime. The alternative he proposed was greater repression and the threat of civil war. He was, in effect, unrepentant and was determined to fight all along to the last bullet, the last man, and the last woman.[18] Abdel Rahman Shalgam, Permanent Representative of Libya to the United Nations, summarized the situation best when he described Qaddafi's position toward the protests by saying, "Qaddafi says to the Libyans: 'Either I govern you or else I'll kill you!'"[19]

It seemed only appropriate to conclude that Saif al-Islam wanted to remind the Libyan people of what his father had said in the early 1970s. Faced with university students in Benghazi who demanded that the military return to their barracks and hand over power to civilians, Qaddafi replied: "I found this country in ruins and will only leave it in ruins!"[20] And to a great extent, Qaddafi kept to his word.

The revolution of February 17: the underlying causes

What happened in Libya was not expected. It initially started as a restricted and specific protest directed towards the particular issue of housing shortages and redressing the victims of Abu Salim prison massacre. Although early January 2011 had witnessed riots that were accompanied by the occupation by squatters of thousands of uncompleted homes in government housing projects, the linkage between these events and the later protests was not yet there.[21] However, it does seem that considerable tension had accumulated in Libya.

What may give the impression of being a sudden and surprising surge of protests and uprisings in fact reflects a cumulative outpouring after four decades of Qaddafi's rule. Although the ideological premises expressed in the *Green Book* were arguably associated with ideals of democracy, justice, and egalitarianism, actual policies revealed a contradiction between ideology and lived experience, obliging Libyans to live in a peculiar confluence of three simultaneously overlapping systems to be expressed as follows.[22]

The first was what may be termed an *ideological system* as outlined in the *Green Book* that focused upon the realization of democracy, justice, equality, and an overall scheme of ethical and moral values that could be shared by humanity at large. This system was utilized as a justificatory mechanism and as a basis for supporting the legitimacy of the regime as well as that of its leadership.

The second was what we might call the *formal system*. This involved the "official" and "*pro forma*" application of the mechanisms recommended by the *Green Book* for structures of government, which took the form of political and administrative institutions, local government, and other units. Accordingly, after March 1977, when the Jamahiriya or the "state of the masses" (as coined by Qaddafi) was announced, a host of "official" institutions came into existence. Theoretically, these institutions were to be created to make the Jamahiriya real in the field of practice, but in reality these institutions and associations were dysfunctional and bereft of any real power. Differently stated, they camouflaged the reality that real power resided elsewhere.

The third system, however, was an informal arrangement of power and influence that Qaddafi was keen to set up at all levels of political, economic, social, and military life. Such informal arrangements brokered real authority and they reflected a pattern of carefully crafted political, military, tribal and economic alliances that in terms of *realpolitik* created a hegemony over and above formal politics that dictated and controlled every major political action or policy. This third system appropriated the other two systems and employed them for various ends. It is in this context that it may be possible to understand the role of Qaddafi's family and the most prominent men of his Qaddadfa tribe in addition to the role played by those who had become to be known as the "men of the tent."[23] This latter term referred to the inner circle of the Qaddafi regime who were in constant consultation with him and who were involved in all matters of consequence. This inner circle was composed of those who typically, and quite literally, gathered in Qaddafi's tent, including his own family, his tribe's leaders and some members of the defunct Revolutionary Command Council that had been organized in the aftermath of the September 1, 1969, *coup* that had brought Qaddafi to power. Others, including some prominent and loyal individuals with personal ties to Qaddafi, heads of the security apparatus, prominent social or tribal leaders, and trusted members of the Revolutionary Committees joined this group.[24]

Although Qaddafi came to power through a military *coup* in September 1969, initially he was able to build a sufficiently wide base of popular support. He successfully managed in the early years of his regime to construct a populist legitimacy based on his responses to the aspirations, hopes, and needs of the population. Yet Qaddafi was keen to remain in power. He was driven towards personal glory and the building a personality cult around himself, resulting in the elimination of every source of potential opposition from any quarter. Many believe that Qaddafi began as a progressive revolutionary who fulfilled the aspirations of ordinary Libyans for a higher standard of living and who achieved accomplishments in the realm of social services and a welfare state.[25] Coupled with a revolutionary pan-Arab and anti-imperialist foreign policy, Qaddafi represented a Third World leader who was prepared to devote a great deal of the country's resources to finance ill-conceived and disastrous foreign adventures that cost the country dearly.[26]

Because Qaddafi wanted to build a state in a way that satisfied his personal aspirations and ego as a self-acclaimed visionary or "prophet" whose ideology or philosophy could resolve all human agonies, he took Libya on an exhaustive odyssey, claiming the application of "direct democracy." The regime he built he claimed was one of "people's power" yet it provided cover for his authoritarian rule that brooked no dissent and rejected freedom of expression. Starting with a speech he made at the town of Zuwarah in 1973, Qaddafi launched his vision and let his imagination run wild in the construction of forms or models for political practice that would theoretically integrate people in politics and would lead to direct participation. In practice, however, Qaddafi was determined to eliminate his opposition.[27]

On the ground the system envisioned and eventually established by Qaddafi grew increasingly repressive and authoritarian. Those who dared to oppose Qaddafi or voice criticism were either hanged in public squares or were tortured and imprisoned. Scores of Libyans were executed. Qaddafi, encouraged by massive oil revenues in the 1970s, and taking advantage of a bipolar geopolitical rivalry between the capitalist West and the communist East, pursued adventures in foreign policy the worst of which were a war with Chad and Libyan intervention in other parts of the world, usually in Africa. These misadventures do not include acts of terrorism supported by Qaddafi on the pretext that he was supporting "liberation movements." Petrodollars made it possible for Qaddafi to play the roles of a self-proclaimed regional leader, bastion of revolution, and champion of Arab, African, and/or Islamic unity and solidarity. Oil power had an enormous impact in affording Qaddafi the means to pursue his various policies with a free hand, and to antagonize the West after periods of some understanding or cooperation, or whenever this suited his purposes.[28]

One of the most important concerns for Qaddafi was to prevent the emergence of organizations or social forces that might impede his Jamahiriya experiment. Accordingly, he embarked on a policy of destroying the private sector and the emerging middle class and depriving these social actors of viable means of potential influence. The state nationalized all economic activities, making the government the sole supplier and employer. Likewise, Qaddafi was as just keen to eliminate any chance for the emergence of political opposition of any kind. This policy involved the adoption and application of methods of repression and terror, leading to violations of human rights, especially as committed by his Revolutionary Committees. Therefore, opposition to the Qaddafi regime began to take various forms, from attempted military *coups* to peaceful expressions of resistance, usually organized by opposition groups abroad.

In the face of opposition, Qaddafi's policy was to introduce greater restrictions on freedom, repression, and extrajudicial trials and summary executions. Overall, there was no willingness to accept dissenting voices and there was even a systematic policy of physically liquidating opposition abroad. The first half of the 1980s witnessed mounting assassination campaigns of Libyan opposition members living abroad whom the regime labeled "stray dogs."[29] Any Libyan who made public his opposition or criticism of Qaddafi was a legitimate target for the Revolutionary Committees or "hit squads," anywhere in the world, or as he had told Libyans in 1978, they were free to travel to either "the North or South Pole" if they wanted, but if they criticized the revolution they would be found "wherever they were."[30]

However, the deterioration of state revenues amid global economic conditions in the 1980s cut short the continuation of such a policy, when the Qaddafi regime was forced to deal with growing internal popular unrest and economic hardship. The government was compelled to adopt austerity measures that were worsened by already bad relations with the rest of the world. Economic conditions played an effective role in provoking anger and fomenting dissatisfaction at the grassroots level; voices were heard demanding better living conditions. Government policies became the target of wider popular criticism that highlighted corruption, which echoed dissatisfaction at all levels.

To deal with this dissatisfaction Qaddafi initiated an economic *infitah* or "opening up" policy in 1987. While instituting the "opening up" policy, he sought to mitigate the negative aspects of these policies that he knew would provoke anger and unrest among the populace.[31] This Qaddafi called a "revolution within the revolution."[32] This initiative temporarily alleviated tensions and, hence, reduced the risk of an uprising against the regime. In the words of Dirk Vandewalle, this was a "safety valve perestroika" that left "intact the rentier economy and the patronage system that fueled Qadhafi's political experiments."[33] The *infitah* proved to be the initiation of a new policy that sought to lay the groundwork for a less confrontational relationship with the people. Luckily enough for Qaddafi, the oil market later improved and the regime was able to proceed with accommodating the economic demands of the people. The fact that Libyan revenues climbed back up to higher levels meant that the regime had resources needed to assuage the demands being made by the population.

At this juncture, because of preexisting animosity to the Reagan administration and because he could now afford to do so, Qaddafi resorted to state-sponsored terrorism that culminated with the bombing of the Pan Am flight over Lockerbie in 1988. Qaddafi had organized the downing of the plane in response to the US-sponsored air raids on his home at the Aziziya barracks in Tripoli in 1986. After the attack over Lockerbie, international economic sanctions were imposed upon Libya, leading to austerity measures, a declining economy, and a renewed set of hardships upon the Libyan people. Libya suffered a great deal because of the sanctions imposed by the US-dominated UN Security Council. The Lockerbie case further revealed just how vulnerable Libya was. A very important implication was that Lockerbie underscored the fragility of internal domestic politics. The sanctions also made clear that Libya's lack of economic diversification had structurally weakened the economy. Because of these events, Qaddafi was concerned about the stability of the state, the survivability of the regime, and the consolidation of its power base. Ideology would remain, however, an important source of political legitimacy and mobilization, but its role in shaping foreign policy options became greatly diminished.[34]

Fluctuating prices in oil markets and the application of international sanctions were underlying causes for the extraordinary concern over regime security and stability, which led to the neglect of other vital aspects of societal security. The regime blamed the international sanctions for a variety of ills and used them as a scapegoat as well as a way of compensating for its poor organization, corruption, and lack of transparency and accountability in the management of economic resources and their uneven distribution. Reference to international sanctions and the need to prepare for the worst served as justification for the continuation of the *status quo*. These were the themes to which Qaddafi resorted so as to deflect growing public dissatisfaction with his regime.

Public dissatisfaction found its way into the discussions of the Popular Congresses. The Libyan people viewed sanctions as indicative of the poor management of the economy. On many occasions the Popular Congresses and the National General People's Congress raised concerns over this issue. Criticism of the "executive branch"—that is, the Popular Committees—became the order of the day leading Qaddafi himself to intervene in the deliberations. To compound problems, the state was effectively abandoning its social obligations, and the welfare system was coming under increasingly heavy pressure because insufficient funds were being directed towards its maintenance or development. The failure to sustain social welfare led to considerable social dissent.

By all accounts, there was a dilemma. Not only did the country have to live with sanctions, it also had to reckon with the grim understanding that the US might decide to use other means, including brute force, to change the regime and its leadership. The domestic situation was in dire need of resources to maintain a reasonable standard of living and public welfare. There was also a need to accommodate a more active role for a younger population that had been brought up under the umbrella of a *rentier* distributive state. Vandewalle notes that the international dynamics had changed and the oil wealth was no longer what it once was, which meant that the regime and its policies were facing manifold dilemmas.[35]

Saif al-Islam and the "Libya of tomorrow": rehabilitation, the domestic context, and an impossible reform

Saif al-Islam Qaddafi tried to convince his father of the need to take measures in the application of policies that would gradually reduce international pressure imposed on Libya. He emphasized the need to address internal issues that could possibly mitigate popular anger.[36] Saif al-Islam's initiative was intended to attract reform-minded Libyans, youth, and moderate elements of the diaspora opposition who, by now, were disenchanted and desperate about the possibility of change within the regime. In particular, Saif al-Islam was keen on recruiting young people to rejuvenate the regime and renew its legitimacy. It is important to understand the possible effects of the demographic phenomenon of the "youth bulge" on the thinking behind Saif's project because in Libya approximately 65 percent of the population was below the age of 40. This new approach confirmed a dire need for the reexamination of the ineffective techniques adopted by the regime as well as the necessity of revising political discourse. The conventional wisdom was that reform was badly needed because of *necessity* rather than conviction.[37]

While all of this was transpiring, a major operation was underway, which entailed a process of quiet economic restructuring. The fallout over the Lockerbie incident and attendant sanctions took place at a time when the world was undergoing radical changes. Libya no longer had friends. Old friends changed camps and ideology proved incapable of resisting globalizing market forces and liberal ideas. Qaddafi had spoken of the irreversible tide of globalization. He saw it as a force to be reckoned with through conversion rather than convulsion. Globalization, in Qaddafi's view, had done away with old dogmas and concepts. Indeed, he argued, globalization had dealt a heavy blow to nationalism and older notions of the nation-state. Only economics was viable in globalization.[38]

Underway was a process of revision and attaching new connotations to yesteryear's dogma within a framework of politics that seemed bent on accepting new boundaries because the security of the regime and the state was at stake. It was in this context that Saif al-Islam Qaddafi embarked on work towards solving Libya's problems with the outside world. In this endeavor he succeeded admirably. Subsequently, he turned his attention to domestic issues through a focus on economic liberalization and restructuring the economy. For this project to succeed, he needed to obtain a reasonable degree of popular acceptance and approval for his program, particularly from youth and other important advocates of political and economic reform. It was not viable to break completely with the existing order, as that would likely have proven a double-edged sword that might have snuffed out the experiment before it even had a chance to begin.

Therefore, the development of a new agency for political action that could serve also as a political platform for Saif al-Islam Qaddafi was indispensable. To this end, the Qaddafi Development Foundation was founded officially in 2003. Through Saif al-Islam's management, the foundation accomplished a number of achievements that contributed decisively towards leading Libya to address many persistent long-standing internal and external issues.

The Qaddafi Development Foundation primarily focused upon the creation of appropriate conditions to render the political system responsive to its priorities while still operating in an environment that effectively narrowed its options. The Libyan economy was beset by crises and structural problems with negative social and political repercussions multiplying every day. Such challenges may be traced back to policies Libya adopted in the late 1970s. That economic approach was marked by excessive state control of the public sector, while marginalizing the private sector. That policy created sharp imbalances that risked development plans. The economy was suffering to the extent that it seemed on the verge of suffocation, and this necessitated a restructuring policy that involved the rationalization of public expenditure that would open opportunities for the private sector to participate effectively in economic activities.[39]

With the economy suffering from numerous structural distortions, reconsideration of many policies was mandatory. This was vitally important because Libya needed to reintegrate into the world community after sanctions were lifted and relations with the West were normalized. In brief, the regime was obliged to embark on economic reform and a proposal known as the National Economic Strategy was prepared. This plan was predicated and drafted on the basis of concepts of competitiveness associated with Harvard business professor Michael Porter of the consultancy firm Monitor Group.[40] However, what resulted in the end was a set of uncoordinated interventions that generally sought to liberalize the economy, develop the business environment, attract foreign direct investment (FDI) while encouraging private business activities and entrepreneurship. Most of the proposals were eventually shelved as Qaddafi discovered that for such ideas to be viable and effective they also needed to be accompanied by an entire range of political and legal reforms. Thus, economic reform could not be implemented because of Qaddafi's reluctance to change the political and legal regimes.[41]

Although some elements of the project were implemented, these only served to highlight the difficulties of establishing the link between economic and political reform. Hence, Libyans' living standards were not immensely improved, while opportunities did open up in the economic reform process that were appropriated by opportunists led by Qaddafi's children and their cliques.[42] The state began relinquishing many of its social responsibilities by withdrawing subsidies and denying employment to new graduates while unemployment rose in the public and private sectors. Economic reform became synonymous with misappropriation of public funds and considerable access for foreign investors who were linked to the regime. Corruption grew widespread and became commonplace.[43] All in all, Libyans lost hope in reform and they questioned both the intentions and policies associated with it. Statements by Saif al-Islam Qaddafi and his numerous political initiatives ultimately led nowhere and proved in the final analysis to be almost purely cosmetic.

The indigenous characteristics of the Libyan revolution

As noted at the beginning of this chapter, the Libyan case at many levels of analysis represented an exception to the other revolutions of the Arab Spring. The Libyan revolution can be partially explained by the failure of both political and economic reform during the four decades of Qaddafi's rule. There were other causal factors for the revolution, which will be addressed next.

Breaking the barrier of fear

When the Tunisian revolution began, Qaddafi addressed Libyans, especially youth, by interpreting what was happening there. He tried to make a point that reform or revolution was ill-conceived in Tunisia because it would replace President Ben Ali with yet another like-minded ruler and that the Tunisian people stood to gain nothing from the process. Worse still, besides repeating threadbare democratic rhetoric, Qaddafi requested that Ben Ali be given more time so as to accomplish for Tunisians what they deserved.[44] The implication was that Tunisians should not have risen up against Ben Ali and hence, by extension, that Libyans who were considerably more affluent should in no way contemplate any similar sort of action. In effect this was reminiscent of a Libyan proverb that commends: "Beat the cat so that the new bride gets the message." Plainly Qaddafi was aiming at convincing young people of the futility of attempting to emulate the Tunisian example. He sought to buy off the youth with the promise of jobs, easy loans, housing, improved living conditions, and increased salaries. Qaddafi also went so far as to hold out the adoption of a constitution and other political reforms long promised by his son Saif al-Islam. In real terms these were preemptive tactics in anticipation of an uprising that, if it were to take place, he asserted, would only reflect Western conspiracies and vested interests.

For youth, such promises fell on deaf ears. They were weary of claims for the sake of reform under the banner of the "Libya of tomorrow" that had been touted by Saif al-Islam for years without any real progress. Therefore, what Qaddafi offered was too little too late. Young people admired Tunisians, Yemenis, and Egyptians who were agitating for change and they began entertaining thoughts that they could do the same. With the first outbreak of clashes and casualties in the eastern regions, Libyans broke the barrier of fear, and the uprising spread across the country.

A revolution for political freedom

All countries of the Arab Spring had experienced dictatorship and authoritarian rule of one sort or another. However, Libya had characteristics that distinguished it from others. Revenues from the country's petroleum and natural gas resources were rising significantly, which buoyed significant growth with a total GDP of $93 billion in 2009.[45] Corruption, however, was also spreading and reaching unprecedented levels with class disparities increasing constantly. Yet, this does not imply that Libyans were suffering from poverty. To the contrary, it is striking to note that Libya still ranked high on indices of human development with high levels of literacy, long life expectancy, and a relatively high *per capita* income of more than $12,000.[46] Nevertheless, average Libyans were comparing their country's wealth on one hand and their relatively small population on the other and they concluded that in contrast with the Gulf countries, for example, they deserved a better life and better standard of living. The discrepancies they perceived were hard to digest.[47] This was especially unacceptable in light of the lack of justice and equitable distribution of wealth that contradicted the regime's discourse of a utopian society of egalitarianism, democracy, and justice.[48]

We might well imagine average Libyans coming to the conclusion that they might be able to bear a continued lack of political reforms and rights if more reasonable economic conditions and standards of living were to be realized. Such sentiments were among the most pervasive in public opinion, particularly given that Libyans were suffering more and more due to the deteriorating condition of the public sector and the failure of various social services. This having been said, by far and away the most distinguishing characteristic of Libya that set it apart from other countries of the Arab Spring, and perhaps Arab countries in general, was the almost complete absence of any active or effective civil society and institutions in any traditional sphere of activity. Qaddafi's government prohibited the formation of such independent organizations along with political parties, free trade unions, or an independent media. After coming to power in 1969, Qaddafi was keen on the destruction of any articulation of political action at any of these levels, and the potential for their independent growth was doomed. Qaddafi's Libya presented something of a corporatist model in dealing with civil society, as M. Zahi Mogheirby explained. Belonging to any political party was considered a crime that merited capital punishment. Libyan trade unions and professional associations were prohibited from any collective action or involvement in politics. The state maintained a monopoly over the right to establish or dissolve these organizations. Thus, civil society organizations did not occupy an independent space in the public sphere; they were subordinated within the corporatist system.[49]

Failure of the tactics of preemption and appeasement: a momentous revolution

The regime and Qaddafi personally thought it was possible to preempt demonstrations and absorb demands by demonstrators and protesters. Qaddafi resorted to employing his trademark style by claiming that top government officials were incompetent and interested only in accumulating personal fortunes. Qaddafi also advised in a speech that Libyans should actually stick to the system of "people's power" and assure its proper implementation because it was capable of responding to their needs.[50] His insistence on displaying his old goods in new packaging was cause for revulsion among the wider strata of Libyans who saw him as a spent force. His exhortations couched in his 1970s rhetoric was detached and far removed from offering any relevant response to the changing circumstances. The divorce from reality was nearly complete, and all the while he claimed that the people still loved him.[51]

When protests first broke out in Bayda in mid-January and later swept to other cities, Qaddafi tried to maintain calm. When nationwide protesters occupied thousands of partially completed housing units, Qaddafi expressed his support for them. In a move apparently designed to circumvent and prevent wider protests, the government announced the allocation of a huge budget to address the housing shortage and lifted taxes and customs duties on many imports, especially foodstuffs.[52]

Rather than achieving their objectives of deflecting rising anger, these steps had the opposite effect. They backfired, with the protesters and youth becoming more confident that the regime might yield to pressures and that it was possible to extract more gains. This was in evidence by the massive popular response to the arrest of Fathi Terbil, the young lawyer representing the victims of the massacre at Abu Salim prison, which sparked the protests in Benghazi that eventually engulfed the whole country. As has been noted, the regime's approach only galvanized people's determination and inspired them to raise the threshold of their demands to include radical political reforms. Significantly, Qaddafi and his advisors grossly underestimated the nature and the scope of the protests and their potential to move from the periphery of politics to its very center. The regime released a group of Islamist political prisoners, hoping to reduce pressures and subdue a volatile situation, but this proved useless and ineffective in defusing protests or placating enraged protesters who were demanding a constitution and civil and political liberties. Popular response to these furtive measures connoted their absolute failure.

These developments were occurring against the backdrop of events in Tunisia and Egypt where protesters were making significant strides on the path of eliminating dictatorship. These successes in neighboring fellow Arab countries played a pivotal role in encouraging Libyans to break the barrier of fear at home. The failure of the system and the inadequacy of its provisions for remedying the situation exacerbated the already confused psyche of the Qaddafi regime. Qaddafi was no longer able to think in a politically rational manner, and this was nowhere more clear than in the failure of Saif al-Islam Qaddafi to resonate with the protesters and particularly the youth and reform-minded Libyans with whom he had for long maintained an affiliation and association. Saif al-Islam appeared noticeably shaken when he spoke on the evening of February 20, 2011. He had decided to abandon political and economic reform to support his father. Saif al-Islam and his father promised confrontation, repression, and bloodshed.[53]

Saif al-Islam's February 20 speech followed the February 17, 2011 protests, which occurred on the fifth anniversary of the killing of demonstrators in front of the Italian consulate in Benghazi. The Libyan opposition in the diaspora was active in spreading the call for nationwide protests for February 17 under the slogan of "Let's make it a day of rage."[54] Social media sites were effective in communicating and networking, while support for protests was growing steadily. When the regime disrupted internet services in the country, cell phone text messaging became instrumental in conveying the message of civil disobedience. Security forces responded violently yet their reaction widened the circle of demonstrations. Saif al-Islam's speech was effective only in severing any possible remaining link between the people and the regime and damaging the chance for rapprochement beyond repair. People began openly demanding the removal of Qaddafi and his family from power and putting an end to his 42-year rule.

Tribes and tribal politics: a double-edged sword

Libya is ethnically and religiously homogeneous to a greater degree than other Arab countries. Most Libyans are Arabs. A minority community of non-Arabs, comprising less than 10 percent of the population includes Berbers (Amazigh), Tuareg, and Tubu peoples.[55] With the exception of a small Amazigh minority who belong to the Ibadi *madhab* or school of jurisprudence, Libyans are Sunni Muslims who follow the Maliki school of jurisprudence that is notable for its moderation and tolerance. Modern Libya has not witnessed incidents or articulations of religious extremism except in the case of some confrontations that took place between the Qaddafi regime and some *jihadist* groups in the Green Mountain region in the east of the country during the mid-1990s. Qaddafi's regime dealt with these hostilities quickly and without any serious repercussions. In general Libyans are characterized by straightforwardness, openness, and a lack of xenophobia. They also tend to practice a moderate and tolerant form of Sunni Islam. Extremist religious organizations have typically failed to attract Libyans in any significant numbers; and, it is worth mentioning here that the country's most radical Islamist group (Libyan Islamic Fighting Group, LIFG) refused to join Al-Qaeda and has expressed disagreement with its ideology.[56]

The revolution against Qaddafi's regime was not motivated by tribalism nor did it witness inter-tribal conflict. Tribalism was, however, invoked by both sides during the conflict. While Qaddafi sought to portray the revolution as confined to the eastern region and involving only specific tribes or areas, the National Transitional Council countered using tribalism in a different way. Qaddafi attempted to misrepresent the revolt as tribal in nature in order to sow discord and conflict; the Council invoked tribalism to suggest that Qaddafi lacked any tribal support at any level, including that of his own tribe. The Council was highly intent on demonstrating that it enjoyed support and legitimacy conferred upon it by consensus of all Libyan tribes, including Qaddafi's own, by virtue of statement of support that was given to it from one of Qaddafi's cousins.[57]

The revolution itself led to the emergence of a kind of a classification of regions along tribal lines. Some tribes were known for taking the initiative in joining the revolution and were conspicuous in supporting and sustaining it. Other tribes, however, were either hesitant or unable to get involved. Yet other tribes such as the Tarhouna and Wirshifanah occupied strategic locations and the regime was keen to impose a virtual siege on them to prevent their joining the revolution. This state of affairs witnessed not only the coming into prominence of particular tribes, cities, or regions—especially Misrata and

Zintan—but also led to what could be described as a process of division and sociopolitical polarization. Libya became manifestly divided between tribes and areas active in the revolution on the one hand and those who were passive or were being recruited by the regime on the other.[58]

In his attempt to counter the revolution, Qaddafi emphasized the issues of identity and national unity. The regime sought to demonstrate that it had the support of all Libyans and that the opposition was the expression of narrow regional or tribal orientations focused upon secession. The regime used this disinformation as propaganda designed to deprive the *intifada* of opportunities for proliferation and expansion. To this end, Qaddafi took the initiative to convene a conference of representatives of the tribes in Tripoli, including representatives from the tribes from the east (among persons residing or available in the vicinity of Tripoli) and the western mountain region. This was a desperate attempt to deny the uprising its national appeal.[59] In response, the National Transitional Council embarked on a counteroffensive on the same front. A conference of Libyan tribes was organized in Benghazi with representatives of all Libyan tribes pledging loyalty to the revolution. The council announced that it had members representing every region and their backing, while at the same time questioning the credibility of those who attended the Tripoli gathering.[60]

Lack of a unified leadership and conflicting ideologies: diverse actors

The February revolution, especially in its early stages, was spontaneous, without prior planning or a unified leadership. It did not express particular partisan political or ideological orientations. This was effective in liberating the revolution from any initial political divisions or ideological confrontations. The uprising involved the work of a wide spectrum of people united by the goal and the desire to overthrow the regime.[61]

Although the National Transitional Council announced that it represented the entire Libyan people, the revolution itself was undertaken by local councils in areas that declared their loyalty to the larger National Transition Council. The conduct of the revolution, however, was a decentralized rather than centralized affair. Local revolutionary councils and coalitions remained independent, while Libya's geography made direct communication with the National Transition Council very difficult. The Libyan revolution was a series of uprisings begun on the periphery and away from central areas of high population density or in the capital.[62] It took a relatively long time and NATO's military assistance and intervention for the revolution to become effective and reach densely populated areas on the coast. The liberation of the coastal city of Misrata became the key battle and the moment when the *intifada* transformed from a revolt on the periphery to a larger and more effective military effort that would eventually reach Tripoli. Educated youth and professionals were prominent actors throughout this movement. From the outset, lawyers, judges, journalists, businessmen, university professors, and other middle-class opponents of the regime were important social figures in this movement.

The revolution was characterized by two fundamentals. First, harmony and cooperation between the leaders of opposition both inside and outside the country was realized effectively. Libyans were united in the goal of overthrowing Qaddafi, and they scrupulously avoided any controversy over ideological or partisan issues.[63] Second, the National Transitional Council, which assumed the leadership role, became the nexus of coordination. Its legitimacy at the broader national levels was pursued through the overt formation of local councils and coalitions in cities and areas liberated from the control of Qaddafi or through secret councils set up throughout the remainder of the country. These councils or committees, composed of professionals and middle-class lawyers, teachers, doctors and university students, etc., handled the task of organizing the revolt and later managing services in liberated areas.[64]

Libyan women: empowerment *par excellence*

After Libya began exporting increasing quantities of crude oil post-1963, it was able to dedicate increasing resources to providing education and employment to graduates of different educational levels, male and female alike. Such policies had the direct effect of linking women to economic activities, which led increasingly to their independence. Enhanced revenues linked to a moderate form of Islam served as a force to liberate women. In the context, the Qaddafi regime practiced polices that sought to restructure Libyan society so women could also be engaged in political mobilization.[65]

The regime adopted policies that encouraged an enhanced role for women and it embarked upon a policy of "feminization" of the education and health sectors wherein women came to constitute the bulk of the workforce.[66] Women-oriented policies were also adopted to promote the inclusion of women in non-traditional areas such as the military, the police, and the judiciary. To add a touch of his own, Qaddafi had a cadre of highly-visible female bodyguards who became iconic of his style.

At the legislative level, with regard to family and marriage laws, changes were introduced to further this orientation, which afforded women more rights, including a virtual ban on polygamy enshrined in the law. Libya scored high on UN indicators related to the empowerment of women.[67] However, as in other areas, reality did not always correspond to expressed policies. Social norms and traditions constrained these developments. Even though legislation did not discriminate against women, reality revealed weaknesses in the regime's *de facto* policies.[68] As far as political participation was concerned Libyan women were marginalized. A study of political participation in Libya concluded that "men controlled most government agencies, departments, and political and economic institutions." Quite often women were unwelcome psychologically and socially. Women's views collided with those of men, making female roles in professional and social entities a rare occurrence. The result was to confine women to teaching and nursing.[69]

Given these developments in Libya, Libyan women were often eligible and able to actively participate in political protests and the *intifada*. Women were active participants in the protests by families of the victims of the Abu Salim prison massacre. Their active role in the revolt was readily observable. Women contributed to the demonstrations by cheering and encouraging protesters. They took to the streets of Benghazi and verbally confronted security forces. Scenes of women shouting at and denouncing security officers were frequently televised, and this was psychologically encouraging for other protestors.[70] A Libyan female writer eloquently summarized the role of women in the February 17 revolution:

> When the revolution came, Libyan women took action. They accomplished far more than simply sending their sons and husbands to the front. They hid fighters and cooked them meals. They sewed flags, collected money, contacted journalists. They ran guns and, in a few cases, used them.[71]

Violence, "civil war," and foreign intervention

From the foregoing analysis it is clear that the revolution in Libya had a popular origin. Libyans embarked on their revolution without political experience, without civil society institutions, and without prior experience in mass movements. The violence that characterized the revolution (on both sides of the divide) was a reflection of the lack of any degree of harmony or viable linkages between society and state. Libyans were impelled to accept NATO's intervention to counter the brutality of Qaddafi's killing machine that mobilized a campaign of indiscriminate slaughter across the country. Qaddafi's elite battalions were characterized by wanton destruction and did not flinch in committing heinous acts in various regions. Their savagery left Libyans with no illusion that a relentless war of extermination was being waged against them, and they had no option but to appeal to the conscience of humanity at large.[72]

The protests began peacefully, being limited in Benghazi and few other towns and initial demands were limited. The failure of the regime to listen to protesters, its lack of any political will to undertake steps that might have satisfied their demands, and its reliance upon force to accomplish its objectives led Western and Arab governments to support the revolt, which transformed the movement from peaceful protest to a full-fledged armed uprising. Soon after the regime embarked on its war against civilians, peaceful protesters discarded their placards and took up weapons. As the formerly peaceful *intifada* shifted to armed struggle, it was assisted firstly by Arab League and NATO air force intervention but secondly yet also importantly by media support provided by Arabic-language television channels (such as Al Jazeera) that provided essential motivational support.

These factors—especially the element of external foreign military assistance—make the Libyan case distinct from other countries of the Arab Spring. The regime's policy of bloody confrontation proved detrimental—and ultimately fatal—in that it left the protesters with no other viable option but to take up arms. This was made easier by the abundance of arms caches the regime left behind in every city or town its forces had been compelled to evacuate. Remarkably, the regime even employed a tactic of leaving numerous arms depots unattended so that people might arm themselves, with the hope that this would lead to a civil war or at least provide the population with the requisite tools for one.

After the first few weeks of largely peaceful uprisings, the situation devolved into a *de facto* civil war, perhaps as Qaddafi may have hoped it would.[73] The fact that this war possessed a prominent international dimension lasting for several months in addition to the factors analyzed above mean that the process of this revolution will have diverse and profound implications for Libya's present and future. The dissemination of weapons, the creation of a huge number of armed militias, and the inability of the TNC and the interim government to control and integrate these militia members into the military and security institutions threatens the stability of the country.[74] Far and away, this was the most important consequence of the internationalization of the conflict.[75] The length and breadth of this war and its entry into bottlenecks and stalemates over a period of eight months with increasing numbers of victims opened the door to outside intervention. At the end the armed revolt was finally made successful by foreign intervention and assistance that, working with local forces, eventually killed Qaddafi and destroyed his regime.

There is no doubt that the Arab League, the United Nations, and NATO responded for various reasons, including humanitarian concerns. The world was not prepared to witness the repeat of another tragedy like Rwanda in Libya or another Srebrenica massacre in Benghazi. Libyans were particularly cautious and anxious to exclude the possibility for large-scale invasion by foreign military forces on the ground, fearing that a boots-on-the ground intervention in Libya would mar the integrity of the popular uprising and give credibility to Qaddafi's propaganda. Despite the circumstances and the continuous atrocities committed by Qaddafi's killing machine and the staggering number of victims and martyrs, the people of Libya voiced no call for a presence of foreign troops on Libya's territory. This may reflect a deep-rooted Libyan sense of patriotism and a sense of pride in Arabism and Islam that restricts alliance with foreigners and/or infidels. It may also have roots in the negative impact the Iraq war had upon the psyche of Libyans who had no desire of transforming their homeland into a "gas station for Westerners" that would be managed by foreign embassies. Libyans, proud of their heroic resistance against fascist Italy, were committed to the legend of this resistance as per Omar Mukhtar's famous maxim: "We do not surrender; either we are victorious or else we die." Minority voices that otherwise might have entertained direct foreign intervention on the ground were forced into silence.[76]

There is no doubt, however, that NATO and other outside intervention gave Qaddafi, and indeed many others, all he needed to cast doubt on the nationalist credentials of the NTC's leadership. Foreign involvement also gave the Qaddafi regime the pretext to engage in violence and destruction upon a scale so large so as to border on war crimes and crimes against humanity. The wide scope of NATO's bombardment of both military and logistical infrastructure and civilian targets resulted in vast material and collateral damage including the killing of civilians.[77] Libya, no doubt, will need to invest heavily in reconstruction, which will render its transition to democracy more cumbersome and costly than it might have otherwise been.[78]

Furthermore, the most adverse effects of this situation can be seen in the social schisms resulting from the political polarization that has ensued from the revolt and foreign intervention. Libyans were divided among those who supported the foreign-backed revolt or those who aligned with the regime. Many tribes faced a conundrum in attempting to determine which side to support. It remains to be seen whether those who took part in the revolt will be able to accommodate and understand the predicament of those who remained on the sidelines or who supported Qaddafi.

Numerous tribes and regions were considered loyal Qaddafi supporters while, in fact, they were under siege by Qaddafi's battalions and were not afforded an opportunity to oppose him. Especially in Tripoli, and except for mass demonstrations on February 20 or various incidents of protest in some quarters of the city later, the citizens of the capital were acutely aware of the regime's capability to control events there; it largely remained quiet.[79] This polarization within Libya will most likely continue. Areas or tribes that were not necessarily pro-Qaddafi but labeled as such are now insulted, scorned, undermined, and denied access to political and economic gains. Inhabitants of some areas have become subject to displacement and have been prohibited from returning to their homes and their towns or villages, making them ghost towns.[80] The fate of other areas or tribes was worse because they were subject to military assaults, violations of their rights, and property confiscation by other tribes. The report of the Commission of Inquiry on Libya reached conclusions attesting to war crimes committed by both Qaddafi forces and revolutionaries. It concluded that "international crimes, specifically crimes against humanity and war crimes, were committed by Qaddafi forces in Libya" and concluded that "the *thuwar* [revolutionaries, i.e., the anti-Qaddafi forces] committed serious violations, including war crimes and breaches of international human rights law, the latter continuing at the time of the present report."[81] Therefore, the tribalism and regionalism that were employed for specific ends during the revolution have begun to assume an active role that threatens peace, social tranquility, and reconciliation, which hinder the attainment of the revolution's objectives.

Mercenaries and immoral belligerent practices

Not only did the Libyan revolution turn to violence but that violence had an additional foreign ingredient this time because of the Qaddafi regime's use of foreign mercenaries. There were reports of the regime's use of mercenaries from some European countries and, for his part, Qaddafi accused the rebels of employing mercenaries. However, such reports were diluted in the heavy reporting about Qaddafi regime's employment of mercenaries from sub-Saharan Africa. Though no conclusive evidence has proved the exclusive involvement of Africans, there is widespread belief among Libyans that they constituted the bulk of mercenary forces resorted to by the regime.[82] Given that Libya was host to more than 2 million African migrant workers, this led to the deterioration of their conditions during the revolution. Poor and helpless African migrant workers were torn between pressing human needs requiring them to remain in Libya and being the object of popular hatred. In the process they were the victims of many violations and they had to flee in conditions of a tragic exodus to neighboring Tunisia.[83] The Libyan–Tunisian border became a theater of a humanitarian crisis. Also, Qaddafi's tactical abuse of migrants led his regime to send thousands of migrants in unsafe boats across sea to the Italian island of Lampedusa, often with many of them losing their lives, as a means of punishing Italy for their participation in NATO's operations in Libya.[84]

In order to explain the predicament of African migrants we must put it in the context of Libyans' resentment of their influx into Libya upon Qaddafi's encouragement. Libyans were critical of Qaddafi's African policy, which they considered a waste of the country's resources, while sectors such as health and education were in shambles. Libyans were dismayed at Qaddafi's policy of freezing their salaries for more than 20 years while the country's wealth was spent lucratively and generously on funding the African Union. To make matters worse, Qaddafi announced in 2010 that he was making available US $90 billion for Africa's development if the continent were to see fit to unite in realization of his vision.[85] This explains, partially at least, why the charges related to mercenaries were basically confined to black Africans. At the same time we must recognize that violence against black Africans manifested not only during the revolution but also before, most notably in 2000, which was an event subject to investigation and condemnation by the United Nations.[86]

No observer would have expected Qaddafi to stoop so low as to resort to unethical practices against people who had decided to revolt. Although Qaddafi's propaganda apparatus widely disseminated video footage and news reports of the rebels' atrocities and unethical practices such as the slaughter or public hanging of pro-regime elements, immolation of dead bodies, rape, drug abuse, alcoholism, theft, etc., these reports had limited effects upon the population. Nevertheless, later reports by human rights organizations validated some of the human rights violations on the part of certain rebel groups, but these paled in contrast to the regime's unethical practices that were tantamount to war crimes and crimes against humanity.[87] For Libyans, Qaddafi's resorting to unethical practices constituted a traumatic shock to the foundations of their moral code; it went so deep as to seem to challenge their value system, and conceptually it posed an insoluble psychological enigma.

News about atrocities committed in many parts of the country and in particular indiscriminate sexual harassment and rape of children and women had a deleterious effect on the psyche of Libyans. Reports of such practices were received with horror and dismay, especially when stories about the torture and rape of eight-year-old children were put into circulation. Reportedly, Qaddafi's security forces and elite battalions employed a unique torture technique whereby children were forced to watch the execution of their parents or family members and where the husband or the father was forced to watch his wife or daughters being raped. This heinous technique was intended to inflict the greatest degree of humiliation and disgrace on the opposition and to suppress popular will to join the rebels. Although rape and sexual abuse have been used historically in many wars, what distinguished the Libyan case from other historical precedents was the degree of interest in the practice and its extensive deliberate use as a military tactic against opponents.[88] Qaddafi's regime went to extremes in using such unconscionable acts as political weapons to prevent the widening of the revolt. The memory of such heinous acts will bear painful scars for generations of Libyans. The fact that Qaddafi himself was subject to physical abuse, killed, and buried in an unmarked grave and that his son Mutassim was killed while in the custody of the revolutionaries, while not justified, are rendered understandable in the context of the revolution's traumatic events.

Qaddafi's legacy and the future of Libya: concluding remarks

Libya after Qaddafi will suffer because of the negative aspects of his policies that lasted for 42 years. What Lisa Anderson wrote more than 20 years ago looks more relevant today: "Qaddafi's own policies have determined the legacy his regime will leave Libya, and any new regime will be required to cope with the economic and social upheavals wrought by ... his revolution."[89] This seems strikingly visible today. Moreover, the policies that Qaddafi adopted rested upon the continued destruction of state institutions and abject contempt for the culture of institutionalism, rule of law, and the sense of community. He undertook to crush all political and civil organizations. In addition to promoting a culture of dependency on the state, the *rentier* economy arguably engendered contempt for work and effort as social values. Corruption became a culture sustained in kinship, political patronage, and clientelism. Coupled with lack of accountability or an independent media or judiciary, contempt for public space and public office became a popular attitude that led to widespread apathy, which destroyed notions of a common good. Taken together Qaddafi's legacy will undoubtedly impinge negatively upon the future of Libya. At least two generations of Libyans were deprived of access to proper education and training. They will have to face a different reality that will make their participation in the new society and economy more difficult.

Libya will need to go a long way before it can adequately address the consequences and effects of Qaddafi's infamous rule that destroyed or impinged upon literally everyone and everything. However, Qaddafi's worst effects were not only those related to human rights violations or war crimes or the squandering of national natural and financial assets. The crimes of Qaddafi exceeded material waste. His destruction of moral values led to the disruption of the culture of political community, which is an essential cultural component for development. His legacy has created enormous challenges that will hinder social reconciliation, which are essential for democratization and the ultimate reconstruction of the society and the state.[90]

As Lisa Anderson presciently noted, Qaddafi's legacy would be even more dangerous when we consider its effects upon tribalism and regionalism and his contempt for trade unions, political parties, and civil society:

> The legacy of the Qaddafi era in the political realm will be a contradictory one. On the one hand, the … regime is in many respects a repressive and manipulative one. Many of its policies are purposely or inadvertently designed to atomize the population and discourage independent organization in civil society … this has had the somewhat ironic result of enhancing the role of kinship ties in political organization … few people are accustomed to the voluntary cooperative behavior with which genuine and productive political participation is associated, and on which a successor regime might hope to draw. On the other hand, Qaddafi's repeated insistence that, "the people rule themselves," and his radically egalitarian policies have politicized segments of the population which were previously quiescent, especially the relatively underprivileged, the young and the lowborn. The experience … however eccentric … has introduced into the political arena claimants to power unlikely to give up their acquired rights without a struggle.[91]

The future Libyan government will have to face the enormous task of managing the high level of expectations that Libyans have.[92] A rush to hasty constitutional arrangements will only make the situation more fragile as was evident in recent calls for federalism, for example.[93] Despite the importance of balancing national expectations and taking into account foreign interests—particularly those of countries that supported the revolution—the real objective remains that of reinventing the Libyan polity that Qaddafi liquidated.

In the future the quality of political leadership and the choices it makes will be very important. The new leaders must be prepared to adopt democracy as a strategic choice and political commitment. The fact that Libya's present leaders are presently more concerned with partisan, regional, and tribal politics suggests the greater need for consensus-building measures. The new leaders confront formidable challenges, which include uniting the country socially, addressing economic problems, and creating a state with viable and effective institutions.

Notes

1 For an interesting analysis about if these were revolutions or revolts, see, Zenonas Tziarras, "New Perspectives on the Sociology of the Arab Spring – Mark II," *The GW Post*, December 1, 2011, http://thegwpost.com/2011/12/01/new-perspectives-on-the-sociology-of-the-arab-spring-mark-ii. Zenonas Tziarras, "The Sociology of the Arab Spring: A Revolt or a Revolution?" *The GW Post*, August 23, 2011, http://thegwpost.com/2011/08/23/the-sociology-of-the-arab-spring-a-revolt-or-a-revolution.
2 Amitai Etzioni, "The Lessons of Libya," *Military Review*, January–February 2012, http://usacac.army.mil/CAC2/MilitaryReview/Archives/English/MilitaryReview_20120229_art011.pdf.
3 Timeline of the events is available in many sources, see, for example, "Let us make it a day of rage," www.facebook.com/17022011libya.
4 "What Qaddafi Said: Excerpts from Libyan Leader Muammar al-Qaddafi's Last Televised Address," *Foreign Affairs*, June 4, 2011, www.foreignaffairs.com/articles/67878/the-editors/what-qaddafi-said.
5 "Libya Revolution 2011," *Global Voices*, September 13, 2012, http://globalvoicesonline.org/specialcoverage/2011-special-coverage/libya-uprising-2011; "Battle for Libya: Key Moments," *Al Jazeera*, November 19, 2011, www.aljazeera.com/indepth/spotlight/libya/2011/10/20111020104244706760.html; "Timeline of the Libyan Civil War," *Wikipedia*, http://en.wikipedia.org/wiki/Timeline_of_the_Libyan_civil_war.
6 For news and archival information on the revolution, see http://topics.nytimes.com/top/news/international/countriesandterritories/libya/index.html?scp=1&sq=libya%202011&st=cse.
7 Barak Barfi, "Who Are the Libyan Rebels?" *New Republic*, April 30, 2011, www.newrepublic.com/article/world/87710/libya-rebels-gaddafi-ntc-saif
8 "Founding Statement of the Interim Transitional National Council (TNC)," www.ntclibya.org/english/founding-statement-of-the-interim-transitional-national-council.
9 "NTC: A Vision of a Democratic Libya," www.ntclibya.org/english/libya.
10 Gilbert Achcar, "Libya: A Legitimate and Necessary Debate from an Anti Imperialist Perspective," *ZNet*, March 25, 2011, www.zcommunications.org/libya-a-legitimate-and-necessary-debate-from-an-anti-imperialist-perspective-by-gilbert-achcar.
11 UNSC Resolution 1970 (2011), www.unhcr.org/cgi-bin/texis/vtx/refworld/rwmain?docid=4d6ce9742; UNSC Resolution 1973 (2011), www.unhcr.org/refworld/country,,UNSC,LBY,4d885fc42,0.html.
12 Ferry Biedermann, "Military Strikes Keep Benghazi in Rebel Hands," *The National*, March 20, 2011, www.thenational.ae/news/world/africa/military-strikes-keep-benghazi-in-rebel-hands.
13 Thomas Seibert, "Turkey Seeks Agreement on 'Road Map' for Qadaffi's Departure," *The National*, July 15, 2011, www.thenational.ae/news/world/europe/turkey-seeks-agreement-on-road-map-for-qadaffis-departure.
14 "Gaddafi Speech Defiant Despite Mounting Unrest," *France24*, February 22, 2011, www.france24.com/en/20110222-gaddafi-speech-rings-defiance-face-mass-unrest-libya.
15 "Gaddafi Speech Defiant."
16 Barak Barfi, "The Sad Saga of Saif the Reformer, as Told by His Right-Hand Man," *New Republic*, September 16, 2011, www.tnr.com/article/world/95001/barfi-libya-saif-qaddafi.

17 Ian Black, "Gadafy's Son Calls for Free Media and Judiciary," *Guardian*, August 22, 2007, www.guardian.co.uk/world/2007/aug/22/libya.ianblack.
18 "Gaddafi's Son Warns of Civil War as Protests Widen," *France24*, March 10, 2011, www.france24.com/en/20110221-libya-benghazi-protests-gaddafi-son-speech-civil-war.
19 Jon Swaine, "Libya's UN Ambassador Denounces Gaddafi," *The Telegraph*, February 25, 2011, www.telegraph.co.uk/news/worldnews/africaandindianocean/libya/8349048/Libyas-UN-ambassador-denounces-Gaddafi.html, Accessed 17/2/2012
20 "Qadhafi's Speech to Benghazi University Students, 1973, World Center," *Speeches and Statements of Leader, Vol. 4* (Tripoli: 1998), p. 344 (Arabic text).
21 Bruce St John, "Libyan Myths and Realities," http://forsvaret.dk/FAK/Publikationer/Research%20Papers/Documents/Libyan_Myths_and_Realities.pdf, p. 5.
22 Youssef Sawani, "Libya After Qadhafi: Interactive Dynamics and Political Future," *Al Mostaqbal Al-Arabi*, 395 (January 2012): 9–11 (Arabic text).
23 International Crisis Group, "Popular Protest in North Africa and the Middle East (V): Making Sense of Libya," Middle East/North Africa Report no. 107, June 6, 2011, www.crisisgroup.org/~/media/Files/Middle%20East%20North%20Africa/North%20Africa/107%20-%20Popular%20Protest%20in%20North%20Africa%20and%20the%20Middle%20East%20V%20-%20Making%20Sense%20of%20Libya.pdf, pp. 8–14.
24 Interesting details in A. Shalgam, *Persons Around Qadhafi* (Tripoli and Beirut: Ferjani and Madarek Publishers, 2012).
25 Achcar, "Libya: A Legitimate and Necessary Debate."
26 Dirgha Raj Prasai, "A Great Nationalist Hero Muammar Gaddafi," *Blitz*, October 24, 2011, www.weeklyblitz.net/1902/a-great-nationalist-hero-muammar-gaddafi.
27 Diederik Vandewalle, "Libya: Post-War Challenges," *AfDB Economic Brief*, September 2011, www.afdb.org/fileadmin/uploads/afdb/Documents/Publications/Brocure%20Anglais%20Lybie_North%20Africa%20Quaterly%20Analytical.pdf.
28 Dirk Vandewalle, "Qadhafi's 'Perestroika:' Economic and Political Liberalization in Libya," *Middle East Journal*, 45:2 (Spring 1991): 216–231.
29 Vandewalle, "Qadhafi's 'Perestroika'," p. 220
30 "Qadhafi Speech to Revolutionary Committees, 8/3/1978," in *Revolutionary Committees* (Tripoli: Green Book Center, 1986), p. 24 (Arabic text).
31 International Crisis Group, "Popular Protest," pp. 15–16.
32 Ronald Bruce St John, "The Changing Libyan Economy: Causes and Consequences," *Middle East Journal*, 62:1 (Winter 2008): 78.
33 Vandewalle, "Qadhafi's 'Perestroika'," p. 217.
34 Youssef Sawani, "Libyan Foreign Policy: Constraints and Opportunities," paper presented at the conference on "Libya, Britain and the US: Problems and Prospects in Moving Towards a New Understanding" organized by the Royal Institute of International Affairs (London), Center of Arab and Islamic Studies (Exeter University) and the Academy of Graduate Studies (Libya). Valetta, Malta, May 25–26, 2001.
35 Dirk Vandewalle, *Libya Since Independence: Oil and State-Building* (Ithaca and London: Cornell University Press, 1998), pp. 132–135, 144–150.
36 Thomas Crampton, "Qaddafi Son Sets Out Economic Reforms: Libya Plans to Shed Old and Begin a New Era," *New York Times*, January 28, 2005, www.nytimes.com/2005/01/28/news/28iht-libya_ed3_.html?_r=1.
37 Saif al-Islam Qaddafi set out his blueprint in his *Libya and the XXI Century* (Beirut; Al Maha Publishing, 2002), especially pp. 39–57, 62–68, 73–75 (Arabic text).
38 M. Qaddafi, *A Lecture at the University of Sirte, August 2000* (Tripoli: Green Book Center, 2006), pp. 2–16 (Arabic text)

39 Youssef Sawani, "Reform and Restructuring the Libyan Economy: Challenges and Policies," *Al Iqtisad wa Al Oloum Al Siasiah*, 2 (2004): 78–92 (Arabic text).
40 Monitor Group, *National Economic Strategy: An Assessment of the Competitiveness of the Libyan Arab Jamahiriya* (General Planning Council of Libya, 2006), pp. 19, 29, 140–148 (Arabic text).
41 M. Zahi Mogherby, "State Building, Transparancy and Corruption: Reflection on Development Thought and Reform Issues," *Libya Forum*, March 13, 2007, www.libyaforum.org/archive/index.php?option=com_content&task=view&id=4215&Itemid=195.
42 International Crisis Group, "Popular Protest," p. 2.
43 See Libya's Ranking on 2009 Transparency Index, Transparency International, http://archive.transparency.org/policy_research/surveys_indices/cpi/2009/cpi_2009_table.
44 Matthew Weaver, "Muammar Gaddafi Condemns Tunisia Uprising," *The Guardian*, January 16, 2011, www.guardian.co.uk/world/2011/jan/16/muammar-gaddafi-condemns-tunisia-uprising.
45 Economy Watch, "Libya Economic Statistics and Indicators for the Year 2010," www.economywatch.com/economic-statistics/country/Libya.
46 World Bank Data on Libya, http://data.worldbank.org/country/libya.
47 International Crisis Group, "Popular Protest," p. 2.
48 Transparency Index, 2009.
49 M. Zahi Mogheirby, www.libyaforum.org/archive/index.php?option=com_content&task=view&id=6359&Itemid=207.
50 Richard Spencer, "Libya: Gaddafi Shows His Determination to Stay in Power," *The Telegraph*, March 2, 2011, www.telegraph.co.uk/news/worldnews/africaandindianocean/libya/8357664/Libya-Gaddafi-shows-his-determination-to-stay-in-power.html; "I Led the Revolution then Retired to my Tent, Gaddafi Says," *Trend*, March 2, 2011, http://en.trend.az/regions/met/arabicr/1838800.html.
51 Christine Amanpour, "'My People Love Me:' Moammar Gadhafi Denies Demonstrations Against Him Anywhere in Libya," *ABC News*, February 28, 2011, http://abcnews.go.com/International/christiane-amanpour-interviews-libyas-moammar-gadhafi/story?id=13019942#.T2OKR4EoGM0.
52 "Libya Set Up a $24bn Fund for Local Development," *Libya2020*, http://libya2020.wordpress.com/2011/01/27/%D9%84%D9%8A%D8%A8%D9%8A%D8%A7-%D8%AA%D9%86%D8%B4%D8%A6-%D8%B5%D9%86%D8%AF%D9%88%D9%82%D8%A7-%D8%A8%D9%82%D9%8A%D9%85%D8%A9-24-%D9%85%D9%84%D9%8A%D8%A7%D8%B1-%D8%AF%D9%88%D9%84%D8%A7%D8%B1-%D9%84.
53 "Gaddafi's Son Warns of Civil War as Protests Widen," *France24*, March 10, 2011, www.france24.com/en/20110221-libya-benghazi-protests-Qadhafi-son-speech-civil-war.
54 "Let us make it a day of rage," www.facebook.com/17022011libya.
55 St John, "Libyan Myths and Realities," pp. 4–8.
56 Noaman Ben Othman, "A Letter to Aiman Dawahiri," November 7, 2007, www.libya-watanona.com/adab/nbothman/nb07117a.htm.
57 Youssef Sawani, "Post-Qadhafi Libya: interactive dynamics and the political future," *Contemporary Arab Affairs*, 5:1 (January–March 2012): 3–4.
58 Youssef Sawani, "Challenges and Prospects in Post-Qadhafi Libya," www.iar-gwu.org/node/368?page=0,2, Accessed 16/3/2012
59 "Libyan Regime: Tribal Meeting Shows Signs of Support for Qaddafi," *Fox News*, May 5, 2011, www.foxnews.com/world/2011/05/05/libyan-regime-tribal-meeting-shows-support-qaddafi.
60 Miranda Leitsinger, "Gadhafi, Rebels vie for Loyalty of Libyan Tribes," *NBC News*, May 18, 2011, www.nbcnews.com/id/43049164/ns/world_news-mideast_n_africa/t/gadhafi-rebels-vie-loyalty-libyan-tribes/#.UU31olc-OpR.

61 Youssef Mohamed Sawani, "Prospects in a Post-Gaddafi Libya," *World Policy*, November 10, 2011, www.worldpolicy.org/blog/2011/11/10/prospects-post-gaddafi-libya.
62 Jason Pack, "Qaddafi's Legacy," *FP: Foreign Policy*, October 20, 2011, www.foreignpolicy.com/articles/2011/10/20/qaddafi_s_legacy.
63 Youssef Sawani, "Libya and Prospects for Democratic Transition," paper presented at the conference on "Revolutions of the Arab Spring: Transition to Democracy: A Road Map," organized by Center for Arab Unity Studies and the Swedish Institute in Alexanderia, Hamamat, Tunisia, February 6–9, 2012.
64 Nicolas Pelham, "Libya, the Colonel's Yoke Lifted," *Middle East Research and Information Project*, September 7, 2011, www.merip.org/mero/mero090711; St John, "Libyan Myths and Realities," p. 10.
65 Alison Pargeter, "Women's Rights in the Middle East and North Africa — Libya," www.unhcr.org/refworld/docid/47387b6dc.html.
66 The UNDP Human Development Report, 2011, states that 55.6 percent of the female population in Libya has completed secondary education, available from http://hdrstats.undp.org/images/explanations/LBY.pdf.
67 Human Rights Council, *Report of the Working Group on the Universal Periodic Review: Libyan Arab Jamahiriya*, www.scribd.com/doc/50053303/Report-of-the-Working-Group-on-the-Universal-Periodic-Review-Libya.
68 Alison Pargeter, "Women's Rights in the Middle East."
69 Ibrahim Abosalah, "Political Participation in Libya," unpublished MA thesis (Tripoli: Graduate Academy, 1992), p. 178 (Arabic text).
70 Yusra Tekbali, "Libyan Women Active Force In Revolution," *Huffington Post*, August 19, 2011, www.huffingtonpost.com/yusra-tekbali/libyan-women-active-force_b_930995.html.
71 Nafissa Assed, "Women's Role in the Libyan Uprising," *Libya Herald*, 9 March 2012, www.libyaherald.com/opinion-womens-role-in-the-libyan-uprising.
72 Youssef Sawani, "Challenges and Prospects in Post-Gaddafi Libya," *International Affairs Review*, December 5, 2011, www.iar-gwu.org/node/368?page=0,2.
73 Michael Calderone, "Associated Press: Libya Conflict A Civil War," *Huffington Post*, June 15, 2011, www.huffingtonpost.com/2011/06/15/associated-press-libya-civil-war_n_877546.html.
74 Amal Obeidi, "The National Security in Libya: Challenges of the Transitional Period," www.arabsi.org/attachments/article/484/%D8%A7%D9%84%D8%A3%D9%85%D9%86%20%D8%A7%D9%84%D9%88%D8%B7%D9%86%D9%8A%20%D9%81%D9%8A%20%D9%84%D9%8A%D8%A8%D9%8A%D8%A7%20%20%D8%AA%D8%AD%D8%AF%D9%8A%D8%A7%D8%AA%20%D8%A7%D9%84%D9%85%D8%B1%D8%AD%D9%84%D8%A9%20%D8%A7%D9%84%D8%A7%D9%86%D8%AA%D9%82%D8%A7%D9%84%D9%8A%D8%A9.pdf.
75 Tim Dunne and Jess Gifkins, "Libya and the State of Intervention," *Australian Journal of International Affairs*, 655 (2011): 515–529, www.tandfonline.com/doi/pdf/10.1080/10357718.2011.613148.
76 Sawani, "Challenges and Prospects."
77 C.J. Chivers and Eric Schmitt, "In Strikes on Libya by NATO, an Unspoken Civilian Toll," *New York Times*, December 17, 2011, www.nytimes.com/2011/12/18/world/africa/scores-of-unintended-casualties-in-nato-war-in-libya.html.
78 *Libya Infrastructure Report 2012*, www.researchandmarkets.com/reports/2077125/libya_infrastructure_report_2012.
79 Anand Gopal, "The Tripoli Uprising," *FP: Foreign Policy*, September 1, 2011, www.foreignpolicy.com/articles/2011/09/01/the_tripoli_uprising.
80 Sawani, "Challenges and Prospects," p. 8.

81 United Nations Human Rights Council, *Report of the International Commission of Inquiry on Libya, A/HRC/19/68*, www.ohchr.org/Documents/HRBodies/HRCouncil/RegularSession/Session19/A_HRC_19_68_en.doc.
82 James Creedon, "Where do Gaddafi's Mercenaries Come From?" *France24*, February 25, 2011, www.france24.com/en/20110225-where-do-gaddafi%27s-mercenaries-come-from-libya-darfur-nigeria.
83 Rebecca Murray, "Migrant Workers Find it Hard to Stay in Libya and Difficult to Return Home," *NTA Newstime*, March 3, 2012, www.newstimeafrica.com/archives/24513.
84 Khalid Koser, "Displacement in Libya: Humanitarian Priorities," *Brookings*, August 15, 2011, www.brookings.edu/opinions/2011/0815_libya_koser.aspx.
85 "Gaddafi: $90bn for US of Africa," *AllVoices*, July 24, 2010, www.allvoices.com/news/6376456-gadfafi-90bn-for-us-of-africa.
86 UN Watch, "Libya Must End Racism Against Black African Migrants and Others," www.unwatch.org/site/apps/nlnet/content2.aspx?c=bdKKISNqEmG&b=1313923&ct=8411733.
87 United Nations Human Rights Council, *Report of the International Commission of Inquiry on Libya*.
88 "Widespread Use of Rape and Other Sexual Violence as Tactical War Weapon," http://libya-al-mostakbal.org/news/clicked/8062.
89 Lisa Anderson, "Qadhdhafi and His Opposition," *Middle East Journal*, 40:2 (1986): 225–237.
90 United Nations Security Council, "Report of the Secretary-General Report on the United Nations Support Mission in Libya," March 1, 2011, http://unsmil.unmissions.org/LinkClick.aspx?fileticket=v_-F2Xr3c9I%3d&tabid=3543&mid=6187&language=en-US; Jason Pack and Barak Barfi, "In War's Wake: The Struggle for Post-Qadhafi Libya," www.washingtoninstitute.org/uploads/Documents/pubs/Policy Focus118.pdf, pp. 15, 40.
91 Anderson, "Qadhdafi and His Opposition," pp. 228–229.
92 *Transitional Constitution*, http://portal.clinecenter.illinois.edu/REPOSITORYCACHE/114/w1R3bTIKElG95H3MH5nvrSxchm9QLb8T6EK87RZQ9pfnC4py47DaBn9jLA742IFN3d70VnOYueW7t67gWXEs3XiVJJxM8n18U9Wi8vAoO7_24166.pdf.
93 "Autonomy Proposal Triggers Libya Clash," *UPI*, March 17, 2012, www.upi.com/Top_News/World-News/2012/03/17/Autonomy-proposal-triggers-Libya-clash/UPI-75981332005384.

6 Morocco

A reformist monarchy?

Mohammed Darif

Introduction

The evolution of the Moroccan political system has depended on the ability of political actors who search for real answers to questions posed by the broader society. One of the most urgent questions this system has faced is whether political reform requires constitutional reform. Demands for amendment of the constitution may not necessarily lead to political reform. Constitutional amendments could be implemented without really changing the structure of existing political institutions or power relations within the state. We therefore find ourselves facing a fundamental question: what is the objective of constitutional reform? Is it just a revision of institutional prerogatives, such as expanding the powers of the prime minister or the parliament, or is it a radical reconsideration of the nature of the relationships among a state's political actors?

The second problem that has arisen out of the revolution relates to levels of constitutional reform. The first stage of such reform concerns the relative power of political actors while the second identifies the decentralization of government as its central mission. Morocco has experienced a shift from the concept of "representative democracy" as originally defined by King Hassan II to "participatory democracy" as demanded by the participants in the 2011 demonstrations. In the Moroccan demonstrations, many voices were raised that rejected the outmoded logic of "representative democracy." These newly energized political actors are demanding the construction of a real "participatory democracy," which involves the renegotiation of the relationship between the central government and its citizens on the one hand, and between the central government and the regional and provincial governments on the other. That second project, known as the "extended regionalism" program, will be discussed later in this chapter.

The third problem of the revolution involves the logic of reform. Should reform stem from political institutions (i.e., the executive, legislative, and juridical institutions), or should it emerge from the political parties? In this context, discrepancies have arisen between the king, who functions as the principal actor of political decision-making in Morocco, and his interactions with both political parties and the new youth movement that has demonstrated its energy in the streets. An additional important issue is that the king and his supporters may not see the advantages of constitutional reform unless the important project of making political parties more effective takes place at the same time. This last concern has necessarily triggered a wide-reaching public debate on the significance and efficacy of the political parties law that was enacted in February 2000.

This study seeks to trace the process of building a reformist monarchy by focusing on Morocco's gradual transition to democracy since the ascent of King Mohammed VI to the throne in July 1999. I will examine this transition to democracy using three perspectives: contexts, backgrounds, and demonstrations.

The context of the transition to democracy: three crucial phases

Ever since his accession to the throne, King Mohammed VI has sent clear signals in support of a gradual transition to democracy. We can identify three key moments in this shift: October 12, 1999; February 4, 2004; and March 9, 2011.

A new concept of power: October 12, 1999

In a speech given on October 12, 1999, in Casablanca, King Mohammed VI outlined a new concept of power for the Moroccan state that would begin with the decentralization of power from the monarchy to the authorities within regional or territorial administrations.[1] This new concept of power provoked questions regarding continuity and rupture with past practices. Through this reconceptualization, Mohammed VI was attempting to express continuity with the political practices of King Hassan II both at a conceptual level and in terms of practice.

On a conceptual level, Mohammed VI stressed four ideas, which he had inherited from his predecessor. The first emphasized the central role of the king as ultimate arbiter of the political system.[2] The second involved his continued status as the *amir al-mu'minin*, or Commander of the Faithful, an identity that has provided religious legitimization of the monarchy's rule, as expressed in Article 19 of the Constitution.[3] The third idea emphasized the necessity of respecting the "ceremonial" nature of the monarchy, as stressed by Article 23 of the Constitution, which states that "the person of the King is sacred and inviolable."[4] Finally, the fourth idea invoked the notion of the "specificity" of the Moroccan society, which is the idea that democracy should be adapted to the realities of Moroccan society.[5]

Continuity was also manifest in Mohammed VI's use of his predecessor's policy regarding "ministries of sovereignty." This policy had long been controversial and led several parties from the democratic *kutla* (bloc) to refuse to participate in King Hassan's October 1993 government. Under this system, the king reserved to himself the right to appoint the heads of four important ministries: the Prime Ministry, the Ministry of the Interior, the Ministry of

Foreign Affairs, and the Ministry of Justice. Later, following an October 1994 royal initiative, the number of "ministries of sovereignty" was temporarily reduced to one: the all-important Ministry of the Interior. However, when the government of Prime Minster Abderrahman el-Youssoufi was formed on March 14, 1998, the policy came back with full force and was now extended to six ministers, who would be appointed by royal prerogative. These royal appointments included the Ministers of the Interior, Foreign Affairs, Justice, and Awqaf and Islamic Affairs, as well as the Secretariat of State of National Defense and the Secretariat General of Government.[6] This contentious issue, which had been opposed by many political actors in Moroccan society, is crucial to our discussion of both constitutional reform and the nation's transition to democracy.

While the policy of ministries of sovereignty remains controversial, the policy of extended regionalism, which involves the decentralization of administrative authority from the central government to regional and provincial governments, has provided a real opportunity for discussion of constitutional and political reform in Morocco. With the introduction of this policy, Mohammed VI aimed to change power relations within the state in a more fundamental way. The objective of this new concept of governance was to establish a more decentralized state that would also reestablish a regime of law with respect for human rights. By proceeding this way, Mohammed VI hoped to address simultaneously the problems of decentralization of power and the "humanization" of the regime through the restoration of respect for human rights.

The extended regionalism policy embraced two seemingly contradictory approaches, one holistic and the other reductionist. The holistic approach was premised on a combination of human rights and democracy. Under this approach, no rule of law or respect for human rights in Morocco would be possible without the decentralization and democratization of the established political system. Decentralization and democratization became related practices in the task of realizing the state's objective of respect for human rights. The realization of human rights required not only a legal framework, but also a new institutional framework that could guarantee these rights.

The death of King Hassan II and the succession of Mohammed VI to the throne created an opportunity to raise issues of political and constitutional reform. At the beginning of his rule, Mohammed continued the authoritarian policies of his predecessor by asserting his determination to exercise fully the king's prerogatives outlined in Article 19 of the Constitution, which placed him as *amir al-mu'minin*, or Commander of the Faithful, in Morocco. Mohammed's adoption of the position of *amir al-mu'minin* created a religious basis for the establishment of his political legitimacy. Like his predecessor, Mohammed VI urged everyone in the kingdom to pledge their allegiance to him (*bayaa*) as king of the monarchy.[7]

Mohammed VI's initial articulation of the monarch's role within the state was premised upon Hassan II's more authoritarian principles. Only later, as

Mohammed's monarchy evolved, did he begin turning toward more democratic principles. Early in his monarchy, however, the king did not call for the forging of a link between democracy and human rights.

Mohammed's initial concept of power dissociated the question of democracy from human rights. He discussed this political formula in the French newspaper *Le Figaro*, on September 4, 2001. Although he initially adopted an authoritarian monarchy model, Mohammed also began opening up the political system when he began the process of "Closing the Years of Lead" by establishing an Equity and Reconciliation Commission.

Closing the Years of Lead: January 4, 2004

Morocco, as a state and a society, undertook significant measures during the process known as Closing the Years of Lead. These measures were adopted in response to the findings of the Equity and Reconciliation Commission, which was created on January 4, 2004, on the initiative of King Mohammed VI. Its proceedings culminated in the publication of a final report at the end of November 2005. That final report contained a set of recommendations for preventing the recurrence of atrocious violations of human rights.

It took Morocco considerable time to reconcile itself to the idea of opening up the official files from the Years of Lead. Persons who had been involved in committing human rights abuses—often under royal command and authority—were apprehensive about the investigation. As the idea of an investigation ripened, considerable controversy arose among Moroccan human rights organizations concerning how to proceed. Two approaches developed: the first semiofficial governmental approach was cautious and sought to preserve the rights of the victims and their relatives without a deep excavation of past events, which they believed would impede the entire process. A second, more radical approach argued that the building of a democratic future required uncovering the whole truth and bringing to justice the perpetrators of human rights abuses. This faction rejected the notion of a government-appointed Equity and Reconciliation Commission and urged the appointment of an independent commission.

Mohammed VI encouraged the creation of the Equity and Reconciliation Commission because he believed that addressing past human rights violations would create a new consensus in Morocco for social and political change. He argued for this commission on two grounds. He first asserted that the radical approach would only widen the gap among the various groups of society, and that this development would undermine the process of reconciliation and the transition toward democracy. Second, he asserted that unless justice was obtained for the victims of human rights abuses and their families, true democracy could not be realized.[8]

Besides these two considerations, Mohammed's approach focused on creating and stabilizing a consensus for change, which revealed a profound awareness of the nature of Moroccan society as a system based on "change within continuity."⁹ Mohammed urged consensus because the objective of his policy was to preserve the memory of human rights abuses while demanding forgiveness.

The recommendations of the final report of the Equity and Reconciliation Commission embodied this consensual approach on two levels. The first level concerned reparations for the harm inflicted on the victims and their families; ultimately, compensation was paid to 9,280 victims. The second level concerned the definition of the procedures and mechanisms that should be adopted constitutionally and institutionally to protect human rights in the future. These recommendations included:

- The constitutional endorsement of the concept of human rights as universally defined.
- Constitutional guarantees of freedom of expression and the right to political action, protest, trade unionism, associative work, and strikes.
- The promotion of separation of powers and preventing the executive from interfering with the judiciary system.
- The introduction of reforms to the security, justice, legislation, and criminal policy systems.
- Amending the statute of the Supreme Judicial Council to strengthen the independence of the judiciary.

After Mohammed VI's ratification of the Commission's final report, three questions arose:

1. To what extent would the work of the commission contribute to the closing of the files of past violations of human rights?
2. Would the consensual approach render justice to the victims and their families and effect reconciliation among involved parties?
3. Was it possible to implement the recommendations of the Commission without also enacting comprehensive public policy reform?

In response to the first question, some human rights activists believed that the Commission would not close the files on past violations, because the full truth had not been revealed in a number of cases. Among the more important of these unresolved cases was the assassination of Mehdi Ben Barka in October 1965. Other human rights activists believed the opposite. Despite criticism, however, the Commission led to the disclosure of many past abuses, identified those persons who were responsible, and appealed to the state to make a public apology to the victims and their families.

Some believe that the Equity and Reconciliation Commission had rendered justice to the victims and their families and effected reconciliation between Moroccans and their past. Others believed that financial compensation and other forms of reparations for the harm inflicted on the victims were not equivalent to true justice, which would have required accountability from the perpetrators of human rights abuses.

Street demonstrations and a new concept of governance: March 9, 2011

Despite the operations of the Equity and Reconciliation Commission, the political opposition in Morocco continued to insist upon the need for a new system of rule that would be expressed through a fundamental revision of the constitution. The Arab Spring that began in Tunisia and Egypt during December 2010 and January 2011 spurred the creation of the February 20 Youth Movement in Morocco that demanded the acceleration of real political and constitutional change. The pressure of regional and local movements in Morocco eventually led to a shift in policies concerning governance that were expressed in King Mohammed VI's speech of March 9, 2011.

What was the February 20 Youth Movement? The movement itself was a gathering of Moroccan youth who were independent of all organizations and political parties and who were motivated by a deep love of country that prompted their demands for change, freedom, democracy, dignity, and social justice. The movement also considered itself a natural extension of previous protest movements in Morocco. Importantly, it was a movement that had been animated and facilitated by the interaction of young Moroccan internet users. The significance and extent of this interaction was manifested by the formation on Facebook and other social media of virtual groups of political contestation, especially the group called "Moroccans Dialoguing with the King."

Before the formation of the February 20 Youth Movement, on January 27, 2011, an internet youth group called for peaceful demonstrations to be held across the country on February 20, 2011. This group called itself the Movement for Freedom and Democracy Now and was built around several demands: (1) the abolition of the current constitution and the appointment of a committee of honest and competent Moroccans to draft a new constitution that would reduce the monarchy to its "natural size"; (2) the dissolution of the parliament, government, and political parties that contributed to political corruption; (3) the adoption of urgent measures to alleviate the suffering of the Moroccan people; (4) the creation of an unemployment compensation fund; (5) the release of all political prisoners; (6) the appointment of a provisional government to run the country until the establishment of a new constitution; and (7) the collaboration of all honest institutions and actors from all classes to address the issue of the new social pact between the monarchy and the nation.[10]

The Movement for Liberty and Democracy Now presented itself as an independent, democratic Moroccan movement that expressed the aspirations of all individuals who believed in loyalty to their country; who wished to preserve their county's geographical and cultural diversity; and who aimed to work within the framework of human rights, freedom, difference, and tolerance. This movement called on the king to keep pace with global changes and to combat and eradicate the influence of obsolete and narrow security approaches.[11] After the call for demonstrations on February 20, 2011, two new movements, the Movement of the People Who Want Change and the Intifada Movement for Dignity, joined the Movement for Liberty and Democracy Now. On February 15, 2011, these three movements issued a joint communiqué in which they referred to themselves as the February 20 Youth Groups. The newly-formed group outlined its position as follows: First, it called for peaceful demonstrations on February 20, 2011, in support of radical constitutional changes that would lead to the creation of a parliamentary monarchy. Second, it issued a statement that the protests would remain peaceful to prevent the protest movement from being hijacked by infiltrators. Finally, it called on intellectuals and nongovernmental organizations to speak out and work for change.[12]

A day after issuing its joint communiqué, the February 20 Youth Groups summarized its demands as follows: (1) the establishment of a democratic constitution that would represent the true will of the people; (2) the dissolution of the parliament; (3) the dissolution of the government and the formation of a provisional transitional government that would be subject to the will of the people; (4) the creation of an independent and fair judiciary; (5) the trial of those who were involved in corruption, abuse of power, and looting of the nation's wealth; (6) the recognition of Tamazigh as an official language of Morocco alongside Arabic; (7) the revalorization of the linguistic, cultural, and historical specificities of the Moroccan culture and historical identity; and (8) the release of all political prisoners and detainees of opinion.[13]

What enabled these youth groups to develop in such a record time into the February 20 Youth Movement? Beginning on February 2, 2011, the Moroccan Human Rights Association, comprising 20 human rights organizations and associations, expressed its critical support of the Freedom and Democracy Now Movement. Two weeks later, this same association reiterated its support of the February 20 Youth Movement and its call for peaceful protest movements demanding rights for the Moroccan people. Jointly, these groups demanded the implementation of a constitutional monarchy. They invited the Moroccan authorities to negotiate with the February 20 Youth Movement and to respect the rights of the people to assemble in peaceful protests.[14]

Besides the support supplied by the Moroccan Human Rights Movement, the Justice and Charity Association, an Islamist organization, also lent its support to the February 20 Youth Movement. This organization urged all Moroccans to take to the street and demonstrate. The Justice and Charity Organization mobilized its youth section to decide upon the appropriate means and forms of supporting the demonstrations of the February 20 Youth Movement.

Questions have been raised about who stands behind the February 20 Youth Movement. Did the group emerge independently from political organizations—as stated in its February 16, 2011, communiqué—or is it an extension of the forces that have long demanded change in Morocco, including Islamist, leftist, or Amazigh groups? Regardless of what the answer may be, the February 20 Youth Movement cannot be dissociated from the forces that preceded it for the following reasons. First, the movement's demands evolved because of the influence exerted by preexisting groups. For example, the youth groups did not initially call for the election of a Constituent Assembly to draft a new democratic constitution; they only demanded that the monarchy be reduced in power to its "natural size." Later, because of the influence of other groups, the February 20 Youth Movement modified its positions to demand comprehensive and fundamental constitutional and political reforms that aimed to establish a constitutionally constrained parliamentary monarchy.

A second reason that the Youth Movement cannot be dissociated from previously existing groups concerns the support provided by the Islamist-oriented Justice and Charity Association and by radical leftists. Despite their differing politics, the Islamists and the leftists merged their demands for constitutional changes to constrain the power of the monarchy. It is therefore necessary to emphasize that one significant achievement of the February 20 Youth Movement was its success in temporarily reconciling the differences between the Islamist-oriented Justice and Charity Association and the radical left to allow political change to be realized. As a result, divergent groups came together to demand the creation of a parliamentary monarchy and vowed to continue the fight against tyranny and corruption. For the moment, the Islamists and the leftists have managed to put aside their ideological differences and place more emphasis on the establishment of a modern civil state that provides dignity and full citizenship to all Moroccans.

Nobody can deny that the dynamic atmosphere created by the February 20 Youth Movement in Morocco was inspired and informed by events in Tunisia and Egypt. These events induced Mohammed VI to accelerate the process of constitutional reform, which he began by delivering a speech on March 9, 2011 that created an advisory committee for the amendment of the constitution and the adoption of other changes that would strengthen institutional mechanisms for the exercise of individual and collective freedoms. These changes included the transformation of the Advisory Council of Human Rights into the National Council of Human Rights, the conversion of the Office of Ombudsman to the Institution of Mediation, and the creation of the Ministerial Cabinet of Human Rights. Additionally, in response to the demands of the February 20 Youth Movement, some political prisoners were released and some persons accused of looting public money were brought to trial.

The process of transition toward democracy was governed by three basic considerations that centered on the issue of legitimacy: the essence of legitimacy, the conflict of legitimacies, and the hierarchy of legitimacies.

The essence of legitimacy

Under King Hassan II and during the initial phase of Mohammed VI's reign, the monarchy's strategy for establishing political legitimacy was premised on the concept of the "supreme representivity" of the monarch and the "subsidiary representivity" of other specially elected political actors. This strategy operated along two axes: one normative, the other political.

When the 1962 constitution was promulgated, it did not contain any reference to the king as the supreme representative of the nation. Article 19 stated:

> The King is the Commander of the Faithful (*amir al-mu'minin*), the symbol of the unity of the nation, and guarantor of the durability and continuity of the State. He is the protector of religion and guardian of the respect of the Constitution.

Reference to the king as the supreme representative of the nation was added later and created significant political controversy. This issue became central to the many conflicts that arose among the various parties after independence, especially when the 1963 parliamentary elections produced a strong opposition bloc formed by the Independence Party and the National Union of Popular Forces. As a result, the issue of representivity became a powerful question that created oppositional logics. One side supported the religious and historical legitimacy of the monarchy and the other supported a system of democracy as defined by republican rather than religious or traditional monarchical standards. The June 1965 declaration of a state of emergency and the subsequent suspension of the Constitution were largely informed by this issue of supreme representivity, as asserted by the monarchy.

The 1962 constitution was followed by the 1970 constitution, which included a new paragraph in Article 19 stating that the "King is Supreme Representative of the nation." This contested article reappeared in the constitutions of 1972, 1992, and 1996.

This new monarchical formulation of the 1970 constitution helps inform a re-reading of Article 3 of Morocco's current constitution, which states that elected political actors and political parties represent the people in a "subsidiary" fashion. When read in conjunction with Article 3, it becomes clear that the Moroccan monarchy intended the new Article 19 to draw a distinction between the "supreme representivity" of the monarch and the "subsidiary representivity" of other political actors, especially political parties.

Hassan II and Mohammed VI's desired to maintain a clear distance between the monarchy and the subsidiary legitimacy of other political actors was manifest in Mohammed's view of the Moroccan monarchy as an "executive" and "performative" monarchy.[15] In this view, the monarchy was not an elected institution; rather, it was an institution with a religious dimension to the construction of its political legitimacy that was linked to an "oath of allegiance," or *bayaa*, that bound citizens in loyalty to the king.[16]

The monarchy's political strategy of confirming the king's legitimacy as the supreme representative of the nation relied on two pillars: one in the parliamentary domain, and the other in the governmental bureaucracy. King

Hassan II considered the members of the parliament to be his counselors, which placed the parliament in a purely consultative rather than politically representative role. This view fits neatly with his idea that all other actors in the political system besides the monarch occupied a position of subsidiary representivity within the political system. The composition of the previous parliaments, including the one that emerged from the elections of September 7, 2007, reinforced this idea.

At the governmental level, the formation of the government of Abbas El Fassi following the elections of September 7, 2007, once again raised debate over the meaning of Article 24 of the Constitution and the meaning of "supreme" and "subsidiary" representivity within the government. Under Article 24, the king appoints the prime minister and the other members of the government as recommended by the prime minister. This article gave the prime minister some power but still reserves the right of appointment or dissolution of the government to the monarch. Article 24 has constantly been subject to two different readings: a textual reading that assigns the king the right to appoint the prime minister and a contextual reading that arose after King Hassan II appointed Abderrahman el-Youssoufi on February 4, 1998, as the prime minister, who then formed a government that became known as the Government of Consensual Alternation. In accordance with more traditional democratic principles, the king should have been obliged to appoint the leader of the party with the largest number of elected seats to the post of prime minister.

Whether we abide by a textual or contextual reading of Article 24, the prime minister should have had the prerogative to propose the members of the government to the king, rather than having the king unilaterally appoint the cabinet ministers. In September 2007, however, Prime Minister Abbas El Fassi was not permitted to name the ministers to his cabinet; instead, that role was undertaken by the king and his counselors. The assertion of power by the monarch at this time elevated the contentious notion of the "supreme representivity" of the monarch and the "subsidiary representivity" of elected officials.

Following the formation of Abbas El Fassi's government in 2007, three types of ministries emerged: ministries of sovereignty, ministries occupied by independents, and ministries under control of ministers affiliated with parties. The government of Abbas El Fassi prompts us to raise questions about the nature of its representivity such as: what and who did this government represent? Political elites and observers became convinced that the third type of government members—those affiliated with political parties—did not represent their parties, but rather the king.

Such a reality made this third category of government members merely "executors" of royal policies. This implies that the party-affiliated ministers did not derive their legitimacy from having been elected, but rather derived a subsidiary legitimacy from the monarchy, which occupied a position of supreme representivity.[17]

The conflict of legitimacies

After Mohammed VI succeeded to the throne on July 23, 1999, he engaged in efforts to strengthen the sources of his political legitimacy, yet he also foresaw and began planning for change. It was clear that he needed to broaden the bases of his legitimacy beyond those he had inherited from his predecessor, leading, for example, to his creation of the title of "Monarch of the Poor." Mohammed shifted the monarchy's priorities to social work and the creation of a culture of solidarity and social cohesion, and adopted the role of leader of an "economic jihad" that enabled him to articulate a new vision of the monarchy.[18]

Mohammed's ideological approach was epitomized by his rhetoric of the "New Era." This approach required the formulation of a new concept of power, which he introduced in a speech at Casablanca in October 1999. In this speech, Mohammed focused on the need to promote economic development as a vehicle to obtain a broader base for his rule. He also raised the importance of "effectiveness" as a central concept of royal discourse. Effectiveness has generally been associated with technocracy, which may have been the impetus for the appointment of Driss Jettou in October 2002 as prime minister. Furthermore, in royal discourse, the rhetoric of effectiveness has been associated with not only the economy, but also politics. This effectiveness has had four orientations. First, this approach has highlighted the need to reform political parties. In many of his speeches, the king has called for the reformation of parties so that they can become more effective and democratic.[19] Similarly, he has called on the political parties to formulate workable and realistic government programs.[20] Second, this approach has required that local communes and professional chambers play more important roles in economic development. Third, Mohammed VI has called for the appointment of competent and qualified candidates to assist the executive in the management of public affairs. Fourth, this approach has required a redefinition of the concept of citizenship. In his aforementioned speech of August 20, Mohammed VI associated citizenship with efficiency, arguing the need for Morocco to provide conditions for economic investment that would contribute to wealth generation, job opportunities, and so on.

King Mohammed VI's challenge was summarized in his motto of the "New Era," which was informed by the fundamental principle of effectiveness. This approach aimed to restore legitimacy in two ways. First, elections would be held within the time requirements specified by the constitution. Second, a House of Representatives would be formed that would reflect the more rational performance of Morocco's political parties.

These were the challenges that King Mohammed VI faced when he consented to the re-formation of the government of Abderrahman el-Youssoufi, known as the Government of Consensual Alternation, on September 6, 2000. This government reflected the monarchy's desire to find an alternate form of political legitimacy based on political and economic effectiveness. This shift almost toppled the government, because it amplified the discourse of effectiveness while falling short in the arena of actual economic performance. Because of its economic shortcomings, this rhetoric of effectiveness was later partially abandoned.

If Mohammed VI's political orientation was informed by his concept of effectiveness in the New Era, the Government of Consensual Alternation was more preoccupied with the concept of a transition to democracy, which involved challenging the monarchy's notion of supreme representivity. This preoccupation explains why the government focused heavily on the need to organize fair elections.

The challenge of the September 27, 2002 legislative elections lay in its differing answers to the search for a missing legitimacy: the valorization of political action on the one hand and the legitimization of the project of political pluralism on the other. The question that faced Morocco was: which argument won—the New Era or the transition to democracy?

Abderrahman el-Youssoufi, the leader of the Government of Consensual Alternation, believed at a certain time in the existence of complementarity between the two ideas, but this conviction disappeared when Driss Jettou was appointed to form a new government in October 2002. The results of the September 27, 2002 elections reinforced a New Era approach that also contained a framework for the transition to democracy.

Those who believed in a transition to democracy thought that the September 7, 2007 legislative elections would lead to a democratic state and society. But the results of these elections and their low 37 percent turnout rate reemphasized the question that the political class feared: Was there an underlying reality to the "transition to democracy" in Morocco?[21]

The hierarchy of legitimacies

Political movements in Morocco have long endeavored to modernize the political system by advocating for a constitutional monarchy while attempting to restrict the power enjoyed by the monarch. Between the years of 1956 and 1962, the Moroccan regime appeared to have adopted this approach to political modernization, especially after the passage of a series of laws and the creation of institutions such as the National Consultative Assembly, the Decree of Public Liberties, and the Fundamental Law of the Kingdom. During this initial postcolonial period, an effort was made to diminish somewhat the religious dimension that underlay the legitimacy of the Moroccan monarchy and substitute a notion of civil or nonreligious legitimacy. This effort was especially prominent after King Hassan II relinquished the traditional title of sultan and adopted the title of king, and it was confirmed with the promulgation of the 1962 constitution. This turn away from religious legitimacy is perhaps why some Western analysts have considered the 1962 constitution to be a monumental event that marked a break with Morocco's political, social, and psychological past.[22] Very soon, however, it became evident that the 1962 constitution created a set of conflicting legitimacies that inhibited the creation of a constitutionally constrained monarchy.

The 1962 Constitution established what Emstard calls a "conflicting coexistence of legitimacies," because it included two types of legitimacy.[23]

The first type was civic legitimacy and was exemplified by Article 2 of the 1962 constitution: "The sovereignty of the nation is exercised directly through a referendum and indirectly through the constitutional institutions." The second type of legitimacy was religious and was exemplified by Article 19 of the constitution:

> The King is the Commander of the Faithful and the symbol of the unity of the nation, and the guarantor of the perpetuation and continuation of the nation. He is the protector of Islam, and ensures respect of the Constitution. He is the protector of the rights and liberties of citizens, social groups and organizations and he is the guarantor of the independence of the Nation and the territorial integrity of the Kingdom within all its rightful boundaries.

Might we then say that a conflicting coexistence of legitimacies was established by the 1962 constitution that derived its authority from Islamic principles? Clifford Geertz has noted that the Islamic system is also characterized by two types of legitimacy: intrinsic legitimacy, in conformity with the principles that provide the Imam with the right to rule in the name of Allah, and contractual legitimacy, which was based on a nation's acceptance of a khalifa's authority as being subservient to Allah.[24] Contrary to Geertz's assumption, we believe that Emstard's theory of the conflicting coexistence of legitimacies cannot be applied to an Islamic system, because Islam has known and recognizes only one form of legitimacy: religious legitimacy, wherein the khalifa derives his right to rule on earth from God. By contrast, what Geertz calls contractual legitimacy—as expressed in the *bayaa*, or oath of allegiance—is not tantamount to a Weberian notion of rational-legal legitimacy for the construction of a state. The construction of political legitimacy in Morocco, as articulated by King Hassan, was at least partially derived from traditional religious practices. In other words, a monarch's demand for an oath of allegiance from his subjects created a form of legitimation derived from tradition or religion, rather than one based on a legal-rational basis, as articulated by the perspectives of either Max Weber or Ibn Khaldoun.[25]

Between 1962 and 1965, the Moroccan political system was characterized by a conflicting coexistence of legitimacies, but this system could not go on indefinitely. In 1965, because of internal dissent, King Hassan declared a state of emergency and put an end to this conflicting coexistence. In the 1970 constitution, he replaced the dual basis of legitimacy with a religiously-based political legitimacy that identified the monarch as the *amir al-mu'minin*, or Commander of the Faithful. Later, in the 1972 constitution, King Hassan sought to expand the scope of his legitimacy beyond this narrower religious concept, resurrecting the notion of civic legitimacy and linking it to the already existing religious legitimacy. This shift is what led Michel Guibal to claim that the 1972 constitution codified monarchical rule in Islam.[26] The 1972 constitution derived its notions of legitimization from tradition and religion, redefining democracy as *shura* (counsel) and the parliament as a *majlis al-shura* (advisory council). This constitution, with its merger of civic and religious legitimacy, realistically led to the creation of a monarchy that leaned toward authoritarianism rather than a constitutionally constrained monarchy.[27]

On the manifestations of the transition to democracy: three basic levels

The reign of Mohammed VI has involved a gradual transition to democracy. This transition has manifested itself in three ways: the reform of political parties; the adoption of the policy of regional governance; and the promulgation of a new constitution.

The reform of political parties: February 23, 2006

The issue of political parties is significant for anyone interested in political and institutional reform in Morocco. Insofar as political parties are tools for political mediation—without which democracy would be meaningless—it has been necessary to reflect on how these mediatory structures operate. A new law for political parties was officially adopted in February 2006 as a framework for initiating a Moroccan transition to democracy. This law aimed to combat two problems that undermined the operation of political parties in Morocco: the phenomenon of political migration, or party switching (nomadism), and a system that permits the existence of an excessive number of parties.

Many political actors have praised Article 5 of the New Political Parties Act, which became effective in February 2006. This article banned members of parliament from shifting their political affiliations during their term of office. During the June 12, 2009, communal elections, several challenges facing the implementation of Article 5 came to the surface. Although territorial administration authorities issued orders regarding respect for this law, the judiciary had a different opinion. A central question emerged from this debate: Were Article 5's constraints that prevented political nomadism a result of judicial interpretation of legal texts, or were they caused by a legacy of politically motivated practices? Regardless of the answer, this law seems to have been incorrectly understood. For example, in the United Kingdom, when a member of the House of Commons decides to change his party affiliation, his parliamentary membership is automatically cancelled and new elections are held in his district. This procedure is based on the principle that the voter does not vote for the candidate but for the party he represents, and that therefore a change in affiliation requires a new election.

The second problem that has plagued the Moroccan political system is its extraordinarily large number of political parties, an issue that was highlighted by the 2009 elections. Twenty-nine political parties participated in this election, with three parties fielding candidates jointly: the Democratic Socialist Vanguard Party, the National Federal Union, and the United Socialist Party. The election process starkly illustrated the political meaninglessness of Morocco's multiparty system in three ways.

The first illustration involved the balkanization of politics. Despite all that has been said about the need to give sense to the multiparty system, the serial reproduction of parties continues. A good example of this chaos is the Authenticity and Modernity Party, which attempted to rationalize the political scene by integrating five parties: the National Democratic Party, the Pact Party, the Environment and Development Party, the Citizenship and Development Initiative Party, and the Alliance of Liberties Party. Three of these parties broke away from the Authenticity and Modernity Party and reestablished themselves with only slight changes to their names. The National Democratic Party became the Democratic National Party, the Pact Party became the Democratic Pact Party, and the Party of Environment and Development became the Environment and Sustainable Development Party. In addition, two new political parties participated for the first time in the elections of 2009: the Unity and Democracy Party, an offshoot of the Independence Party, and the Democratic Society Party.

The second indicator of the Moroccan political system's meaninglessness is the phenomenon of "nomadism" or "electoral traveling," which refers to the transfer of a large number of candidates from one party to another.

The third indicator involves the so-called independents who participated in the June 12, 2009, elections. There was a major discrepancy between the number of seats that independents won in communal elections (72 seats, or 0.3 percent of the total), which should have left them ranked 20th in results, and their first-place showings in provincial council elections (25 percent of seats), regional council elections (24 percent of seats), and the presidential elections for the Provincial and Regional Council. This paradox can be explained by the fact that most of the independent candidates were actually affiliated with parties but failed to secure their party's official nomination, leading them to enter the elections as independent candidates.[28]

These three indicators reveal that the electoral process in Morocco has given rise to a multitude of political parties that are devoid of political significance, and that the project of rationalizing the political party system has been deferred. They also prove that the 2006 New Law of Political Parties has not yet achieved its objectives, and that other alternatives need to be found.

The decentralization of power to the regional level: January 3, 2010

The second decade of Mohammed VI's rule began with the launch of a program of institutional reform called "extended regionalism." During the first decade of his reign, Mohammed VI occasionally referred to the importance of devolving some power to regional governments with the inauguration of this program[29] in a royal address on January 3, 2010, and the formation of an Advisory Committee on Regions.

One question regarding this program arose immediately: did the introduction of a policy of extended regionalism indicate a move from a first generation of reforms in Morocco to a second? There was a widespread belief that the focus on the decentralization of power and the policy of extended regionalism did indicate a second generation. However, this does not imply that Morocco has completely closed the chapter of first-generation reforms. The extended regionalism policy will certainly profoundly change the nature of the relationship between the center and the periphery, as well as the nature of the state in Morocco. The real question to be resolved is the extent of that decentralization.

We should distinguish between the priorities of the state and the priorities of the monarchy in promoting extended regionalism. Currently, extended regionalism is seen as an opportunity to deepen institutional reforms and modernize the state. The state's objectives appear to relate to the implementation of democracy and the accomplishment of economic objectives through a focus on sustainable development.

Patience is necessary because these challenges and objectives will determine the manner and extent to which extended regionalism is implemented. The project of extended regionalism will involve three stages. The first was launched by Mohammed VI in his speech of January 3, 2010, which created the Advisory Committee of Regionalism.[30] This stage is concerned with the formulation of policy vision and what the king has referred to as the "Moroccan model." In his January 3 speech, Mohammed VI spoke of the need to invent a national model for extended regionalism that takes into consideration Moroccan specificities. The second stage concerns the realization of this vision. It is not sufficient to put forth a vision—measures that can be applied on the ground must also be put into practice. Finally, the third stage involves the assessment of the program's effectiveness. We have not yet reached the stage of evaluating extended regionalism, because the policy has not fully been put into practice.[31] Morocco still remains at the first stage of elaborating its vision.

We must also identify the primary reasons that prompted Mohammed VI to initiate the extended regionalism program. The reasons were certainly related to the territorial problems with which Morocco has struggled since its independence, particularly in peripheral regions such as the Western Sahara that were formerly under Spanish colonial rule. Having withstood political, economic, and security pressures in the 1960s, 1970s, and 1980s, Morocco has now reached a pivotal moment of political stability that enables it to focus on issues of economic development and decentralization of power.

When we talk about extended regionalism, we are speaking in the context of consolidating the foundations of a modern state that can bring about a break from the traditional state. Such a rupture requires a new approach to the management of the relationship between the central authority and its peripheral regions, as well as a vehicle for achieving democracy while facing the challenges of economic development.[32]

At the constitutional level: July 1, 2011

In Morocco, the project of creating a modern and democratic society has always been informed by the need to reconcile the two major cornerstones on which the Moroccan monarchy has been based: the king as the *amir al-mu'minin*, or Commander of the Faithful, and the king as the principal architect of the Moroccan political system. This system of rule has involved a blend of Islam and politics.[33] Here a question arises: to what extent are the two concepts reconcilable?

The need for reconciliation sometimes means that political discourse risks falling into binaries and favoring one interpretation over another. Uncertainty about the vision informing this project can be attributed to the nature of this theoretical construct, which is guided by these reconciliatory drives. The push for political and social reform presents Morocco as a country seeking to attain Western achievements at the legal and political levels, while establishing respect for human rights and a democratic model and taking into account the specificity of its cultural and historical identity, which is rooted in a particular interpretation of Islam.

It is this theoretical foundation of a modern and democratic society that frames the problem of political and institutional reform. This foundation therefore consists of two levels: first, ideological and cultural reform, and second, sectorial reform. On the first level, it is important to examine the extent to which Morocco really possesses a culture of reform. Do Moroccans have a motivation for reform? Moroccan society is generally described as conservative and traditional. Consequently, a cultural barrier may exist that prevents rapid advancement on issues of reform. And if the society does not sufficiently embrace the culture of reform, any discussion of specific sectorial reforms quickly becomes meaningless.

Moving on to the second level, sectorial reform is based on two main principles. The first is related to legal texts. Legal texts play an important role in creating dynamism in any particular sector. But these legal texts are useless unless they are placed in an environment that is conducive to their implementation. There have been numerous legal texts in Morocco, but they have lacked meaning because of an inappropriate environment, which reveals the need for a culture of reform.

To approach the question of whether Morocco possesses a culture of reform that deals with sectorial reforms, we need to ask whether or not constitutional reforms are the gateway to real reform. If the answer is yes, then what should be the subjects of reform? The constitutions promulgated between 1962 and 1996 never really affected the essence of the monarchy's political power; regardless of the constitution, this institution remained centrally powerful in the Moroccan political system. All proposed constitutional amendments in the past have affected institutions such as the parliament or have demanded the transformation of the constitutional chamber into a constitutional assembly or have expanded the prerogatives of the prime minister. They have not essentially constrained the power of the monarchy.

But when conditions have matured socially and culturally, constitutional reform can focus on the nature of the political system. In most democratic countries that are not republics, the monarchy is a constitutionally constrained parliamentary monarchy. When Mohammed VI refers to an "executive monarchy" or a "performative monarchy," his description should not be interpreted as an endorsement of a constitutionally constrained parliamentary monarchy, which would necessarily include strong and effective (but not too numerous) political parties. To the extent that the monarchy is focusing on political party reform, it may be moving toward more real reform of the political system.

The process of reaching a consensus on the desired political system should be guided by a vision that creates a balanced political system in which power is shared between the monarch and a popularly mandated government that enjoys a parliamentary cover—that is, by adopting a semi-presidential system. This formula takes into account the transformations that Morocco, the region, and the world are undergoing by recognizing that the two fundamental bases of democracy: the ballot box and the accountability of rulers.

In addressing the question of how the constitution should be drafted, some political and human rights activists have called for the adoption of a constituent assembly to draft a new constitution. What the advocates of this approach fail to realize is that the writing of a new constitution has been historically associated with uprisings leading to the fall of an existing regime and its substitution with an alternate regime. Those who call for a constituent assembly in Morocco forget this historical reality. In contrast, Morocco is attempting to reform rather than depose its monarchical system. Its people are advocating for a new era rather than a new regime, reform not revolution; in short, they seek "change within continuity."

Consciousness in Morocco has evolved and conditions have matured. Both of these factors are creating a consensus that change can only be effected through negotiations and mutual understanding among the major political forces and social groups. Hence, there is an emerging consensus—even among the Islamist and leftist parties—in favor of the elaboration and production of a comprehensive charter that would include all political forces that desire change and a common agreement that would save the country from crisis.[34] This need for consensus led to Mohammed VI's speech of March 9, 2011, which was followed by the drafting of a new constitution, and the presentation of its major outlines to the nation in the speech of June 17, 2011. This new constitution was officially adopted on July 1, 2011, in a referendum. What are its provisions?

Concerning its philosophy of governance, the new constitution marks a clear break from the general vision of the previous constitutions of Morocco.

Morocco's previous constitutions identified the monarch as the source of legitimacy for the government, the parliament, and the judiciary, and positioned the monarchy above the constitution.

The new constitution grants many rights and freedoms to the Moroccans, endorses the concept of citizenship, and seeks to build a system of government based on the principles of separation of powers and participatory and citizenship-based democracy (Article 1, Part I). The powers of the king have become more explicitly defined than in previous constitutions. The new document also provides a clear definition of the powers and expansion of the judiciary. The judiciary will enjoy autonomous authority. At this stage, it is important to ask: does the new constitution establish a system of parliamentary monarchy in Morocco?

Not yet. Even with a constitution that enlarges the powers of the prime minister, the legislature, and the judiciary, the monarchy still wields considerable power. In effect, the king still "reigns" and "rules." But at another level, the new constitution establishes a legal regime of fundamental rights and freedoms, enlarges both the rights and the duties of Moroccan citizens, and attempts to create the conditions necessary for the emergence of the pillars of a democratic system. The first of these pillars is the existence of political parties that play the role of representing citizens. The new constitution urges parties to adopt democratic mechanisms for the conduct of their activities, their representation of citizens, and their political training (Article 7). The second pillar is the existence of a civil society. The new constitution makes considerable provisions to ensure the inclusion of civil society in the process of determining, promoting, implementing, and evaluating public policies. One of these provisions formally creates the new Consultative Council on Youth and Associative Action, which was formed to respond to the demands of the February 20 Youth Movement (Article 169).

The challenge of the 2011 Constitution is to secure the conditions of a democratic transition, whether by conferring credibility on political parties and making them an embodiment of true political pluralism or by strengthening the role of civil society. The 2011 Constitution should be understood not so much as a constitution that inaugurates a democratic era, but as a constitution that frames the next stage in the transition to democracy.

Acknowledgment

This chapter was translated from Arabic into English by Khalid Bekkaoui.

Notes

1 Scott Macleod, "The King of Cool," *Time*, June 26, 2000, www.time.com/time/magazine/article/0,9171,997285,00.html; Mohammed VI, "Throne Speech," July 30, 2000, www.map.co.ma.
2 Ibid.
3 Mohammed VI's speech, August 20, 1999, www.map.co.ma.

4 Ibid.
5 Macleod, "King of Cool."
6 These appointments were effected in Second Youssufi Government, September 6, 2000.
7 Mohammed VI, "Throne Speech," August 20, 1999.
8 Mohammed Darif, "Hayaat al Insafwa al Musalahaattawsiyyat al hadir-atwaattanfid al ghaib al Masaa" ["Equity and Reconciliation Commission: Present Settlement and Absent Implementation"], *Al Masaa*, March 3, 2011.
9 Mohammed VI's speech, January 6, 2006, www.map.co.ma
10 First communiqué of Liberty Now Movement, January 27, 2011, www.20fev.wordpress.com.
11 Second communiqué of Liberty Now Movement, January 30, 2011, www.20fev.wordpress.com.
12 Communiqué of Groups of February 20 Youth Movement, February 15, 2011, www.20fev.wordpress.com.
13 Communiqué of Groups of February 20 Youth Movement, February 16, 2011, www.20fev.wordpress.com.
14 Communiqué of the Moroccan Human Rights Association, February 14, 2011.
15 See *Le Figaro*, September 4, 2001; Mohammed VI's Speech, July 30, 2003, www.map.co.ma.
16 Mohammed Darif, "Ishkaliyat at-Tamthiliyya fi an-Nasaq as-Siyassi al Maghrebi" ["Problematic of Representativity in the Political Structure of Moroccan Politics"], *Al Massa*, May 26, 2010.
17 Ibid.
18 See Mohammed Darif, *Ad-Din wa as-Siyassat fi al Maghrib* [*Religion and Politics in Morocco*] (Casablanca: Manshurat al Majallat al Maghribiyya li Ilm al Ijtimaa as-Siyassi, 2000).
19 Mohammed VI's speech, August 20, 2002, www.map.co.ma.
20 "Throne Speech," July 30, 2003, www.map.co.ma.
21 Mohammed Darif, "Bayna Makulat al Ahd al Jadidwa al Intiqal ad-Dimuqrati" ["Between the concept of the new era and democratic transition"], *Al Masaa*, July 7, 2010.
22 J. Aveille, "Le Maroc se Donne une Monarchie Constitutionnelle," *Confluent*, 27 (January 1963): 6.
23 Jacques Lagroy, "La le'gitimation," in M. Grawitz and J. Leca (eds) *Traite de Science Politique*, vol. 1 (Paris: Presses Universitaires de France, 1985), p. 475.
24 Ibid., p. 435
25 Mohammed Darif, "Ishkaliyat Al Mashruiyya fi al Maghreb" ["Problematic of Legitimacy in Morocco"], *Al Majallat al Maghribiyya li Ilm al Ijtimaa as-Siyassi*, 1:4 (1984): 46.
26 Ibid.
27 Ibid.
28 Mohammed Darif, "Fi amrad al Jism as-Siyassi al Maghribi" ["The Ailments of the Moroccan Political Body"], *Al Masaa*, December 15, 2010.
29 Mohammed VI's speech, November 6, 2008, www.map.co.ma.
30 Mohammed VI's speech, March 9, 2011, www.map.co.ma.
31 Mohammed VI's speech, August 20, 2010, www.map.co.ma.
32 Mohammed Darif, "Hawamishala Matni al Jihawiyya al Muwassaa" ["Footnotes on Extended Regionalism"], *Al Massa*, September 23, 2010.
33 Mohammed VI's speech, July 30, 2003, www.map.co.ma.
34 Mohammed Darif, "Fi ar-Ru'ya al Muattiralil Mashru' ad-Dimuqrati al Hadathi" ["On the Vision Informing Democracy and Modernity Project"], *Al Massa*, June 23, 2010.

7 Algeria

Untenable exceptionalism during the spring of upheavals

Azzedine Layachi

Thousands of youths suddenly took to the streets in many Algerian cities demanding immediate political and economic change. High unemployment, substantial dissatisfaction with a failing educational system, highly restricted access to policymakers and policymaking institutions, and very limited leisure and sports facilities and activities led to dismal living conditions and created a profound sense of hopelessness and helplessness. They rebelled against an authoritarian system led by a much older generation. This aging leadership had been condescending. It abused its authority. Youths rebelled against injustice and what they called *hogra* (the abuse of power demonstrated by agents of public authority, especially the police, the military, and state bureaucrats).[1]

Youth riots quickly engulfed key Algerian cities. The army harshly repressed these disturbances, leaving 500 dead within a few days. These violent events were the most serious that had occurred in the country since Algeria obtained independence from France in 1962. Almost immediately thereafter, after realizing the seriousness of the revolt, state leaders decided to enact major political changes, including ending the one-party system, opening up the electoral system, and enacting new laws that allowed the birth of new parties along with freedom of association and independent print journalism.

With these and other measures, and at a heavy cost in human lives, Algeria had a "spring" of its own. However, this spring did not take place in 2011, but more than two decades earlier. The triggering riots took place in October 1988 and in early 1989. As is discussed in this chapter, Algeria experienced important political changes during 1988 and 1989 but authoritarian rule was not seriously undermined.

In the early days of what has been termed the "Arab Spring," Algeria also had its share of street riots, which occurred during January 2011. These disturbances were short-lived and were politically inconsequential. Since then, Algeria has been sitting out the dramatic changes that have engulfed the region despite a *malaise* that plagues the country.

After 50 years of independence from colonialism, Algeria is today at a major crossroads that is characterized by important social mutations, economic uncertainty despite oil and gas wealth, and a dangerous political sclerosis. The question being asked nowadays is whether the current leadership will heed calls for substantial change or will it try to sail through the regional winds of change without serious reform, hoping to buy people's silence by pumping more hydrocarbon dollars into populist projects and by pointing to the chaos and uncertainties in post-Qaddafi Libya, post-Mubarak Egypt, and post-Saleh Yemen.

This chapter, which focuses on Algeria during the 2011 Arab Spring, will examine this and several other questions, including the reasons why the country does not seem to have been affected by the social upheavals that occurred in the Maghreb and the Middle East, especially given that Tunisia and Libya, countries with which Algeria shares borders and regional culture and customs, were able to overthrow systems of authoritarian rule that had been the norm for decades in the region.

A conceptual clarification may be in order before the chapter proceeds. Very few people have taken a moment to define "Arab Spring" beyond simply meaning "popular revolt against authoritarian rulers." The use of this expression will be limited in this chapter because the phenomenon to which it refers has been misconstrued by many observers. Also, the word "Arab" in the expression implicitly excludes those who have rebelled but do not share the Arab identity, such as some Berbers of North Africa. For these reasons, other expressions are preferred here, such as "popular revolts," "mass protests," and "social upheavals." If the expression "Arab Spring" were to be used, it will be done but with this working definition in mind: a mass protest (peaceful or violent) against existing political and economic systems, against rulers and policies in some Middle East and North Africa (MENA) countries, demanding fundamental change. Such protest is persistent, vocal, and sometimes violent. They either challenge the governing political leadership or end its tenure. In Tunisia, Libya, Egypt, and Yemen, the rulers were overthrown and new political forces claimed the state authority in order to pursue substantial change in a variety of spheres (political, economic, social, judicial, and even cultural). In Bahrain, the protest movement was met with harsh repression, while in Syria, at the time of this writing, the peaceful protest has turned violent yet it has not succeeded in overthrowing the existing order. In the Arab Gulf states, the authorities doled out billions of dollars and promised some reform in the hope of buying social peace and keeping the Arab Spring at bay. Fearful of the winds of changes blowing in their region, the less rich monarchies of Jordan and Morocco changed government personnel and enacted some institutional reforms which, for now, have postponed the showdown.

Algeria took a different path. It chose to use its substantial oil and gas income to satisfy immediate social demands, it promised political reform, and it pointed to instability in Libya, Tunisia, Egypt, Syria, and Yemen as a reason for not falling "victim" to the Arab Spring. Of course, the story is somewhat more complicated than this. This chapter will try to elucidate this case of Algerian "exceptionalism."

To understand where Algeria stood in the midst of the Arab Spring, how it reacted to it, and whether it will eventually be affected by it, it is necessary to go back to the political and economic order that the country's early leadership designed and implemented. This will include describing and analyzing how such a political system emerged and how it failed to live up to its own promises because of an inadequate economic development strategy that was overly reliant upon hydrocarbons as a source of income and a closed one-party political system. This chapter will also examine the outcome of the quasi-liberalization of the economy that took place during the 1980s and the ensuing social explosion of 1988. The 1988 riots resulted from economic hardship due to a sharp drop in hydrocarbon revenues (a decline that began in 1986) and an authoritarian leadership that was in disarray.

The second section of this chapter will analyze the nature and limits of the political liberalization that took place during the late 1980s, which was termed by some as a "big bang political liberalization" and by others as the "Algerian Spring" —a "Spring" that occurred well before the 2011 "Arab Spring." This section will also analyze the events that followed, mainly the rise of political Islam and its 1991 landslide electoral success, which was annulled by a 1992 military *coup*, and the ensuing decade-long internal war that devastated the country and its people. A third section will address the economic conditions and reforms.

Once this necessary background is established, the Algerian reaction to the Arab Spring may be then more adequately contextualized and explained in the fourth part of this chapter. In this part, the May 2012 parliamentary elections and their significance in the context of the regional dynamics will be analyzed. A final section will look into what might be in store for Algeria in the near future in light of the prevailing socioeconomic conditions, as well as domestic and regional dynamics.

Systemic failures and the riots of 1988

Following independence, and after eschewing capitalism as an economic model because of its association with inequality, injustice, and colonialism, Algeria opted for a socialist mode of development, which put all social and economic development responsibility in the hands of the state. The state became responsible for production, employment, welfare, and social protection. By the end of the 1970s, the country had a consolidated state, a stable political system, a rapidly industrializing economy, a state-centered socialist program, and an expanding petroleum and gas export industry. However, by the early 1980s, the development strategy had proved incapable of dealing with an economic decline that was caused by several factors, including an inefficient and oversized complex of heavy industries that had not stimulated economic growth as had been planned. Meanwhile the agricultural sector had been neglected, which led to steady declines in output, the growth of dependency upon food imports, which resulted in frequent food shortages that were exacerbated by substantial migration to cities. Adding to this combustible mix, during this period of high population growth, state revenue—which was highly reliant upon the export of hydrocarbons—fluctuated wildly and eventually declined during the late 1980s (a 40 percent drop).

Initial economic reforms during the 1980s not only failed to halt the decline but also exacerbated an already dismal situation and they did not diminish the country's vulnerability to external shocks. Unemployment continued to increase along with uneven urbanization, reduced industrial output, and a substantial increase in consumer prices. The economic reforms were ill-conceived, incoherent, and poorly implemented. They contributed to worsening the economy and social conditions. Industrial investment fell by 21 percent between 1980 and 1981 alone, and imports decreased by 35 percent. Many industrial projects were shelved and several international contracts were canceled.

By the late 1980s, Algeria had highly polarized economic conditions that included rapidly declining export revenues that eroded the state's capacity to meet its social welfare needs and its ability to maintain security and stability. The state had a massive foreign debt that was causing a heavy strain on the state's finances and a high level of dependency on both food imports and hydrocarbon exports left the country dangerously vulnerable.

The worsening social and economic conditions discredited the state, which could no longer support the generous services and subsidies it had previously provided. The relative disengagement of the state from the economy caused more strain and did not halt economic decline. When oil prices fell by 40 percent in 1986, the situation became even more critical. By 1988, the industrial output had dramatically declined and public enterprises had a total deficit of $18.5 billion.[2] The state was close to bankruptcy due to a major decrease in hydrocarbon revenues and rising external debt. Social inequality increased to a point where 45 percent of the national income went to 5 percent of the population while less than 22 percent of such income was shared by 50 percent of the population.[3] Inflation hit an annual rate of 42 percent and 22 percent of the work force had become unemployed. The social conditions worsened when 125,000 more workers—mostly in the public sector—were laid off by 1991.[4] Furthermore, corruption spread and became endemic throughout state institutions and bureaucracy,[5] and the external debt reached $26,557 billion by 1991, with an export-earnings ratio of 193 percent and a debt service ratio of 73.7 percent.[6]

As a result of the botched liberalization reforms of the early 1980s and a major decline of national income by the end of that decade, the living standards of ordinary citizens degraded dramatically; a substantial black market developed; illegal activities and crime rates increased; and corruption set in. In this context, uncontrolled Islamist groups began imposing moral and behavioral restrictions in public places.

Over the years, the ruling elite consolidated its political power through its access to economic rents generated by the hydrocarbon industry. Because of this fact, political elites resisted economic reform. Resistance came also from public company managers, top bureaucrats, and powerful civilians and military officers who benefited from economic protectionism and from the *de facto* monopolies they had created for themselves in the lucrative import–export sectors. It was in this context that the country experienced the worst riots since independence during the month of October 1988. Just like in the popular protests of 2011, the 1988 Algerian rioters demanded the end of a system that was self-serving, condescending, unresponsive, and authoritarian.

By the end of the 1980s, misguided economic policies, the negative effects of major socioeconomic transformations, and restricted political freedoms led to a gradual disintegration of national solidarity, which produced an alternate revolutionary religious discourse and a popular rebellion that eventually turned violent throughout the 1990s.

Political liberalization of the late 1980s: limits and outcome

As indicated above, the riots of October 1988 were followed by a sweeping program of political liberalization that, unfortunately, did not turn into either a democratization process or democracy. Political liberalization is a process that gradually allows political freedoms and establishes some safeguards against the arbitrary state action, while democratization, which involves a higher level of political opening, is a process through which state control over society is slowly diminished to a point where the state becomes less arbitrary and more prone to bargaining with key groups who represent differentiated social, economic, and cultural interests. At this stage, the state progressively resorts to governing less by top-down command and more by negotiated public policies.

Democracy is a set of institutions, a process, and a political culture, which allows individuals and groups to have a regular input in the policymaking process. The authoritarian reflexes of political leaders are restrained by participatory politics. The political system is characterized by accountability and regular turnover of leaders and by the transparency of political and economic transactions. At this stage political culture is characterized by a belief in free debate, tolerance of differences, transparency and accountability in governance, and bargaining-produced public policies. Democracy involves enabling citizens "to pursue their happiness" within the confines of what society, through its representative institutions, decides freely to be in the interest of all.

On the basis of the definitions given above, the political opening in Algeria after the riots of October 1988 was the start of a political liberalization process that ended the one-party system and opened avenues for the creation of a variety of political organizations and for an unprecedented level of freedom of expression and association. However, this sudden and substantial political opening lasted only from 1989 to 1991. It did not amount to democratization, democracy, or regime change.

Despite its limits, this brief period of political liberalization brought about an irreversible transformation of Algeria's political map. Civic associations proliferated and became a vibrant part of Algerian political life. Many organizations—mainly those involving journalists, women, human rights advocates, and independent trade unions—played a significant role during the years of political liberalization. Despite setbacks during the 1990s due to political violence by Islamist groups and state repression, these organizations became a permanent fixture in Algeria's political environment and constitute today a source of regular challenge to the government and they remain an imposing element in the country's political dynamics.

Besides formal parties and associations, another kind of social mobilization for political action was born in 2001 in the wake of a tragic event in the Kabylie region, east of Algiers. The "Citizen Movement," as it became known, demanded, among other things, the recognition of the Berber language (*Tamazight*) as a national and official language. This was a unique movement started by grassroots traditional leadership structures called the *aarch*, which were revived because of failing formal institutional outlets for popular expression of demands and grievances. Notwithstanding its cultural demands, this movement was mostly directed against the entire system of governance and its failure to deal adequately with the serious social and economic problems people across the country were encountering. Twenty years earlier the Berber cultural demands prompted a major showdown with the state in what became known as the "Berber Spring."[7]

Political Islam: from politics to violence and to politics again

Islamist movements and parties, which quickly became the main aggregators and articulators of popular grievances and demands during the late 1980s, took the lead in the first multiparty municipal elections in 1990 and were poised to win overwhelmingly in the 1991 parliamentary elections. However, a military intervention in January 1992 prevented them doing so with a succession of acts: the army cancelled the second round of the parliamentary elections and then the entire vote; it pushed the sitting president (Chadli Bendjedid) to resign; it banned the leading political party, the Front of Islamic Salvation (FIS); and it instituted a temporary collective leadership of the country from 1992 to 1995. The Islamists reacted by forming several armed groups that waged an all-out war against the state and anyone in society deemed an enemy.

The state and radical Islamist groups became entangled in a very complex and deadly struggle. New armed organizations, mainly the Armed Islamic Group (GIA), the Armed Islamic Movement (MIA), the Islamic Salvation Army (AIS, the armed wing of FIS), and the Salafist Group for Preaching and Combat (GSPC), perpetrated a series of killings of not only military and police personnel, but also, and mostly, of civilians. The civilian victims included simple citizens who refused to help them or were suspected of cooperating with the state, and many journalists, professors, poets, doctors, opposition party leaders, and foreigners. Approximately 200,000 people were killed by the rebels and the state between 1992 and 1999; even more were injured, and 1.5 million people were displaced as a result of the insurrection.[8] The Islamist violence destroyed much of the non-hydrocarbon economic and social infrastructure and threw more people into poverty; it also isolated the country in the international arena. However, it also drastically reduced the popular support that religious movements had formerly enjoyed. By the end of the 1990s, the Islamist rebellion was tamed thanks to several factors, including "military (increase in the number of security forces, 80,000 gendarmes, 200,000 militia), political (civil concord [amnesty program]), and social (loss of popular support for the guerrilla following the massacre of civilians)."[9]

Controlled political integration of Islamism

While radical Islamist challengers were met with harsh state repression, moderate Islamists (so called because they rejected violence) were tolerated, coopted, or included via elected representation in state institutions after parliament was restored in 1997. The state's leaders did this through a carefully managed process of inclusion of the moderately oriented Islamist opposition into the political sphere. In the June 1997 elections for the 380-member assembly—the first national election since the one that was aborted in 1992—two Islamist parties, the *Harakat mujtam'a al-silm* (Movement of Society for Peace or MSP) and the *Harakat al-nahda* (known as Nahda) respectively won 69 and 34 seats. A newly-formed party, the National Democratic Rally (RND), was created to support incumbent President Liamine Zéroual and it won 115 seats while the FLN won only 64 seats. The 1997 local and municipal elections continued this trend as government-backed candidates won the majority of seats. In a paradoxical turn of events, the MSP eventually ended up being part of a coalition government with the FLN and the RND. The Islamists were awarded up to seven ministries in the government.

It is worth noting that a year before the 1997 elections, a constitution that was approved by referendum declared that Islam was the state's religion. Yet the constitution prohibited the creation of parties on a "religious, linguistic, racial, gender, corporatist or regional" basis or the use of partisan propaganda based on these elements. The new constitution also created a second parliamentary chamber, the "Council of the Nation," one-third of which would be appointed by the president and the rest by indirect suffrage. Finally, constitutional amendments reinforced the powers of the president while diminishing those of parliament and the prime minister.

The Algerian ruling elite—both civilian and military—followed a three-track policy aiming to reestablish the legitimacy and authority of the state and resolving the crisis without surrendering to Islamist demands. First, it waged an all-out campaign of physical eradication of the armed Islamist rebellion by mobilizing the army and police and arming thousands of civilians; second, it resumed political life through multiparty elections for both the presidency and parliament; and, third, it resumed a program of political liberalization but this time with more control over who would be included—in contrast to the first "big bang" liberalization of 1989–1991.

Since 1992, four presidents and several prime ministers and their respective cabinets took turns in trying to solve the multidimensional crisis. The first three presidents were: Mohamed Boudiaf who was assassinated in June 1992 by one of the members of his security detail barely six months after being invited to lead the country; Ali Kafi, the leader of the national liberation war veterans' organization; and, Liamine Zéroual, a retired general, who ended up resigning before his finishing his term. Zéroual was the first person in independent Algeria to be elected through a multiparty contest. Although he resigned before ending his term, he managed to start truce talks with one of the major armed Islamist groups, the Islamic Salvation Army (AIS), which agreed to lay down its weapons in exchange for full amnesty. The fourth president (who is still in office) is Abdelaziz Bouteflika who finalized the truce with the AIS. Bouteflika came to power in 1999 and immediately submitted the amnesty program, known as the Civil Concord, to popular approval by referendum. Five years later, yet another amnesty program was implemented and more armed Islamists benefitted from it. After the Armed Islamist Groups (GIA)—the deadliest of all the armed Islamist groups—withered away due to infighting and infiltration by governmental security services, the Salafist Group for Preaching and Combat (GSPC) remained as the last armed group that rejected the government's offer of amnesty and vowed to continue fighting. In 2006, the GSPC joined the Al-Qaeda network. It changed its name to Al-Qaeda in the Islamic Maghreb (AQIM), and it extended its scope of activities from northern Algeria to the rest of the Maghreb and the Sahel region. AQIM remains a serious security threat to Algeria and the region but its violent campaign has declined in the north while it has accelerated in the Sahel.

Political Islam in Algeria seems to have been tamed for now by strong state repression of its radical fringe and a successful strategy that induced and coopted its moderate wing (MSP and Nahda) to participate in electoral politics. It is safe to say that this policy succeeded in attaining its objectives of ending the mass rebellion led by the Islamists and controlling political Islam by incorporating its non-violent and less threatening expressions into the political process.

Starting in 2000, insecurity and political instability began to diminish. The terrible decade of civil war in the early 1990s became a memory but scars remained deep. Relative peace and stability finally returned to Algeria after a long, nightmarish, and unrelenting era of vicious political violence. However, the country has been unable to deal effectively with serious socioeconomic problems and a lasting political *malaise* that is due to reforms that have not brought undertaken about effective change. Real reform is still resisted by those who hold power and the opposition still lacks the ability to mount a coordinated challenge against the regime.

The institutional changes and elections that have taken place since the mid-1990s have not fundamentally changed the political system. The nature of the ruling regime has remained unaffected as the power configurations within the governing elite and between them and society have not changed substantially. The state has continued to exclude Islamist and secular political figures who demanded radical change, who asked for the reinstatement of the FIS, or who sought direct negotiations with the government for a comprehensive political solution to the country's problems. As a result, Algeria's management of its multidimensional crisis has not moved beyond a semblance of controlled political liberalization.

As indicated above, non-violent political Islam entered the political arena as a set of legal and legitimate political parties, starting with the first multi-party presidential election in 1995 and parliamentary elections in 1997. However, after initial respectable results at the polls, the Islamist parties—mainly the MSP—have started declining in electoral results. During the last three parliamentary elections, (2002, 2007, and 2012) the Islamist political parties have witnessed a marked decline that is due partly to the general irrelevance of opposition parties within the political system and partly to *intra*-party conflicts. In 2007, the MSP lost 31 of its 69 seats in parliament. However, a new party, the Movement for National Reform or MRN (known as the *Harakat al-iIslah al-watani* or Islah)—a breakaway party from Nahda—won 43 seats. Overall, the number of seats controlled by the Islamists declined from 103 to 60. In the May 2012 parliamentary vote, the number of parliamentary seats held by these Islamist parties declined further to 49—all held by the "Green Algeria Alliance" which included combined candidates from MSP, Islah, and Nahda.

Algerian sociologist Nasser Djabi suggested that one of the reasons for this Islamist decline is because "unlike in Tunisia or Egypt, Algeria's Islamist parties do not have deep roots in society and their middle class activists cannot mobilize people the way the Muslim Brotherhood can."[10] Another way of looking at this evolution of political Islam in Algeria is that "the regime has successively neutered ... the main Islamist parties, allowing them to participate in elections and including them in governing coalitions, tempting them with the fruits of power, and then watching their support slump as they compromise to stay in Parliament."[11] According to Khemissi, Larémont and Taj Eddine, this strategy has also been employed at the level of municipal councils where Islamist parties were allowed to participate: "When these councils failed to deliver positive results, youth became further distanced from Islamist parties. In this process, Islamist parties have acquired the same level of disdain or skepticism that secularly oriented political parties have encountered."[12]

Economic conditions and failed reforms

At the end of 1993, and while the armed Islamist rebellion was underway, Algeria was in a precarious economic situation. Its only option to deal with a rapidly declining economy was to abide by the commands of international financial institutions and their most influential members, mainly France and the United States. After much delay, and quite reluctantly, Algeria agreed in 1994 to an IMF and World Bank-sponsored Structural Adjustment Program (SAP). This led the government to devaluate its currency by 40 percent and to lift remaining subsidies on basic consumption items. The government had to tighten monetary and credit policies and reorganize its financial institutions while liberalizing its foreign trade, lowering its budget deficit, and privatizing some public enterprises. Within a few years, the country's aggregate economic indicators improved markedly and the general environment slowly started to attract modest levels of domestic and foreign investment.

Inflation was brought down from 30 percent in 1995 to less than 3 percent in 2005; the state budget and the trade balance recorded a surplus; hard currency reserves increased from $1.5 billion in 1993 to $90 billion in 2007 and $182 billion by December 2011; and most of the external debt, which stood at $35 billion in the early 2000s, was almost entirely paid off by December 2011.[13]

The "shock therapy," however, did not fulfill its overall promises for a variety of reasons. One was a strong resistance to the mandated reforms from various forces, including political elites who feared the social cost; groups with vested interests in the *status quo*, including the largest labor union (the General Union of Algerian Workers or UGTA), civil and professional associations, public enterprise managers, big private import/export businesses that had substantial informal business monopolies, and small private entrepreneurs who benefited from protectionism; and, an overvalued currency. More than 500,000 workers were laid off by 1998 following the restructuring or closing of public enterprises (815 public enterprises were dissolved and the economic units that survived had to lay off 60 percent of their workers).[14] Unemployment climbed to 35 percent in the 1990s before falling to 17.7 percent in 2004 and 11 percent in 2011; and the number of people living below the poverty line increased substantially, reaching 23 percent in 2006,[15] before falling to 18.95 percent in 2008. Social inequality increased markedly, as indicated in the country's security services' report on poverty that showed that less than 20 percent of the population controlled more than 50 percent of the country's wealth.[16]

Algeria's biggest paradox, as indicated above, has been that on one hand the country's overall financial standing had improved during the last decade, but, on the other hand, that the social and economic conditions of most of its citizens had worsened during the same period of time. This resulted from the absence of a coherent development strategy and the inadequate management of the oil rents that failed to stimulate non-hydrocarbon economic development. Furthermore, Algeria, which relies upon oil and gas exports for revenue, remains vulnerable to international oil price fluctuations and other conditions that affect its revenue substantially.

Algeria 135

Just like other rentier states, the Algerian state

> appears strong when oil revenue is rising but it becomes weak, sometimes abruptly, when oil revenue can no longer sustain growing social entitlements. There is a mismatch between the scale of economic reform required to restore economic growth and the limited capacity of a state that lacks political legitimacy to execute painful reform.[17]

This scenario was experienced at the end of the 1980s and throughout the 1990s and yet Algeria remains hostage to the oil rent mentality and seems unable to design and implement a viable long-term strategy of economic development.

The government's most important response to social unrest during the past decade has been the infusion of large amounts of cash into the economy in the form of infrastructure investments that do not generate long-term income and employment. Between 2000 and 2011, approximately $500 billion went primarily to highway construction, new low-income housing construction, and agriculture. It is feared, however, that this massive injection of capital in the economy may not have the expected effects in employment creation.[18] During recent years, some public investments have been earmarked for manufacturing cement and fertilizer or for developing telephony and tourism. Other funds were allocated as micro-credits to help young people find jobs or create their own businesses. However, these efforts have fallen short of the estimated 300,000 new jobs that are needed per year to absorb current and future employment demands. The official unemployment rate is hovering around 10 percent but in reality is closer to 25 percent with many of the jobless being young and university graduates.

An important impediment to sound economic reforms has been the existence of a "parallel economy" that represents approximately 40 percent of non-hydrocarbon activities. This parallel economy escapes state control and taxation. Some individuals in high public offices and the bureaucracy, as well as some retired military officers with major business interests, have vested stakes in the informal sector and do not welcome the transparency and accountability of financial transactions being required by economic reform and privatization.

The current economic regulations, institutions, and practices discourage overall reform and private investment and they block the growth of a formal productive private sector, while encouraging thriving predatory private behavior that continues to extract benefits from the rent-based and subsidized formal system. In this context, corruption at high levels of public companies and the bureaucracy became in recent years a major problem that hurt not only the end-goal of public investments but also the legitimacy of the state. Two recent big corruption cases involved the construction of the East–West highway and the national hydrocarbons company, Sonatrach. High-level managers and even government ministers were brought down by these corruption scandals.

Algeria and the Arab Spring

On the eve of the 2011 social upheavals across North Africa and the Middle East, Algeria was finally enjoying a return of political stability, relative security, and some economic prosperity—again due to increased hydrocarbon revenues—after a long period of turbulence and uncertainty. However, beneath this image of stability and prosperity there was—and still is—a continuing social, economic and political *malaise* due to high youth unemployment rates, rising inflation, lack of government responsiveness to people's pressing demands, a stagnant political liberalization process, and an aging and disconnected top leadership. When the upheaval in Tunisia began in December 2011, the social situation in Algeria had already been tense. "The country's dire socioeconomic conditions, coupled with the governmental paralysis mainly owing to President Abdelaziz Bouteflika's illness, made Algeria the best contender for revolt."[19]

The January 2011 riots: limited, short and apolitical

On January 3, 2011, riots broke out in Algiers, the capital, and other major cities following rumors that the price of basic food staples (semolina, sugar, and cooking oil) were about to rise again due to new regulations intended to reign in the substantial informal market. The riots were spontaneous and were not primarily about overturning the regime. They focused on the rising cost of living due to increases in the cost of food within the global food market (Algeria imports close to 75 percent of its food), diminished state subsidies, and a stagnant low minimum wage. The rioters were also angry at the state for acute shortages of affordable housing, failing educational and health systems, rampant corruption, and cronyism and nepotism in the bureaucracy and in the public companies. Their demands included the improvement of the living conditions, lower food prices, jobs and respect. However, "the riots ... never took on a directed political character; the mobs of rioters did not become protesters. There were no marches, no shared slogans and no coherent demands."[20]

As the labor market proved unable to absorb them and as immigration laws in Europe and North America tightened, much of the Algerian youth found themselves trapped in a desperate situation. They had little faith in formal politics and political parties, which, for them, only served the well-connected. Having few means of peacefully expressing their grievances and getting a response, they resorted instead to street violence.

The January 2011 riots were not an isolated event without precedent. Riots in Algeria have become such a regular occurrence that not a single day passes without more than one riot occurring somewhere in the country. Nowadays, whenever people face a problem that neither the local authorities nor the state addresses, people often and promptly take to the streets and attack government buildings, block traffic on main roads, and organize sit-ins and even hunger strikes.

The riots of January 2011 were not limited to a single locality but took place simultaneously in several cities across the country; all were triggered by the rumored impending price hikes and they were inspired by the unfolding Tunisian mass protests. However, in contrast with the Tunisian and Egyptian protests, the rioting Algerian youth did not obtain the support of labor unions, political parties, or civic associations. Also, the riots did not last more than four days and the protesters did not present political demands; they ended as soon as the government announced a low price ceiling on basic food, tabled impending market regulations, and provided for "temporary and exceptional exemptions on import duties, value-added tax and corporate tax for everyday commodities."[21] These measures stopped the riots in their tracks but they did not resolve the underlying problems.

Three hundred young people were invited on January 19, 2011, to a parliament session where they were allowed to freely state their complaints and wishes. Surprisingly, the issue of the price of food was the last item on their list, even though many people spend on average 40–55 percent of their income on nutrition. Instead, their key grievances were related to jobs, housing, their marginalization in the political and economic systems, and the contempt (*hogra*) shown towards them by bureaucrats and state security agents.

Addressing the country for the first time almost a month after the riots of early January, President Bouteflika promised on January 30 many new jobs, the lifting of the 19-year-old state of emergency law, and more political freedom. His speech was received with cynicism by an incredulous audience because similar past promises were recanted or did not address the fundamental problems that in fact were embedded in the entire political and economic system. Furthermore, the lifting of the state of emergency did not mean the end of the arbitrary curtailment of liberties because many restrictive regulations remained in place.

Political protest in 2011: limited, repressed, and ephemeral

A peaceful movement of political protest was finally underway in Algiers on February 12, more than a month after the January riots, which was an indication of how hard it had become to mobilize the masses for concerted mass political action against the government. The protest that began in February 2012 was short-lived for several reasons. It was led by the National Coordination for Change and Democracy (known by its French acronym CNCD), which was an organization created on January 21 by small political parties, the National League for the Defense of Human Rights, the National Association of Families of Missing Persons (those who "disappeared" during the internal war of the 1990s), an association of the unemployed, and many other groups. The CNCD protest movement was led by the Rally for Democracy and Culture (RCD), an opposition party with a narrow constituency of Berber-speaking people in Algiers and the nearby Kabylie region. It demanded democracy, and end to the state of emergency, the liberalization of the political and media fields, and the release of people arrested during the January 2011 riots.

The CNCD called for a massive rally in Algiers on February 12 against the entire ruling system and those who lead it—known to most Algerians as *le pouvoir*. However, the government prevented the rally by using an overwhelming number of police to disperse the gathering, by closing off streets and erecting checkpoints, by halting all bus and train services, and by blocking access to Facebook. Several other attempts to organize rallies and demonstrations did not succeed and attendance declined.

Several reasons may explain the inability of the political opposition to mount and sustain mass demonstrations against the government. The first and often-cited reason is that the traumatic 1990s decade is still fresh in people's memory and its wounds have not yet healed; as a result, most people may not be willing to fight another battle, even one that is peaceful, because it may degenerate into violence. Another reason is that people believe that the Algerian security forces will not hesitate, as they did in 1988 and in the 1990s, to use violent means to subdue a popular movement that they deem a high risk to stability. A third reason is the known fact that the most powerful institutions in Algeria are the military and security services (known as DRS). The civilian leadership has only nominal authority. Taking on the political system would thus entail either having the acquiescence of the military (as in the 2011 Tunisian mass protest) or risk harsh repression (as in the 1990s Algeria or Syria during 2011–2012). A fourth reason is the inability of the opposition to create a wide and sustained coalition that can become a mass movement of protest or revolt against the ruling regime. The leaders of the regime have become adept at neutralizing the opposition through cooptation, infiltration, manipulation, or just plain elimination, making it very difficult for political dissenters to organize and act in unison. Another reason for the failure of the February 2011 protest was that—just like the riots of a month earlier—it was not supported by the General Union of Algerian Workers, significant political parties, and professional associations.

The National Coordination for Change and Democracy, as a coalition of less powerful independent unions, civic associations, and opposition parties, did not articulate clear objectives beyond vague denunciations of the regime and a vague call for democracy. Also, the CNCD protests did not target the head of state as had been done in Tunisia, Egypt, Libya, Yemen, and Syria. Rather, it attacked a more elusive and ambiguous *pouvoir* – the real, unelected power holders in Algeria. Furthermore, the legitimacy and attractiveness of the National Coordination seemed compromised by the fact that its key figure was Said Saadi, the head of the RCD party, who was recognized as a coopted opposition leader who had supported the military's cancellation of the 1992 parliamentary elections and who had applauded the repression of the Islamists who had been poised to win that election. After a few weeks of attempting, in vain, to recruit more protesters and to break through the overwhelming police presence in the capital, the protest movement led by the CNCD died out. It has not yet been replaced.

However, other types of protests and localized riots over limited issues have continued and intensified at times throughout 2011 and 2012. These actions have affected several towns and villages and many professional sectors. Several strikes led by independent unions (i.e., those not affiliated with the UGTA) have had an impact upon the education and health sectors, the civil service, the legal sector, and several industries. The strikers' demands have included either pay raises to keep up with inflation or parity with salaries in the public sector, which have recently benefited from pay increases of 25–50 percent, improved work conditions, or better health insurance and retirement compensation programs.

Another form of protest has also recently become prevalent: suicide, especially by immolation. Throughout 2011 and 2012, such an act has, unfortunately, became a recurring phenomenon in seeming emulation of the self-immolation of Mohamed Bouazizi, the man from the Tunisian town of Sidi Bouzid where the whole Arab Spring began in December 2010. However, the increasing rate of these suicides or suicide attempts by self-immolation has generated neither public interest nor the concern of government officials. The final form of protests involves the growing phenomenon of illegal migration to Europe by way of the sea. Commonly known as *Harga*, this dangerous form of exit has caused many deaths yet it remains an attractive alternative for many people with no hope of ever having a decent life in Algeria.

Algeria's reforms to circumvent the region's spring of upheavals

Feeling the heat of the social pressure generated by collective and individual acts of protest and fearing a contagion effect from the popular upheavals in the region, the Algerian government has been trying to buy peace and stability by promising economic and political reform. On the economic front, it announced a new round of public investments in the social and economic sectors. In spring 2011 it announced that $280 billion will be injected in the economy in an effort to create new jobs in the industrial and service sectors. That money would support micro-credit programs and paid internships for the youth, finance public works that generate some employment, and increase the salaries of public workers.

> The government regularly buys off social discontent by providing relative social welfare on the back of windfall gains from hydrocarbon exports. Whereas this approach provides the government political leeway in the short term, it sidesteps the need to seriously tackle a number of weaknesses in Algeria's economy and political system.[22]

On the political front, President Bouteflika announced on April 15, 2011, a plan for a series of reforms that would affect, among other things, the constitution itself, the electoral system, gender balance in political institutions, and the media.[23] At the outset, he created in May 2011 a National Commission of Consultation on Political Reforms (CNCRP),[24] which, after consulting key individuals and organization, would submit recommendations for reform to the president and parliament. Sidestepping a popular debate on the nature of the reforms, the commission, which handpicked the individuals it wished to consult, lacked credibility and independence, but it nevertheless provided recommendations in June 2011 that were approved by the government and parliament. These recommendations did not amount to much in terms of democratic change even though they were intended as such.

In pursuance of the reform recommendations, 21 new parties were legalized, which further diluted the power of both the secularist and Islamist parties. A new quota system for women's presence on the electoral lists and in parliament brought in 145 female members of parliament who constituted approximately 31 percent of the 462 deputies of the National Assembly—up from a mere 7 percent in the previous parliament.[25] This constituted a tremendous change in the female representation in parliament but one wonders how this will affect the overall level of women's participation in politics and public policies affecting women.

As for constitutional reform, the government rejected the opposition's call for the creation of a constituent assembly that would draft a new constitution; instead constitutional changes would be debated and voted on by the new parliament. Among the rumored reforms there is the possible return to presidential term limits, which had been eliminated in 2009.[26] Overall, the enacted reforms and those still being discussed "constitute no real breakthrough and are unlikely to change the fundamental nature of the political system put in place 50 years ago. The regime seems to be reproducing the scheme it devised following the riots of October 1988."[27]

The 2012 parliamentary elections and the liability of inertia

On May 10, 2012, Algeria held parliamentary elections in a very tense socioeconomic climate compounded by a pronounced political *malaise*. The vote was boycotted by the vast majority of eligible voters. The official voter participation rate was 43.14 percent but most observers agree that in reality it was less than that, probably somewhere between 20 and 30 percent. Most of those who voted were believed to be members of participating parties, civil servants, the military, the police, clients of power holders, and people who needed to be well perceived by the ruling system.[28]

The elections, which were preceded by the legalization of 21 new parties, produced results that made most contenders unhappy while an apathetic society looked on almost with a yawn. The lack of popular interest in the parliamentary elections declined to the worst level since political liberalization began in 1989. People did not find it useful to vote for a parliament that had been generally unresponsive to people's demands and grievances, that was powerless *vis-à-vis* other centers of authority and power, and was full of individuals who seemed attuned more to their personal wellbeing than on that of society.

Prior to the vote, President Bouteflika and the FLN and RND leaders[29] presented these elections as a plebiscite on security and stability in the country in light of what had been happening in Libya, the Sahel region (especially the crisis in Mali), Egypt, Yemen, and Syria. Prime Minister Ahmed Ouyahia explicitly expressed his dismay at the Arab Spring, which he characterized as a foreign conspiracy against the Arab states.

In the wake of an internal dispute over leadership, the FLN became divided over the leadership of its secretary general, Abdelaziz Belkhadem.[30] The MSP decided three months before the vote of May 2012 to withdraw from the pro-government coalition and join the opposition, with the hope of an electoral victory that would resemble those of Ennahda in Tunisia, the Muslim Brothers in Egypt, or even the Party of Justice and Development (PJD) in Morocco. However, that move proved to be almost fatal to the party as its weak results showed.

The results of the 2012 elections surprised many and contributed to deepening the political *malaise*, if not crisis, in the country. Instead of placing Algeria on a track for helpful change, as some people had hoped, these elections indicated the regime's intention to avoid what it perceived as the pitfalls of the Arab Spring. With the state coffers awash with substantial hydrocarbon income, Algeria's leaders opted for the *status quo* as a guarantor of stability and a defense against the tidal wave of Islamist electoral victories in the region.

The FLN had the strongest results since its demise in the aborted 1991 elections and the elections of 1997. It won 208 seats of 462 in the 2012 parliamentary vote, while the RND received 68 seats, up from 61.[31] According to press commentary, "the low [voter] turnout (43.14 percent) helped the FLN. Its traditional supporters—the elderly, the military, and public servants—were the most likely to turn up and vote, while those who could have countered them stayed at home."[32] After its initial defeats in the 1991 and 1997 elections, winning only 15 and 69 seats respectively, the FLN rebounded in 2002 with 199 seats. In the 2007 elections, the FLN and the RND lost 49 of the combined 246 they held—due to FLN losses (from 199 to 136 seats)—but they still remained the two dominant political parties.

Between 2002 and 2007, the process had come full circle with the FLN back in a dominant position and extending full support to President Bouteflika. The FLN's position was further enhanced by the 2012 elections. Both the FLN and the RND obtained control of the majority of the seats (276 out of 462) and could create a majority in parliament without Islamist participation.

At the time of this writing, the configuration of parliament has not been established. One of the many questions prompted by the election results and by the controversies they generated concerning voting fraud and other irregularities was what would happen to the Islamist parties of the Green Alliance that won merely 49 seats? The three-party Islamist alliance, which

Table 7.1 Select results of Algerian parliamentary elections from 1997 to 2012

Parties	1997	2002	2007	2012
	Seats	Seats	Seats	Seats
FLN (Front de Libération Nationale)	69	199	136	208
RND (Rassemblement National Démocratique)	156	47	61	68
MRN/Islah (Mouvement de la Réforme Nationale)	-	43	3	-
MSP/HMS (*Harakat Moujtama'a al-Silm*)	69	38	52	-
MRI/Nahda	34	1	5	-
Alliance Algérie Verte (MSP, Islah, Nahda)	-	-	-	49
PT (Parti des Travailleurs)	4	21	26	24
FFS (Front des forces Socialistes)	20	-	-	27
Indépendents	11	30	33	19
Front pour la Justice et le Développement (Addala/FJD)	-	-	-	7
RCD (Rassemblement pour la Culture et la Démocratie)	19	-	19	-

Notes: The total seats in the National Assembly was: 380 in 1997, 389 in 2002, and 462 in 2012. MRN/*El-Islah* was created in 1998. RCD boycotted the 2002 and 2012 elections, while the FFS boycotted the 2002 and 2007 vote. Alliance Algérie Verte is a new alliance of three Islamist parties MSP, Islah, and Nahda, which presented a common list of candidates. The FJD party of Abdallah Djaballah is new.

had hoped for a victory similar to those of other Islamist parties in the region, seemed in shock when the results were published. Its leaders accused the government of electoral irregularities and fraud. Abdallah Djaballah, the leader of the newly-created Islamist party, the *Front pour la Justice et le Développement* or Addala/FJD, which won only seven seats, created the Political Front for the Safeguard of Democracy (*le Front Politique pour la Sauvegarde de la Démocratie* or FPSD) with 15 other party leaders. The FPSD called on parties to boycott the parliament, demanded the establishment of a transitional government, and asked for the creation of a national body that would draft a new constitution. Back in February 2012, Djaballah had declared in a speech that

> the Algerian *pouvoir* should heed the lessons of the [Arab] Spring led by the youth who broke the myth of 'undethronable' Arab dictators. If it does not want to know the same fate as the regimes of Ben Ali or Mubarak, it must, for once, bow to the will of the people that has been confiscated since 1962.[33]

The 16 parties of the FPSD have small constituencies and little political weight, which means that their calls for action are unlikely to affect the course of events that are largely determined by the top leadership of the country. That leadership will most likely continue its policy of cooptation of opponents, which has been largely successful.

The risk of uncontrollable political opposition and possibly instability lies elsewhere, outside of the formal institutions. It is in the streets where the potential challenge to the *status quo* resides. This is amply reflected in the numerous strikes and riots that have been taking place with increasing intensity. As the institutional setting remains fairly closed to political dissent and protest, people have decided to take matters in their own hands.

In what was probably his best work, the late Samuel P. Huntington warned us in 1968 in *Political Order in Changing Societies* of the problems that arise when there is a lag in the development of political institutions in countries that are experiencing rapid social and economic change. For Huntington, "violence and instability" can be "in a large part the product of rapid social change and the rapid mobilization of new groups into politics coupled with the slow development of political institutions."[34]

Algeria has changed in major ways during the past two decades, especially within society where a new generation is in the process of replacing the post-independence leadership. As indicated by Algerian sociologist Nasser Djabi in a study of the political significance of generational shifts in Algeria, the current generation's preoccupations are more economic and social and less ideological and political. This generation seems to have less taste for past ideological battles and is more concerned with its own immediate needs in terms of education, jobs, housing, and social mobility.[35] It is also more willing to fight for these needs outside of the failing institutional framework.

Using Huntington's reasoning, it can be said that the expansion of political participation in Algeria during the late 1980s, which had origins in both socio-economic mutations and political liberalization, was not matched by the required level of political institutionalization. A consequence of this mismatch between the expansion of political participation and a low level of political institutionalization is "political instability and disorder."[36] In short, a weak level of political institutionalization may thus be one of the reasons why "the street" may matter more than the failing institutions of representation and of public policymaking.

Instead of being channeled through political institutions that aggregate, articulate, and respond to popular grievances, people's frustration with the state and its leadership is expressed through strikes, street protest and rioting.

> For many Algerians, blocking the road, burning a tire, closing a city hall, participating in a rally or any other protest action is a political act. The stage has been set for more than a year where protest movements take place every day. This is to say that these are all political acts that take place in the street.[37]

However, these acts are limited, localized, isolated, and usually are of short duration. Most do not even have political slogans. They are driven by demands for water services, low-income housing, jobs, new labor contracts, and similar matters. Once some of these demands are somewhat satisfied with a new infusion of public money, the protests usually end. Of course, this state of affairs cannot last for long, especially if the oil and gas prices fall drastically and the state can no longer fully meet its obligations.

The state's policy of putting out fires, one at a time, avoids the necessary discussion over a new social contract between state and society. The limitation in avenues and occasions of peaceful, regular, and institutionalized interactions between state and society over public policies has created distance, along with mistrust and suspicion, which keeps the ruling elite and the citizenry apart, except for the occasional violent clashes that result partly from such distance.

One has just to look at recent opinion surveys conducted in Algeria to see the extent of disconnection that exists today between society—especially its young component—and the governing institutions and leadership. A survey conducted by the Arab Barometer in April and May 2011 found that 62 percent of Algerian respondents are not satisfied with the work of the government. More than 50 percent do not have confidence in political parties at all and close to 30 percent have no confidence in civic associations. The survey indicates also that 54 percent of respondents have no confidence in the judicial system.[38]

The apathy and mistrust felt toward the political institutions and processes reflect a substantial legitimacy deficit that cannot be ignored or dismissed simply because hydrocarbon rents provide for the short-term provision of populist spending projects. Things can easily turn for the worse if there is a substantial decrease in the oil and natural gas income, or if the state and its agents commit a major blunder that would serve as the match that would light yet another armed rebellion. Unfortunately, short of such an unsettling shock, the current governing system and top leadership are likely to persist with current policies, even until the 2014 presidential election that is expected to usher in a replacement for President Bouteflika.

In the medium term, Algeria's "exceptionalism" is untenable in the wake of the upheavals that have rocked the region. To avoid an almost certain conflagration, the country needs a genuine institutional overhaul, a meaningful change of civilian leadership at all levels, and sound economic reforms that aim to lessen the economy's dependency upon the sale of hydrocarbons, which would undermine the predatory behavior of civilian and military high office holders and would absorb hundreds of thousands of young job seekers. Algeria has resources that could provide for a positive transformation of the country in the interest of its citizens. These factors include abundant natural resources; a high level of export income and of cash reserves; a large pool of highly educated people and a sizeable force of technocrats; a thriving independent print press and an already existing multiparty political scene that can be rendered more meaningful by democratization.

These assets can be put to good use only if important institutional changes are made. The powers of all state institutions need be revised by ending the overwhelming and unproductive dominance of the presidential office; by allowing parliament to exercise legislative, investigative, and oversight functions; and by making the judicial system truly independent and able to guarantee basic freedoms and protection against abuse of power and retribution for political reasons. The military's role in politics,[39] which was somewhat curtailed under the pressure of President Bouteflika, must be further diminished so as to allow accountable and regularly alternating civilian leaders who would steer the country towards genuine political and economic development. These measures will not happen overnight but it is necessary to start comprehensive reform endeavors now with the hope that they would help avoid the almost certain explosion that would end Algeria's exceptionalism in an era of sweeping changes in both the region and the world.

Notes

1 For an excellent discussion of the origin and meaning of the purely Algerian notion of *hogra*, see Amel Blidi, "C'est l'injustice et l'humiliation de tous les jours: La hogra, un mal algérien," *El Watan*, June 7, 2012. There is also a website dedicated to this notion: Hogra en Algerie at http://hogra.centerblog.net/#.
2 Abed Charef, *Octobre* (Algiers: Laphomic Editions, 1990), p. 16.
3 *El Moudjahid*, January 29, 1990.
4 Zakya Daoud, "L'Economie du Maghreb en Difficulté," *Le Monde Diplomatique* (June 1991), p. 26.
5 The 2011 Transparency International Report ranked Algeria 112 out of 183 countries with a score of 2.9 over 10 (10 being free of corruption). The Algeria Report is available online at www.transparency.org/country#DZA.
6 The World Bank, *World Bank Report 1993* (New York: Oxford University Press, 1993).
7 The Berber Spring started on March 10, 1980, when the police prevented Mouloud Mammeri, a renowned writer, from giving a lecture on ancient Berber poetry at a university in Tizi Ouzou, the main city of the predominantly Berber region of Kabylie, east of Algiers. This action was followed by student strikes, demonstrations and repression, which lasted until June.
8 Global IDP Project, "Algeria: More Than One Million Internally Displaced People Ignored By The International Community," March 5, 2004. See also "Profile of Internal Displacement: Algeria." A report compiled from the Global Internally Displaced Populations Database of the Norwegian Refugee Council, www.idpproject.org.
9 Luis Martinez, "La sécurité en Algérie et en Libye après le 11 septembre," EuroMeSCo Paper, May 2003, www.euromesco.net/euromesco/media/euromescopaper22.pdf.
10 Nasser Djabi quoted in Paul Schemm, "Algerian Islamists Fall To Govt Party In Election," *The Associated Press*, May 11, 2012.
11 Jack Brown, "Algeria's Midwinter Uproar," *Middle East Research and Information Project* (MERIP), January 20, 2011, www.merip.org/mero/mero012011.
12 Hamidi Khemissi, Ricardo René Larémont and Taybi Taj Eddine, "Sufism, Salafism and State Policy Towards Religion in Algeria: A Survey of Algerian Youth," *The Journal of North African Studies*, 17:3 (June 2012): 553.
13 In December 2011, Algeria owed $4.4 billion only, as announced by the governor of Algeria's Central Bank in February 2012. See "Les réserves de changes atteignent 182,22 milliards de dollars en 2011," Algérie Presse Service, February 23, 2012.
14 "*Rapport" Préliminaire sur Les Effets Économiques et Sociaux du Programme d'Ajustement Structurel,* Conseil National Économique et Social (CNES), (Algiers: CNES, November 1998).

15 "Algeria," *CIA World Factbook*, May 2012.
16 "Pauvreté en Algérie: Rapport Alarmant Des Services De Sécurité," *Le Soir d'Algerie*, May 11, 2006.
17 Richard M. Auty, "Third Time Lucky for Algeria? Integrating an Industrializing Oil-Rich Country into the Global Economy," *Resources Policy*, 29 (2003): 38, www.elsevier.com/locate/resourpol.
18 Florence Beaugé "L'Algérie va lancer un 'plan Marshall' pour doper son économie," *Le Monde*, June 24, 2005.
19 Yahia H. Zoubir and Ahmed Aghrout, "Algeria's Path to Reform: Authentic Change?" *Middle East Policy*, XIX:2 (Summer 2012): 66.
20 Jack Brown, "Algeria's Midwinter Uproar," *Middle East Research and Information Project* (MERIP), January 20, 2011, www.merip.org/mero/mero012011.
21 "BTI 2012 Algeria Country Report," Bertelsmann Stiftung's Transformation Index (BTI) Gütersloh: Bertelsmann Stiftung, 2012, p. 23, www.bti-project.de/fileadmin/Inhalte/reports/2012/pdf/BTI 2012 Algeria.pdf
22 "BTI 2012 Algeria Country Report," p. 64.
23 "Bouteflika annonce des réformes politiques en Algérie," *L'Express.fr*, April 15, 2011, www.lexpress.fr.
24 The commission was chaired by Abdelkader Bensalah, speaker of the Council of the Nation (Conseil de la nation, upper house of parliament) and co-chaired by retired General-Major Mohamed Touati and Mohamed Ali Boughazi, two close advisors of President Bouteflika.
25 The size of the lower house was increased in 2012 from 389 to 462.
26 In 2009 a constitutional amendment did away with the limit of two five-year terms for the presidency in order to accommodate President Bouteflika's wish to serve a third term. He was re-elected for the third term in that year.
27 Zoubir and Aghrout, "Algeria's Path to Reform," p. 66.
28 Dominique Lagarde, "Algérie: des élections et des questions," *L'Express.fr*, April 15, 2011, www.lexpress.fr/actualite/monde/algerie-des-elections-et-des-questions_111 3831.html.
29 The RND is headed by the three times prime minister Ahmed Ouyahia. The FLN is headed by Abdelaziz Belkhadem who was prime minister from 2006 to 2008. Right before the 2012 election, his leadership was strongly contested by a faction of the party, known as the "redresseurs" (rectifiers).
30 The intra-FLN division was not new; it dates back to when Ali Benflis was a prime minister who challenged his president, Bouteflika, in the 2004 elections and tried to take over the leadership of the FLN, but succeeded only in creating deep rift that has not yet healed.
31 The results published by the government a few days after the vote were revised in mid-May after more than 60 complaints of irregularities and fraud were filed by participating political parties and individual candidates who were not pleased by the results. The revised numbers are in Table 7.1. After an investigation, the FLN lost 13 seats from 220 to 208; the RND lost two seats, 70 to 68, the Islamist three-party Alliance Verte gained two seats, from 47 to 49; the FFS gained six seats, from 21 to 27; and the PT gained seven, from 17 to 24.
32 Christian Lowe and Lamine Chikhi, "Algeria Ruling Party Snubs Arab Spring To Win Election," *Reuters*, May 11, 2012.
33 Abdallah Djaballah, quoted in Kamel Beniaiche, "Abdallah Djaballah: 'Même les morts ont des cartes d'électeur en Algérie'," *El Watan*, February 26, 2012 (my translation).
34 Samuel P. Huntington, *Political Order in Changing Societies* (New Haven, CT: Yale University Press: 2006 [1968]), p. 4.
35 Nasser Djabi, "The Impasse of Political Transition in Algeria: Three Generations and Two Scenarios," *Research Paper Series* (Arab Center for Research and

Policy Studies, Doha, Qatar, April 2012), http://english.dohainstitute.org/release/9d3fd57b-e368-42d5-bd7b-aadb74f9017e.
36 Huntington, *Political Order in Changing Societies*, p. 5.
37 Karim Aimeur, "Ne voulant pas des structures officielles les Algériens font la politique autrement," *L'Expression*, January 18, 2012, www.lexpressiondz.com/actualite/146555-les-algeriens-font-la-politique-autrement.html.
38 The Arab Barometer numbers were relayed by Fayçal Metaoui et Mehdi Bsikri, 'Démocratie, gouvernement, religion, partis, économie, citoyenneté : Ce que pensent les Algériens, ' *El Watan*, January 17, 2012.
39 Officially, the military establishment is committed to a democratic project and a republican form of government. However, most people believe that it is the backbone of the Algerian political system; it plays the role of kingmaker, watches over the security and stability of the country, and has an overwhelming place in the high state institutions.

8 Moving past revolution and revolt
Transitions to democracy in North Africa

Ricardo René Larémont

Introduction

The revolutions, revolts, and protests that occurred in North Africa during 2011 considerably disrupted political arrangements as we had known them. At a minimum they led to the deposition of authoritarian leaders in Tunisia and Egypt, the execution of another in Libya, and the acceleration of constitutional reform in Morocco. The significant exception among these trends was Algeria. In Algeria there were large yet short-lived protests; politics there, however, were not fundamentally disturbed. After these series of revolts and demonstrations all five countries in North Africa held elections during 2011 and 2012. These elections provide indications about whether these societies and states are transitioning towards becoming pluralist democracies. As a result of these elections, one country (Egypt) had Islamist parties win a preponderant majority of the vote and two others (Tunisia and Morocco) had results in which Islamist parties won pluralities rather than majorities; the Islamist parties in Tunisia and Morocco then formed coalition governments with secular parties. Our two remaining countries (Libya and Algeria) had secular parties as victors. Two years after the "Arab Spring" or the "Arab Awakening" where are we in North Africa? What has happened to the authoritarian state? Are we experiencing movements towards greater societal and political pluralism? Or is authoritarianism returning in different, newer forms?

Egypt and Tunisia: two transitions; one flawed and the other fragile

Egypt and Tunisia give us opportunities to examine two very different transitions to democracy. Of the two, the organization of the transition in Tunisia was structurally superior but it is still troubled; it has a greater probability of success because of attempts by Islamists and secularists to share power. Egypt's was deeply flawed because the Islamist parties and the military there have proceeded to negotiate the terms of the transition without the participation of secularists or Coptic Christians. The Egyptian transition has fundamentally fractured Egyptian society, putting the transition and the possibility of the unity of the country in considerable doubt.

Scholars have articulated various factors that contribute to the success or failure of transitions from authoritarianism to democracy.[1] For our analysis of the transitions in Egypt and Tunisia, we focus on five that we believe are essential: (1) *elite coherence* on the objectives of the democratic transition; (2) the *sequencing* of elections and the drafting of constitutions; (3) the *role of the army*; (4) the role of *sharia* in the constitution; and (5) the protection of *minority rights*.

Elite coherence

When examining the transitions to democracy in Egypt and Tunisia, the first distinction between the processes in these two countries has involved the role and the potential unity of purpose among political elites who have undertaken the task of guiding the transition. For Egypt and Tunisia we need to ask: (1) To what extent have political elites in both countries arrived at consensus regarding the ultimate objectives of their democratic transition? (2) To what extent have political elites collaborated and compromised to accomplish those objectives? (3) Have political elites successfully communicated to the masses that they are committed to a pluralist democratic project despite their ideological differences? (4) To what extent have these political elites agreed upon subsidiary issues, including notably the *sequencing* of elections and the drafting of constitutions; the *role of the army*; the role of *sharia* in the constitution; and the protection of *minority rights*?

The theoretical literature regarding transitions to democracy repeatedly emphasizes that *elite consensus* regarding the ultimate objectives of the transition may be among the most important factors that will lead to either the success or failure of the transition. Beginning with Dankwart Rustow's seminal article in 1970 to Samuel P. Huntington's 1984 analysis and others, democratic theorists have emphasized that elite consensus along with elites' interaction with the masses are essential for the success of transition to democracy.[2] Spain and South Africa provide two excellent examples that demonstrated a high degree of elite consensus regarding the ultimate objectives of the transition.[3] In those two cases political elites, despite holding widely disparate views concerning political and economic objectives and ideology, obtained a high degree of consensus regarding the desirability of pluralist democracy and also the desirability of protecting minority rights (South Africa) or regional rights (Spain).

It is precisely upon this issue of elite consensus that we observe real and substantial differences in the transitions to democracy in Tunisia and Egypt. After the fall of President Ben Ali and the holding of elections in Tunisia, one Islamist party (Ennahda) and two secular parties (the Congress for the Republic and Ettakatol) united to create an *interim coalition government* that has collaborated to govern the country. By evident contrast, after the deposition of President Mubarak in Egypt, the principal organizers of the Egyptian transition (the military and the Muslim Brotherhood) chose an exclusionary rather than inclusionary path for the transition that did not provide for the participation of either the secularists who had initiated the original movement to depose President Mubarak or minority Christians. From the very beginning of the Egyptian transition, the military and the Muslim Brotherhood chose to negotiate between themselves while substantively shunting aside leaders from minority secular and Coptic Christian communities. Although they were minorities within Egyptian society, the leaders of the transition should nevertheless have recognized these communities as relevant political actors in order to obtain social cohesion for the transition. The exclusion of secularists and Coptic Christians at a very early stage in the Egyptian transition created an atmosphere of distrust at the outset that has worsened over time and has left Egypt as a fractured and divided society.

It is important to remember that secularists and Islamist youth organized and led the January and February 2011 demonstrations that forced President Mubarak to resign. After their victory, however, elders from within the Muslim Brotherhood turned away from the leaders of the revolt and the Coptic Christian community, choosing instead to negotiate more directly with the military regarding the future course of the Egyptian transition. The Muslim Brotherhood's policy of exclusion, begun from the inception of the transition, was an important flaw. It will be very difficult to rectify.

While recognizing this procedural, tactical, and strategic error, we can at the same time understand why the Muslim Brotherhood would have chosen to negotiate directly with the military without substantive collaboration from secularists or Coptic Christians. When the results of the November and December 2011 elections were announced on January 21, 2012, it became clear that two Islamist parties (the Muslim Brotherhood's Freedom and Justice Party (FJP) and the Salafist Al-Nour Party) had captured approximately two-thirds of the seats in the parliament with the FJP winning 43.4 percent of the vote and 225 seats in the 489-seat parliament while Al-Nour finished second with 21.8 percent of the vote and 109 seats.[4] The two leading Islamist parties had won 65 percent of the vote. With this overwhelming majority, these two parties believed that they had obtained a mandate to negotiate on behalf of the Egyptian people, even if this meant marginalizing the smaller secular and Coptic Christian communities. Nevertheless, the Brotherhood's decision to exclude these communities in their negotiations with the military created distrust and pushed them to join the opposition.

By contrast, the managers of the Tunisian transition operated differently. When elections were held there during October 2011 to create a Constituent Assembly that would draft a new constitution, the Islamist Ennahda party won a plurality (41 percent) rather than a majority of the vote, which enabled them to obtain 90 seats in the 217-person Constituent Assembly. Two secular parties (the Congress for the Republic or CPR and Ettakatol) followed Ennahda in the voting with the CPR winning 30 seats and Ettakatol obtaining 21. Under these rather different circumstances, because no party had obtained an absolute majority of the vote in the election, Ennahda, the CPR, and Ettakatol began collaborating in a political context that created real inducements for them to form a coalition government.[5] This new coalition government, locally known as the "troika," has governed Tunisia on an interim basis since that election. The collaboration of this troika in governance has demonstrated that Islamist parties and secular parties can work together in Tunisia. Islamist-secularist collaboration is not limited to Tunisia. It is also observable in Morocco as well where another Islamist-secularist coalition government has been formed.[6]

With the benefit of a retrospective perspective, we can now understand how the first set of electoral outcomes in Tunisia and Egypt had critical consequences in determining the future course of the transitions in those two countries. The Muslim Brotherhood in Egypt, because of its overwhelming electoral victory, believed that it had the legitimate authority to negotiate directly with the military concerning the future direction of Egypt's transition to democracy, even if it meant substantially ignoring the secular and Coptic Christian communities. By excluding these two communities, however, the Brotherhood created a permanent opposition who could criticize the Muslim Brotherhood's leaders as being "majoritarian democrats" rather than "pluralist democrats" who were intent upon implementing a political program without regard to their concerns. The electoral outcome in Tunisia created a different context and a contrasting political logic for the transition. Because Ennahda won a *plurality* rather than a *majority* of the vote, Ennahda had incentives to negotiate very early in the transition process with the two minority secular parties that led to an environment of dialogue and compromise. During the very early stages of the transition to democracy an environment of compromise and collaboration among relevant political actors is extraordinarily important as the theoretical and empirical work of Juan Linz, Alfred Stepan, Guillermo O'Donnell, Phillipe Schmitter, and Laurence Whitehead have previously demonstrated.[7]

The sequencing of elections and the writing of the constitution

Elections have important consequences in transitions to democracy. As we analyze the role of elections in the Egyptian and Tunisian transitions, three issues arise: (1) the sequencing of elections and the writing of the constitution; (2) the type of election held (for a legislature versus a constituent assembly); and (3) the type of electoral law used within the election. For our analysis here, we believe that the first two factors are more important: the sequencing of elections and the writing of the constitution and the type of election held.

The leaders of the transition in Tunisia designed a process that was procedurally superior to what was undertaken in Egypt. The critical flaw in Egypt was that the transition leaders (the military and the Muslim Brotherhood) held elections *before* writing a constitution whereas the leaders of the Tunisian transition chose instead to simultaneously elect a Constituent Assembly that would be charged with writing a constitution and an *interim government* that would rule temporarily. By choosing to hold their elections for the parliament and the presidency *before drafting and enacting a constitution* that would define the powers of government, the leaders of the Egyptian transition introduced considerable chaos into the transition. The Egyptian sequencing of elections and constitution writing was illogical and created a political and legal situation in which both the elected parliament and president could not know the writ or the boundaries of their authority, simply because a constitution did not exist. By proceeding as they did, the parliament and the presidency began operating in a legal fog of doubtful authority at the very beginning of the transition, which made their decisions ultimately subject to challenges in court. Procedural, legal, and constitutional logic would have required the election of a legislature and president only after their powers had been defined in the context of a constitution.

The leaders of the Tunisian transition by contrast proceeded logically. They decided to form an *interim government* in Tunisia that would lead the country on a temporary basis and a separate Constituent Assembly that would draft and enact a constitution before the eventual election of a *permanent government*. The election for that permanent government is scheduled for December 2013.

The process in Egypt seemingly was organized without reference to other transitions that had taken place elsewhere, notably in southern Europe, Latin America, eastern Europe, and South Africa. A long record of democratic transitions with concomitant successes and failures has been established and they were available for reference by the leaders of the Egyptian transition. Nevertheless, despite the availability of these examples, the organizers of the transition in Egypt focused upon the exclusion of minorities from participation in the transition and they sequenced the elections and the drafting and enactment of the constitution in a procedurally illogical way. The illogical sequencing of the elections and constitution writing created a political space in which the Egyptian judiciary—many of whom had been appointed by President Mubarak and who were often opposed to the Muslim Brotherhood's political objectives—were institutionally poised to frustrate and countermand the Brotherhood's political advances by judicial decree. In summation, a legislature and a president cannot be logically elected without having their powers defined beforehand in a constitution. From a retrospective perspective we now see that the *sequencing* of the elections and the drafting and enactment of the constitution had profound consequences, leading to the stability of the transition in Tunisia while creating instability in Egypt.

The most recent case of a successful transition was that of South Africa. In contrast to the rushed processes in Egypt and Tunisia, the organizers of the South African transition had the advantage of time. Their transition was well-planned, negotiated among the relevant political actors over a longer period of time, and elite consensus was reached about the desirability of a pluralist democracy after considerable negotiations among the relevant parties had been conducted. Also, the writing of the constitution took place *before* the holding of elections and that constitution assured the protection of minority Afrikaner economic and political rights. This planning and logic led to constitutional, political, and democratic success. The organizers of the Egyptian transition by contrast suffered considerably from operating under the compression of time. This deficiency of time, however, neither accounts for nor forgives the organizers' failure to sequence the elections logically nor their failure to include minority secular or Coptic Christian communities in the negotiation process. The Tunisians were similarly compressed for time. They nevertheless sequenced the elections more logically and they took more care to create an inclusive process that enabled the realization of elite consensus for their transition.

The role of the military

In Tunisia and Egypt the military played two contrasting roles in the transition. In Tunisia, the military consciously decided to revert to a more traditional function within a democratic state: it submitted itself to civilian political authorities. In Egypt, the situation has been altogether different: the army there continued to play an essential role in politics as it has ever since it deposed King Farouk in 1952. It intends to play that role into the foreseeable future.

The Egyptian transition has two major players (the military and the Muslim Brotherhood) and the three minor players (the secularists, the surviving representatives of Mubarak's *ancien régime*, and the Coptic Christian community). The minor players have less capacity to effect political outcomes, which are negotiated by the two major players. The number of secularists in Egypt are comparatively small, which means that they can be marginalized to quasi-irrelevancy by the military and the Muslim Brotherhood. The second set of minor players, the left-over representatives of Mubarak's *ancien régime*, detest the Brotherhood. They have mostly been able to exert power through the operation of the judiciary, which has intermittently frustrated the Muslim Brotherhood's aspirations for expanded power by judicial decree. The third community, the Coptic Christians, has had their percentage of the population dwindle over time (from 20 percent of the population in the 1970s to 9–10 percent of the population now). It is not politically influential at this moment in time but the community does continue to play an important role in the economy.

With President Hosni Mubarak's resignation on February 11, 2011, Egypt's military leadership assumed control of the state under the aegis of the Supreme Council of the Armed Forces (SCAF), which was headed at the time by Field Marshal Mohamed Hussein Tantawi. Field Marshal Tantawi was eventually forced to resign on August 12, 2012.[8] The military, through the SCAF, declared that it was intent upon controlling a process that would attempt a transition from President Mubarak's authoritarian political system towards something new. What has become clearer over the passage of time was that the SCAF did not intend to guide the country towards a freewheeling pluralist democracy; its objective was the creation of a newer, less authoritarian system (in league with the Muslim Brotherhood) that would assure that its essential economic and institutional interests would not be substantially diminished. It is quite likely that at the beginning of the Egyptian transition the SCAF did not have either a grand strategy or clear set of tactics regarding the future construction of the government. Its behavior during the transition was substantially improvisational. It did, however, have a core interest: it wanted to assure that a new government would not substantially oversee or interfere with its essential economic and institutional interests. For the military to accomplish that objective, it chose to negotiate directly with the Muslim Brotherhood while intermittently and covertly collaborating with the judiciary that was intent upon frustrating the Brotherhood's efforts to expand its power.

The military first asserted itself and consolidated its power in Egyptian politics during the Nasser regime. After Nasser's demise, it developed substantial *economic* interests during the neoliberalizing regimes of Presidents Anwar Sadat and Hosni Mubarak. The military, because of the outsized role that it plays in economics and because it still wields important symbolic capital in society will remain a key player in politics. The Egyptian military's ultimate objective is the creation of a new government that will lightly supervise its affairs and that would not exercise real control over the military budget. It seems that at the present moment in the Egyptian transition it has accomplished that objective with the leaders of the Muslim Brotherhood having entered into pragmatic compact with the military wherein it has left the military to operate without extensive civilian supervision. With that compact now in place and with military's economic and institutional needs having been met, the military, at least within the short term, has been willing to provide some institutional support to the Muslim Brotherhood government. This compact between the Brotherhood and the military, however, fundamentally contradicts positions taken by most democratic theorists who insist that the military must subordinate itself to civilian leaders, especially in the critical areas of budgeting and finances, if a democratic state is to exist.[9]

To understand why the military would arrive at this particular compact with the Muslim Brotherhood, we need to comprehend that the military in Egypt is an oversized social and economic force. First, the Egyptian military is large. It is the tenth largest in the world with more than 450,000 active soldiers and millions of reservists; in Tunisia the army there comprises less than 50,000 soldiers. The military also plays a large role in the Egyptian economy.[10] It is active in all aspects of the economy—from heavy industry to light industry and agriculture. On the high end it is involved in aerospace, missiles, electronics, and avionics industries; in light industry it manufactures washing machines, heaters, clothing, stationery, and pharmaceuticals; on the low end it is involved in dairy farms, milk processing facilities, cattle feed lots, poultry farms, and fish farms.[11] Furthermore, it has substantial interests in land-ownership in Egypt, which is a significant source of wealth that is difficult to calculate.[12] Besides its substantial role in the economy, the military has also received considerable military aid from the US government. In 2011 it received $1.3 billion in military aid.[13]

With these considerable economic interests, we understand why the military would seek the formation of a government that would not closely monitor its affairs. To preserve its economic prerogatives, the military decided to negotiate the terms of the transition with the most important player in civil society (the Muslim Brotherhood) while still maintaining alliances with key bodies within the judiciary that could intermittently stymie the Muslim Brotherhood's efforts to expand its power. These judicial bodies at varying moments have been successful in frustrating the Brotherhood's political agenda. The collaboration between the military and the judiciary was primarily played out in the context of two institutions: the Presidential Election Commission and the Supreme Constitutional Court.[14]

Elections for the first post-Mubarak legislature were held on November 28 and December 14, 2011. The election results were announced on January 21, 2012. Those results revealed that the Muslim Brotherhood's Freedom and Justice Party (FJP) and the Salafist Al-Nour party were the principal winners. After the election of legislature, the next election that was planned involved the selection of a president, which became a confused adventure with numerous and unexpected twists and turns, all of which demonstrated how the military could covertly collaborate with the judiciary either to affect or frustrate the outcome of the elections.

The first example of judicial intervention in the Egyptian transition took place within the operations of the Presidential Election Commission. On April 14, 2012, the Commission ruled on various grounds that ten of the candidates who were running for the presidency would be unable to stand for election. Among the persons that they dismissed were three leading candidates: Khairat el-Shater, Omar Suleiman, and Hazem Salah Abu Ismail.[15] Khairat el-Shater had been a leading strategist and financier for the Muslim Brotherhood and Hazem Salah Abu Ismail represented *ultra*-conservative Islamist forces. Omar Suleiman was notorious, having served as President Mubarak's vice-president and chief of intelligence. By simultaneously striking el-Shater, Suleiman, and Abu Ismail from the field, the Presidential Election Commission could claim that it was being even-handed in its approach of eliminating both Islamists and remnants from the *ancien régime* from the list of presidential candidates. By relying on questionable grounds for the elimination of the candidates—for example, Abu Ismail was denied eligibility because his mother claimed American citizenship towards the end of her life and el-Shater was denied because of a previous criminal conviction during the Mubarak regime—the Commission diminished its credibility and it displayed considerable judicial legerdemain by unilaterally narrowing—perhaps on specious grounds—the field of candidates that Egyptians could consider.

Having narrowed the number of candidates who were eligible to run for the presidency, the first round of the presidential election was held on May 23, 2012. The outcome of that first round resulted in two finalists who would be eligible to participate in a run-off election. They were Mohamed Morsi, representing the Muslim Brotherhood's Freedom and Justice Party, and Ahmed Shafiq, a retired general who had served as prime minister towards the end of the Mubarak regime.

The final round of the presidential elections were scheduled for June 16 and 17, 2012. However, just three days before the election (June 13) the military decided to act unilaterally. On that day the army restored martial law—the very same martial law that had been the object of scorn for those who had led the revolution.[16] On the next day—June 14—the Supreme Constitutional Court in apparent collaboration with the military invalidated the parliament that had been elected by the Egyptian people by declaring that approximately one-third of the elected parliamentarians had been unconstitutionally elected.[17] While the court's decision was ambiguous and difficult to interpret, the court dismissed the entire parliament rather than the one-third that had been unconstitutionally elected.[18] By dismissing the entire parliament, the court injected a degree of cynicism within the transition that substantially eroded public confidence in the overall legitimacy of the transition. The evening of the court's decision, army tanks rolled up in front of the parliament and barred entry to elected parliamentarians.

Three days later the SCAF acted again. On June 17, 2012, the SCAF issued amendments to the operating Egyptian constitution that stripped the presidency and the parliament of any real power and transferred legislative and war-making powers to the SCAF. The military then agreed with the Supreme Constitutional Court's decision to annul the parliament and it declared that henceforward the SCAF would legislate. Furthermore, the military declared that it and not the president would have authority to declare war or send the army into the streets to quell domestic disturbances. The SCAF also announced that it had the power to appoint unilaterally the members of the 100-person committee that would draft the constitution. (The now dissolved parliament had previously been charged with that responsibility.) Last, the army declared that any prospective constitution would not have any provisions wherein the parliament or the president would have the authority to oversee military operations or the military budget.[19] After this military intervention, the election of the president was held.

The presidential election was held on June 16 and 17, 2012. The results were announced on June 24, 2012. On that day the Presidential Election Commission declared that Mohamed Morsi, the Muslim Brotherhood's candidate, was the winner, having garnered 51.7 percent of the vote. Ahmed Shafiq, his opponent, obtained 48 percent of the vote.[20] President Morsi was elected to office, however, without a constitution being in place. Because of the absence of a constitution, his powers were ill-defined. He nevertheless continued to act as president and he continued to negotiate with the military concerning the terms of the transition. Needless to say, this process remained rather chaotic with President Morsi even declaring one month before the referendum and the eventual enactment of the constitution that he had quasi-dictatorial powers.[21] The constitution was finally ratified by referendum and enacted into law on December 26, 2012.[22]

During the period between his election in June 2012 and the eventual enactment of the constitution in December 2012, President Morsi and the military continued to negotiate the terms of the transition and the outlines of their comparative power. Throughout this six-month process the military's objective remained safeguarding its economic interests and possibly obtaining assurances from the emerging government that military officers would be immune from prosecution for past crimes. That second objective may have been accomplished during the month of August 2012 when on August 12 President Morsi first dismissed Field Marshal Tantawi and Army Chief of Staff Lieutenant Colonel Sami Anan from their responsibilities, yet two days later awarded both men with Egypt's highest honors. (Field Marshal Tantawi received Egypt's Order of the Nile and Lieutenant Colonel Anan received the Order of the Republic.)[23] Although it was not explicit, it seems that the awarding of these honors provided a sufficient signal to the military leadership that they would be treated with dignity and that would avoid prosecution within the eventual state when it would be constituted.

Now that the Egyptian constitution has been ratified and enacted, the next stage of the transition can now proceed with greater clarity because the powers of government have now been defined. As mentioned earlier, it would have been more logical if the Egyptian constitution had been enacted *before* the holding of parliamentary and presidential elections. A substantial amount of the chaos of the Egyptian transition would have been avoided if that had been the case. However, because the Egyptian transition process was undertaken with reverse logic, confusion was unnecessarily introduced into the transition and deep seeds of social division have been sown. The Islamists in Egypt have won various elections since the ouster of Mubarak and they have apparently brokered interim agreements with the military that have assuaged the military's concerns. Relevant minority actors in Egypt's political system, however, notably the secularists who initiated the Egyptian revolt and Coptic Christians, remain suspicious of the Islamist's capabilities for taking their concerns into account. If President Morsi and his government can now successfully reach out and reincorporate these dissident elements into the society and the state, then the prospects for stability, progress, and pluralist democracy in Egypt will be enhanced. If President Morsi and his government fail to assuage the concerns of substantial minority communities, however, Egypt will remain socially riven, with destabilizing consequences for the emerging Egyptian state and for the region.

Now that time has elapsed we can now reflect upon the contrasts between the Egyptian and Tunisian transitions. In Tunisia the military was not deeply involved in politics over the long-term history of the Tunisian republic and it more easily returned to a traditional role, which involved its submission to civilian authority. Civilian leaders have been able to manage the Tunisian transition without military interference. In Egypt the role of the military was entirely different. The Egyptian military had been deeply involved in running the politics of the nation for decades and it was determined to continue to do so. The military seized an opportunity after the resignation of President Mubarak. It engaged in direct negotiations with its principal civilian rival the Muslim Brotherhood and it successfully brokered a deal in which its essential economic and institutional interests would not be affected. With the deal in place, it could grant its benediction to the continuation of the transition.

Sharia

One important issue that has emerged in the Tunisian and Egyptian transitions concerns the role that Islamic law or *sharia* will play in these new states. A second issue is the extent to which clerical institutions will play roles in reviewing governmental legislation or policy.

On March 26, 2012 in Tunisia the Constituent Assembly responsible for drafting Tunisia's new constitution published Article 1. That article defined the role of Islam in the state. Much to the relief of Tunisia's liberal and secularist communities, the Constitutional Assembly decided not to revise the 1959 constitution on this matter. The new Article leaves verbatim the language of the preexisting constitutional language that "Tunisia is a free, independent and sovereign state. Its religion is Islam, its language is Arabic, and its type of government is the Republic."[24] With the reiteration of the 1959 constitution's language, a contentious debate on the role of *sharia* in governance was avoided.[25] Indeed Rachid Ghannouchi, the leader of the Islamist party Ennahda, revealed in an interview with the author that introducing a divisive debate on the role of *sharia* in Tunisia would have served as a distraction from focusing upon solving Tunisia's economic and social problems and would have been inconsistent with Tunisia's juridical and governmental traditions.[26]

By contrast, the Muslim Brotherhood in Egypt addressed this question differently. With its solid control of the committee that was drafting the constitution, the Brotherhood in Egypt during December 2012 drafted Article 2 of the constitution that declared that *sharia* would be the main source of legislation. It also drafted a new Article 4 that declared for the first time that clerical authorities (most likely officials at Al-Azhar University) would be consulted on the application of *sharia* throughout the government. Article 2's statement on the role of *sharia* as a source of legislation did not depart substantially from the text of the 1971 constitution. The new Article 4, however, which provides for clerical review of legislation, governmental policy, and judicial decrees is a considerable innovation from the 1971 constitution. This new article creates the possibility for clerical review of governmental policy, which would create a quasi-theocracy unless other checks and balances are introduced into the Egyptian constitutional system. Article 4 has provoked considerable criticism from both the Coptic Christian and liberal secularist communities in Egypt, both of which remain unconvinced that *sharia* has a liberating orientation.

Protection of minority rights

Our analysis of the Tunisian and Egyptian transitions reinforces the notion that besides elite consensus, the sequencing of elections, and *sharia*, the incorporation of important minority groups in the transition is important for the eventual success of the transition. It is particularly in the context of elections that particular attention should being given to assuring minority communities that their interests will be addressed.[27] For example, we need only remember how the poorly designed March 2010 Iraqi parliamentary elections, which failed to address the interests of minority Sunnis and Kurds, led to further disintegration of the social fabric of that country. In contrast to bungled electoral processes such as in Iraq and arguably in Egypt, we could offer the alternative of the very well-planned 1994 South African elections that provided economic and political assurances to the Afrikaner minority community that had formerly held power there. The African National Congress' provision of assurances to the Afrikaner community stabilized the South African transition and made it successful.[28] Our references to failure in Iraq and success in South Africa help us appreciate the particularly fragile environment that is created after the fall of an authoritarian regime. In this rather vulnerable environment, elections need to be very carefully planned so as to assure that the interests of minorities (who will clearly lose the election) will be addressed.

Despite this necessary objective, from the outset of the transition the Muslim Brotherhood and their allies in the Salafist Al-Nour parties marginalized liberal secularists and the Coptic Christian community. For example, when the committee to draft the constitution was first established, it was dominated by Islamists, which provoked considerable criticism and consternation from Coptic Christians, liberals, and women who argued that their interests were not being adequately represented.[29] Somewhat belatedly on June 7, 2012, the Brotherhood recognized this criticism and added numbers of Copts, women, and liberals to the committee. However, the Brotherhood's initial decision to limit the participation of liberals, Coptic Christians, and women marginalized these groups and inhibited the possibility of collaborative politics at the very beginning of the transition.

Moving forward, President Morsi will need to adjust his policies to include the heretofore excluded liberal secularists and Coptic Christians if the transition to democracy in Egypt is to be stabilized. If policies are not adjusted, what may occur in Egypt is what has occurred in Iraq: a majority will rule and the excluded minorities will exercise their options of either resistance or exit from the country.

More on the Tunisian transition

While the leaders of the transition in Tunisia have done much that is procedurally superior to what has occurred in Egypt, the future success of Tunisia's democratic experiment also depends upon the extent to which secular parties will remain viable. The Ennahda party in Tunisia is a highly disciplined party. It is also is party that has an extensive social and political infrastructure and it has substantial financial resources being supplied by Qatar and Saudi Arabia. The leaders of the secular parties by contrast have not displayed the same level of party discipline nor do they have at their disposal adequate financial resources that would enable them to convert themselves from elite parties to mass parties.[30] These factors weaken the prospects for secular parties in Tunisia.

Also, the existence of a proportional representation electoral system in Tunisia creates a set of incentives and a logic that induces the secular parties to divide into smaller multiple parties that compete among themselves, which strengthens the power of Ennahda, which remains united and disciplined.[31] The secular parties have continued to splinter into smaller parties. Ennahda, despite its structural advantages and unlike the Muslim Brotherhood in Egypt, has chosen not to dominate the political stage and has opted to share power with secular parties.[32] Ennahda hopes to sustain this grand coalition comprising Islamist and secular parties. Despite this desire, however, Ennahda may nevertheless dominate the political scene in the future simply because of its higher level of organization, its discipline, and its better financing. Meanwhile the secular parties in Tunisia, again because of the logic of the electoral system, will most likely continue to splinter, which may likely diminish their role in Tunisia's political future.

Libya: the state, security, and the transition

The regime of Muammar Qaddafi came to an end when members of a rebellious Libyan militia called the Zintan militia captured and killed Brother-Leader Qaddafi on October 20, 2011. His death ushered a new era for Libya, one that is at the very early stages of a transition to what hopefully will be a democracy. Before a democracy can be realized, however, a state with formal institutions must be created. Security, which is an essential function that should be monopolized by the state, must be reestablished rather than shared with militias. The new government's inherited problem is that Brother-Leader Qaddafi quite consciously created a state with informal institutions so that he could disperse power and responsibility among his familial and clan networks. He also purposefully created a decentralized military so that it would be less capable of staging a *coup d'état* against him. With Qaddafi now gone the new government needs to correct his legacy. It needs to create a formal state and reestablish the state's monopoly in the security domain. These two issues distinguish Libya's transition from the others discussed in this chapter.

Since Qaddafi's demise Libya has held regional and national elections. It has also constituted a new national parliament. The holding of a national parliamentary election has created electoral legitimacy for this new body. However, besides holding elections, the more urgent tasks remain of creating a state with formal institutions and having that state reexert a monopoly in the security domain. Of what use is electoral democracy if Libya's citizens and residents continue to live in a state of insecurity?

The Libyan transition has been guided by two entities. The first to try to accomplish that task was the National Transition Council (NTC), which was established on February 27, 2011.[33] The NTC managed governmental affairs until August 8, 2012 when Libya's new parliament was invested.[34] Libya's new parliament has 200 members: 120 of those members have been elected as individuals without official party affiliation; the remaining 80 were elected from party lists (in Libyan parlance a "political entity" list). The July 2012 parliamentary election yielded an electoral victory for the Alliance of National Forces, which is a conservative yet secular coalition of civil society organizations that is being led by former interim Prime Minister Mahmoud Jibril. That coalition won 39 of the 80 party list seats. Running second in the electoral competition was the Muslim Brotherhood-affiliated Justice and Construction Party (JCP), which won 17 seats. Libya's first post-revolt election revealed voters' initial preferences for a secular yet conservative leadership provided by the Alliance rather than the Islamist alternative that was proposed by the JCP. The electoral result in Libya contrasted with those in Tunisia and Egypt where Islamist parties won either pluralities or overwhelming majorities. Libya's new president is Mohammed Magarief and its prime minister is Ali Zidan.

Now that a parliament is constituted and operative, that body is now charged with accomplishing three essential tasks that are necessary for the continuation of the transition: (1) creating a state with formal institutions; (2) reestablishing a governmental monopoly on the question of security and dismantling local militias; and (3) writing a constitution.

While the new national government undertakes what will be the longer-term objective of creating a state with formal institutions, its more immediate responsibility involves the reassertion of a governmental monopoly over security and dismantling independent militias that are in operation. The present government, like its predecessor the NTC, has not yet accomplished this important objective. The new government still shares responsibility in the security domain with powerful militias. As long as militias continue to operate independently of state authority, they will, by their very existence and operations, impede and destabilize the transition towards a stable state and a democracy.

The government's ultimate objective requires the integration of these militias into a state-controlled, centralized army. As long as militias continue to resist submission to state authority, the creation of a stable state would be still at considerable risk, even though the government has obtained some electoral legitimacy by having successfully staged elections. If militias continue to operate in a parallel fashion with the national army, then Libya's leaders will be put in the position of accepting two clearly less preferable alternatives. The first would the Lebanon option: the creation of a national army that exerts some authority but that negotiates arrangements with local militias for power sharing. The second course of action would be worse: Libya could follow the example of a state such as Somalia, where young men wielded weapons and operated beyond the scope of the law and the state.

Qaddafi's legacy of creating a decentralized military fundamentally differentiates Libya from either Tunisia or Egypt where the militaries were centralized and cohesive. From the viewpoint of the comparative analysis of militaries in transitions, we need to remember that the Tunisian and Egyptian militaries were centralized before the revolts that took place there. Because they were centralized and cohesive, they held together during the revolt and during the post-revolt period. (Even as we remember that the Tunisian army submitted to civilian authority while the Egyptian army still has not.) Qaddafi's creation of a decentralized military made it a weaker force and facilitated the creation of militias both during the revolt and in the post-revolt environment.

Obviously the best result moving forward would be for the government to merge the militias into a new national army. That outcome, however, will be rather difficult to attain because the militia members became armed during the revolt and now they effectively wield considerable power. Militia members have obtained "battlefield legitimacy" as opposed to "electoral legitimacy" because they fought on the front lines of the revolt. Now that they are armed, they will surrender their arms only hesitatingly. Additionally, considerable bonds of solidarity exist among militia members, which cause them to remain more loyal to their militias than to the government. For these reasons they will resist integration into the emerging Libyan state.

Between 100 and 300 militias operate in Libya. Their members total 150,000 persons or more.[35] Of the hundreds of militias that exist, three are arguably more important than the others. The first (but not necessarily the most important) is the Tripoli militia that is led by Abdelhakim Belhadj. Two other important militias operate in Tripoli and elsewhere: they are the Misrata and Zintan militias, which emerged during the revolution.[36] The Misrata militia is led by Faraj al-Swehli and the Zintan militia is led by Mukhtar al-Akhdar. Smaller militias exist, destabilizing the situation further. The last actor on the security scene is what is called the National Army, which is staffed primarily by officers and soldiers from eastern Libya where the revolution began.[37] Given the staffing, the arms, and the yet to be developed trust for the government, from an operational point of view we can expect that the dismantling of the militias will take considerable time and that creative incentives will have to be created to encourage them to integrate into the national army.

Besides the resolution of this important security question, the other issue in the Libyan transition involved the sequencing of elections and the writing and enactment of the constitution. Like Egypt, Libya complicated its transition by deciding to elect a parliament without having written and enacted a constitution beforehand. Libya had an interim rather than permanent constitution that had been created by the unelected NTC, which meant that that interim constitution lacked validity. From a constitutional and legal point of view it would have been much better if the planners of the Libyan transition had followed the Tunisian example, which involved writing and enacting a constitution *before* electing a parliament.

One additional and important factor involving the institution of the judiciary differentiates the Libyan transition from the one taking place in Egypt. Egypt for decades has had a very well-developed and a quasi-independent judiciary and that judiciary has played an important role during the Egyptian transition by issuing numerous decrees that have redefined or changed its course. Libya, by contrast, because Qaddafi created an informal state, does not have a well-developed or even quasi-independent judiciary that could play an intermediary or defining role in the transition. Like other needed state institutions, the judiciary in Libya will have to be rebuilt.

The 2012 parliamentary elections in Libya empowered a secular yet conservative coalition of political forces and it has temporarily relegated the Muslim Brotherhood-led Islamist party to a secondary position. The leadership of the conservative coalition seems intent to follow a path first whereby it intends to enact a constitution that is secular in orientation, which means more specifically that it does not want to authorize the creation of a clerical body that will review the laws or decrees of parliament. The emerging Libyan constitutional position differs from that in Egypt that restores a role for Al-Azhar University in clerical review of legislation and governmental policy.[38] The new conservative leadership in Libya has publicly declared a preference for a new constitution in which the constitution, laws, and legislation will not "contradict or conflict with Islamic Sharia or its interpretations" yet it prefers that the new constitution follow the Tunisian model.[39]

While conservative but secular leaders have temporarily taken charge of the Libyan transition, Islamist elements remain. Regarding the configuration of Islamist organizations and parties in Libya, the patterns there mirror those that are observable elsewhere in the Muslim world. The Islamists in Libya have two branches: a more pragmatic Muslim Brotherhood branch and more conservative Salafi wing. The differences between these two branches revolve around two central issues: their contrasting flexibility concerning the role of Islamic law or *sharia* in government, constitution-making, and legislation and their different degrees of willingness to impose their views upon other members of society at large who disagree with their views. The members of the Muslim Brotherhood have often demonstrated considerable pragmatism and flexibility regarding the centrality and interpretation of *sharia* in governance, using it as a starting point but not an exclusive basis of governance and legislation. They also have relied upon *dawa* (counseling or preaching) to correct what they perceive as immoral or impious behavior on the part of others. Many Salafi organizations, by contrast, have usually insisted upon more strict adherence to *sharia* in matters related to legislation, constitution-making, and governance and they have often demonstrated frequent intolerance on matters of religious conformity, personal conduct, and questions of probity.

The Libyan parliamentary election results revealed that the most important Islamist group was the Libyan Islamic Group, which comprises the local branch of the Muslim Brotherhood. It was founded in the 1950s and since the onset of the revolution its membership has burgeoned.[40] Its leader is Suleiman Abdulkadir.

Besides the more dominant Libyan Islamic Group, the second but less important group has been the Islamic Movement for Change (*al-haraka al-islamiyya l'l-taghyir*) or LIMC, which was formerly known as the Libyan Islamic Fighting Group (*al-jama'a al-libiyya al-islamiyya al-muqatilah*) or LIFG. Its leader is Abdelhakim Belhadj. The LIMC, like its predecessor the LIFG, has had a more militant orientation towards politics than the Muslim Brotherhood. The LIFG originally had approximately 800–1,000 members who took up arms against the Soviets in Afghanistan during the 1980s.[41] After their success in Afghanistan, members of the group returned to Libya where they waged an insurrectionist campaign against the Qaddafi regime, only to find themselves brutally repressed by his regime during the late 1990s. After Al-Qaeda's 9/11 attacks upon the United States, the United States and Qaddafi collaborated to pursue and persecute members of the LIFG because they believed that LIFG members were linked to Al-Qaeda and Osama bin Laden. In a joint intelligence effort undertaken by Libya, the United Kingdom, and the United States, the LIFG's leader Abdelhakim Belhadj was arrested at the Kuala Lumpur airport in Malaysia, transferred to a secret detention center in Thailand, held there for several days and tortured, and then was transferred back to Libya. In press interviews and in court documents Belhadj has alleged that he was arrested upon information provided by MI6 and the United States Central Intelligence Agency. Belhadj now is a key figure in Libya. Belhadj has publicly proclaimed his commitment to democracy and pluralism but these declarations must be rigorously examined in the light of his past activities and his life experiences, which included public allegiance to Osama bin Laden and Al-Qaeda and his memory of torture at the hands of the Thais (with perhaps British and American complicity).

Morocco: evolution rather than revolution

Soon after the success of the January 2011 Tunisian revolt, large demonstrations demanding economic and political change began in Morocco, with the first demonstration taking place on February 20, 2011, in the capital Rabat. That first demonstration led to the creation of the February 20 Movement, which was an *ad hoc*, youth-led, web-inspired movement that made demands for the end of corruption, initiatives to improve employment, constitutional reform, and the curtailment of the power of the king. Quickly after the beginning of these demonstrations in late February, King Mohamed VI responded on March 9, 2011, by calling for the creation of a commission that would suggest changes in Morocco's constitution.[42] A referendum to approve or disapprove the constitution was held on July 1, 2011. With voters participating at a 73 percent rate, Moroccans approved the constitution with 98.5 percent of voters voting in favor.[43] King Mohamed VI's reaction to the large-scale protests, which led to the successful promulgation of a new constitution, was a masterful exercise in state management of dissent.

The proposed constitution provided for the following reforms: (1) it gave the prime minister the power to appoint a larger number of officials within the government without direct monarchical intervention regarding these appointments; (2) it designated that the future prime minister would be the leader of the party that obtained the greatest number of votes in an election rather than being appointed by the king (as had been the case in the past); and (3) it provided for greater independence for the judiciary. Despite these constitutional reforms, the king still reserved substantial powers to himself. He remained in total control of the armed forces and foreign policy and he continued to rule as Commander of the Faithful (the head of the Muslim community in Morocco), which was a position of considerable symbolic capital that helped bolster his political legitimacy. Over time we will need to see whether these more recent constitutional reforms will advance in Morocco's transition to a fuller constitutional monarchy/democracy. If these most recent constitutional reforms are meaningfully implemented, they will provide evidentiary support to the contention that King Mohamed VI has continued a program of evolutionary reform towards a constitutional monarchy, which was a process that began shortly after his ascension to the throne.

With the new constitution in place, Morocco set elections for a new parliament that were held on November 25, 2011. The election for the new legislature experienced a much lower voter turnout than that observed for the constitutional referendum. Thirty-seven percent of eligible voters participated in the vote with 395 parliamentary seats being contested. Of those 395 seats, 305 were elected from party lists and 90 from a "national" list of candidates. Thirty parties participated in the election and 18 won seats. The three lead parties were the Justice and Development Party (PJD) (a moderate Islamist group), the Coalition for Democracy comprising eight separate parties (led by Morocco's former Minister of Finance Salaheddine Mezouar), and the Koutla or Coalition alliance (led by former Prime Minister Abbas El Fassi). The PJD won 107 of the seats within the new parliament, giving it the largest bloc and giving the PJD the right to have its leader, Abdelillah Benkirane, appointed as the Prime Minister of Morocco. Benkirane formed a coalition government on February 7, 2012.[44]

The creation of a coalition government in Morocco composed of an Islamist party and secular parties was a significant achievement that mirrors the coalition arrangement that was obtained in Tunisia. Both Tunisia and Morocco provide positive examples that Islamist parties can share governance with secular parties. These two coalition governments have disabused notions that Islamist parties are intent upon monopolizing the political space. Also, the successes at compromise in both Tunisia and Morocco have bought a modicum of social peace while advancing the objective of creating a pluralist rather than majoritarian democracy. By contrast the Islamist party in Egypt has not yet followed the Tunisian and Moroccan Islamist examples of building bridges to secular parties. The Islamist party there has taken a majoritarian rather than a pluralist path. If it can somehow change course and emulate the Islamist parties in Tunisia and Morocco, it may be able to reconcile the divergent ideological inclinations that exist not only in Egypt but in every state and society.

Algeria: the exception

Protests against the Algerian government began on December 28, 2010, shortly after the self-immolation of Mohamed Bouazizi in Tunisia. These protests may have been partly inspired by what was taking place in Tunisia but there were already considerable grievances within Algeria involving steep rises in the cost of food, high unemployment, and lack of confidence in the ruling government. The Algerian government reacted to these demonstrations partly by using the police to repress them, partly by using its considerable natural gas generated economic resources to increase governmental subsidies for basic commodities (flour, milk, cooking oil, sugar) and to invest in public investment projects that would ameliorate unemployment, and partly by calling for elections for a new parliament.

As Azzedine Layachi recounted in Chapter 7, protests were endemic in Algeria throughout 2011 and 2012. Protests seemingly take place on a daily basis. There is much to protest in Algeria: high unemployment; a bleak future; and a continuing authoritarian government that does not provide much opportunity for participation. An important difference with Tunisia, Egypt, Libya, and Morocco, however, is that while protests have been constant in Algeria, mass protests were infrequent (except for the months of January and February 2011). And when mass protests do occur, they are quickly and effectively repressed by the police.

The lower turnout for protests in Algeria is explicable because that country suffered an extremely costly, approximately ten-year civil war that began in 1992 and involved the deaths of approximately 200,000 people. Algeria seems to suffer from a case of mass post-traumatic stress disorder, which inhibits calls for mass protests that may lead to violence. The country is fatigued. For example, a survey conducted by this author in conjunction with the University of Algiers in 2011 revealed that most youth in Algeria were disillusioned with both governmental and religious institutions.[45] Despite mass disillusion, large movements of social protests simply have been very difficult to organize because of the expectation among the masses that change will occur is quite low. When low public expectations combine with war-weariness and effective police measures to suppress demonstrations, we have a formula for understanding why demonstrations did not lead to a mass revolt in Algeria.

Also, besides the effective use of the police, the government has used its considerable economic resources to lower the cost of basic commodities (flour, milk, cooking oil, sugar) when necessary and to invest in public infrastructure projects that periodically lower unemployment in the construction sector. These measures further dampened enthusiasm for mass social protest.

Last, to suffuse public discontent further, the government held elections for a national parliament, which took place on May 10, 2012. According to the government, voter participation in the May election was 42.9 percent of the population, which would constitute an 8 percent increase in voter participation from the last set of parliamentary elections that were held in 2007.[46] Islamist parties and some secularist parties disputed the results of the May election because the former ruling party, the FLN (*Front de Libération Nationale*), won 220 of a total of 462 seats in the parliament while another party that was close to the government, the RND (*Rassemblement nationale démocratique*), finished second with 68 seats.[47] An alliance of Islamist parties called the Green Alliance (*Alliance de l'Algérie Verte*), which was led by the Movement of the Society for Peace (*Mouvement de la société pour la paix*) and Ennahda, did particularly well in the city of Algiers but performed poorly elsewhere. The Green Alliance won 15 of 37 seats in Algiers and 59 seats nationally, which made them the third most popular party after the FLN and the RND. The remainder of elected parliamentarians were represented by the *Front des forces socialistes* (21 seats), the *Parti des travailleurs* (20 seats), and the *Mouvement populaire algérien* (six seats). Independent candidates without party affiliation won another 68 seats.

Critics of the electoral processes in Algeria remain skeptical of these results because they believe that the government regularly manipulates electoral outcomes to its advantage. In Algeria political parties can participate in elections only if they have been certified by the government, which inhibits the registration of parties that inimically oppose the regime. Furthermore, electoral fraud is widely suspected, which suppresses voter participation. The alleged manipulation of elections, along with governmental policies of cooptation that have involved the distribution of governmental largess to certified "opponents" of the regime, leads to electoral results that usually benefit the existing government and regime. These various arrangements in Algeria are democratic in form rather than in substance; they ultimately serve to preserve a "soft" authoritarian regime in which the military and security apparatus collaborate with a quasi-independent civilian president. In Algeria in the final analysis, the military and the intelligence community remain as key players in politics, as they have since Colonel and then President Houari Boumediene initiated his *coup d'état* in 1965.

Notes

1. Scott Mainwaring, "Transitions to Democracy and Democratic Consolidation: Theoretical and Comparative Issues," www.undp.org.eg/portals/0/int%20forum/democratic%20consolidation_mainwaring.pdf; Guillermo O'Donnell, Philippe Schmitter, and Laurence Whitehead, *Transitions from Authoritarian Rule, Vol. 4: Tentative Conclusions about Uncertain Democracies* (Baltimore, MD: Johns Hopkins University Press, 1986); Juan J. Linz and Alfred Stepan, *Problems of Democratic Consolidation* (Baltimore, MD: Johns Hopkins University Press, 1996).
2. Dankwart Rustow, "Transitions to Democracy: Toward a Comparative Model," *Comparative Politics*, 2 (April 1970): 337–363; Samuel P. Huntington, "Will More Countries Become Democratic?" *Political Science Quarterly*, 99 (Summer 1984): 193–218.
3. Josep M. Colomer, *Game Theory and the Transition to Democracy: The Spanish Model* (Cheltenham, UK: Edward Elgar, 1995); Daniele Conversi, "The Smooth Transition: Spain's 1978 Constitution and the Nationalities Question," *National Identities*, 4:3 (November 2002): 223–244; Richard Gunther (ed.), *Politics, Society, and Democracy: The Case of Spain* (Boulder, CO: Westview); Paul Preston, *The Triumph of Democracy in Spain* (London: Routledge, 2001); Javier Tusell, *Spain: From Dictatorship to Democracy* (London: Blackwell, 2007); J. Barkan, "Protracted Transitions Among Africa's New Democracies,"*Democratization*, 7:3 (2000): 227–243; M. Bratton and N. van de Walle, *Democratic Experiments in Africa* (New York: Cambridge University Press, 1997); L. Diamond and M. Plattner (eds), *Democratization in Africa* (Baltimore, MD: Johns Hopkins University Press, 1999); S. Huntington, *The Third Wave: Democratization in the Late Twentieth Century* (Norman: University of Oklahoma Press, 1993); G. Hyden, *African Politics in Comparative Perspective* (New York: Cambridge University Press, 2006); S. Lindberg, *Democracy and Elections in Africa* (Baltimore, MD: Johns Hopkins University Press, 2006); M. Salih, *African Democracies and African Politics* (New York: Pluto Press, 2001); R. Sandbrook, "Transition Without Consolidation: Democratisation in Six African Cases," *Third World Quarterly*, 17:1 (1996): 69–88; L. Villalon, and P. Von Doepp, *The Fate of Africa's Democratic Experiments* (Bloomington: Indiana University Press, 2005).
4. BBC News, "Egypt's Islamist Parties Win Elections to Parliament," January 21, 2012, www.bbc.co.uk/news/world-middle-east-16665748.
5. BBC News, "Tunisia's Islamist Ennahda Party Wins Historic Poll," October 27, 2011, www.bbc.co.uk/news/world-africa-15487647.
6. BBC News, "Islamist PJD Party Wins Morocco Poll," November 27, 2011, www.bbc.co.uk/news/world-africa-15902703.
7. Linz and Stepan, *Problems of Democratic Consolidation*; O'Donnell, Schmitter, and Whitehead, *Transitions from Authoritarian Rule, Vol. 4*.
8. BBC News, "Egypt Leader Mursi Orders Army Chief Tantawi to Resign," August 12, 2012, www.bbc.co.uk/news/world-africa-19234763.
9. Samuel Huntington, *The Soldier and the State* (Cambridge, MA: Belknap Press, 1981); S.E. Finer, *The Man on Horseback: The Role of the Military in Politics* (Boulder, CO: Westview, 1988).
10. Robert Springborg and Clement M. Henry, "Army Guys," *The American Interest*, May–June 2011, www.the-american-interest.com/article.cfm?piece=954.
11. LTC Stephen H. Gotowicki, "The Role of the Egyptian Military in Domestic Society," Institute of National Strategic Studies, National Defense University, 1997, http://fmso.leavenworth.army.mil/documents/egypt/egypt.htm; "One-Third of Egypt's Economy Under Army Control," *Business Report*, February 20, 2011, www.iol.co.za/business/business-news/one-third-of-egypt-s-economy-under-army-control-1.1029129#.T9IV8Y4UiaE; Shana Marshal and Joshua Stacher, "Egypt's Generals

and Transnational Capital," Middle East Research and Information Project, www.merip.org/mer/mer262/egypts-generals-transnational-capital.
12 Interview with Abdallah Helmy, Political Advisor to the People's Assembly, June 9, 2012, Cairo.
13 Robert Springborg, " Egypt's Cobra and Mongoose," *Foreign Policy*, February 27, 2012, http://mideast.foreignpolicy.com/posts/2012/02/27/egypt_s_cobra_and_mongoose; Kristen Chick, "Why Egypt May Not Care About Losing US Aid," *Christian Science Monitor*, February 10, 2012, www.csmonitor.com/World/2012/0210/Why-Egypt-may-not-care-about-losing-US-aid.
14 The author would like to acknowledge Ibrahim Youssri, former judge and diplomat for the government of Egypt, who informed him of the inner workings of the judiciary and its relationships with the military. For insight into the role of the Supreme Constitutional Court in this transition process I would like to thank Professor Nathan J. Brown of George Washington University.
15 David D. Kirkpatrick, "Authorities Bar 3 Leading Candidates in Egypt Race," *The New York Times*, April 14, 2012, www.nytimes.com/2012/04/15/world/middleeast/ten-candidates-barred-from-egyptian-election.html.
16 David D. Kirkpatrick, "Egypt Reimposes Martial Law, Ahead of Closely Watched Ruling", *The New York Times*, June 13, 2012, www.nytimes.com/2012/06/14/world/middleeast/egypt-extends-martial-law-before-election-ruling.html?ref=egypt.
17 David D. Kirkpatrick, "Blow to Transition as Court Dissolves Egypt's Parliament", *The New York Times*, June 14, 2012, www.nytimes.com/2012/06/15/world/middleeast/new-political-showdown-in-egypt-as-court-invalidates-parliament.html?pagewanted=2& ref = global-home; Borzou Daragahi, "Egypt Court Orders Parliament Dissolved," *Financial Times*, June 15, 2012, www.ft.com/intl/cms/s/0/02c5e588-b61c-11e1-a511-00144feabdc0.html#axzz1xkf0nUMv.
18 BBC News, "Egypt Supreme Court Calls for Parliament to be Dissolved," June 14, 2012, www.bbc.co.uk/news/world-middle-east-18439530.
19 Al-Ahram Online, "English Text of SCAF Amended Egypt Constitutional Declaration," June 18, 2102, http://english.ahram.org.eg/News/45350.aspx.
20 *Guardian*, "Muslim Brotherhood's Mohamed Morsi Wins Egypt's Presidential Race," June 24, 2012, www.guardian.co.uk/world/middle-east-live/2012/jun/24/egypt-election-results-live.
21 David D. Kirkpatrick and Mayy El Shekih, "Citing Deadlock, Egypt's Leader Seizes New Power and Plans Mubarak Retrial," *The New York Times*, November 22, 2012, www.nytimes.com/2012/11/23/world/middleeast/egypts-president-morsi-gives-himself-new-powers.html?hp_r=0 *Al-Jazeera*, "Egypt's Morsi Assumes Wider Powers," November 23, 2012, www.aljazeera.com/news/middleeast/2012/11/20121122161830842641.html.
22 David D. Kirkpatrick and Mayy El Sheikh, "As Egypt Constitution Passes, New Fights Lie Ahead," *The New York Times*, December 23, 2012, www.nytimes.com/2012/12/24/world/middleeast/as-egypt-constitution-passes-new-fights-lie-ahead.html?emc=rss&partner=rss.
23 Kareem Fahim, "In Upheaval for Egypt, Morsi Forces Out Military Chiefs," *The New York Times*, August 12, 2012, www.nytimes.com/2012/08/13/world/middleeast/egyptian-leader-ousts-military-chiefs.html?pagewanted=all&_r = 0; *Al Jazeera*, "Crowds in Cairo Praise Morsi's Army Overhaul", August 13, 2012, www.aljazeera.com/news/middleeast/2012/08/201281215511142445.html; Henry Shull and Ingy Hassieb, "Egypt's Morsi Decorates Generals He Dismissed," *Washington Post*, August 14, 2012, http://articles.washingtonpost.com/2012-08-14/world/35492887_1_military-chiefs-military-rule-morsi.
24 Duncan Pickard, "The Current Status of Constitution Making in Tunisia," *Carnegie Endowment for International Peace*, April 19, 2012, http://carnegieendowment.org/2012/04/19/current-status-of-constitution-making-in-tunisia.

25 Interview with Rachid Ghannouchi, the leader of the Ennahda Party, May 22, 2012; BBC News, "Tunisia's Islamist Ennahda Edges Away from Sharia," March 26, 2012, www.bbc.co.uk/news/world-africa-17517113.
26 Interview with Rachid Ghannouchi, the leader of the Ennahda Party, May 22, 2012.
27 Jack Snyder, "Elections as Milestones and Stumbling Blocks for Peaceful Democratic Consolidation," *Friderich Ebert Stiftung*, International Policy Analysis, September 2010, http://library.fes.de/pdf-files/iez/07438.pdf; Malcom MacLaren, "'Sequentialism' or 'Gradualism'? On the Transition to Democracy and the Rule of Law," Swiss National Science Foundation, National Centre of Competence in Research, Challenges to Democracy in the 21st Century, Working Paper No. 38, October 2009, www.nccr-democracy.uzh.ch/publications/workingpaper/pdf/wp38.pdf; Jason Gluck, "Constitutional Reform in Transitional States: Challenges and Opportunities Facing Egypt and Tunisia," *Peacebrief*, 92 (May 2011), www.usip.org/publications/constitutional-reform-in-transitional-states-challenges-and-opportunities-facing-egypt-.
28 Eghosa E. Osaghae, "What Democratization does to Minorities Displaced from Power," *Forum for Development Studies*, 2 (2002).
29 Mariam Fam, "Egypt Constitution-Drafting Committee Starts Work Amid Divisions," *Bloomberg Business Week*, March 28, 2012, www.businessweek.com/news/2012-03-28/egypt-constitution-drafting-committee-starts-work-amid-divisions.
30 Interview with Abdel Raouf Ayadi, former secretary general of the CPR and founder of the breakaway party, the CDI or Congress of Independent Democrats, April 17, 2012; Michael Buchanan, "Qatar Flexing Muscle in a Changing World," BBC News, December 28, 2011, www.bbc.co.uk/news/world-middle-east-16348250.
31 Maurice Duverger, *Les partis politiques* (Paris: Armand Collin, 1951).
32 Interview with Riadh Chaibbi, Member of Ennahda's Executive Bureau, May 21, 2012.
33 "Founding Statement of the Interim Transitional National Council," www.ntcli-bya.org/english/founding-statement-of-the-interim-transitional-national-council.
34 CNN, "Libya's Transitional Council Hands Over Power," *CNN*, August 9, 2012, http://edition.cnn.com/2012/08/08/world/meast/libya-power-transition/index.html.
35 International Crisis Group, "Holding Libya Together: Security Challenges After Qadhafi," Middle East/North Africa Report No. 115, December 14, 2011, www.crisisgroup.org/en/regions/middle-east-north-africa/north-africa/libya/115-holding-libya-together-security-challenges-after-qadhafi.aspx.
36 Ibid.
37 Ibid.
38 See especially Articles 219 and Article 4, which read together empower Al Azhar with the power of judicial review. See analysis by Zaid al-Ali, "The New Egyptian Constitution: An Initial Analysis of its Merits, and Flaws," www.opendemocracy.net/zaid-al-ali/new-egyptian-constitution-initial-assessment-of-its-merits-and-flaws.
39 See Sami Zaptia, "National Congress Leader Magarieft Says Libya Should be a 'Secular State'," *Libya Herald*, October 1, 2012, www.libyaherald.com/2012/10/01/gnc-head-magarief-uses-the-s-word.
40 See Paul Cruickshank and Tim Lister, "Energized Muslim Brotherhood in Libya Takes Prize," CNN, March 25, 2011; Reuters, September 14, 2011.
41 International Crisis Group, "Holding Libya Together."
42 BBC News, "Morocco's King Mohammed Unveils Constitutional Reforms," June 18, 2011, www.bbc.co.uk/news/world-africa-13816974.
43 BBC News, "Morocco Approves King Mohammed's Constitutional Reforms," July 2, 2011, www.bbc.co.uk/news/world-africa-13976480.
44 Morocco News Agency, "Morocco: First Formal Meeting of New Democratic Government," February 8, 2012, http://morocconewsagency.com/morocco-first-formal-meeting-new-democratic-government-2-9-12.html.

45 Hamidi Khemissi, Ricardo René Larémont, and Taybi Taj Eddine, "Sufism, Salafism, and State Policy Towards Religion in Algeria: A Survey of Algerian Youth." *The Journal of North African Studies*, 17:3 (2012): 547–558.
46 Cherif Ouazani, "Algérie: La surprise FLN," *Jeune Afrique*, 2679 (May 13–19, 2012), p. 10.
47 Al Jazeera, "Is Algeria Immune to the 'Arab Spring'?" May 14, 2012, www.aljazeera.com/programmes/insidestory/2012/05/201251465357500445.htm.

Index

Page numbers in italic type refer to figures, those in bold type refer to notes and those including an n refer to notes.

Abu Salim Prison Massacre (Libya) 75, 90, 94
African Union 97
Al Arabiya 5, 11, 15
al-Ghad (Tomorrow) Party (Egypt) 57
Al Jazeera 5, 11, 15, 45, 70, 76
al-Nahda 36
Al-Qaeda 164
Al-Qaeda in the Islamic Land of the Maghreb (AQIM) 132
al-Wasat (Center) Party (Egypt) 57
Al Watad Movement of Democratic Patriots 44
Aleya-Sghaier, Amira ix, 30–52
Algeria: amnesty programs 132; apathy and mistrust for political institutions and processes 144; Berber language 130; cell phone subscriptions *26*; Citizen Movement 130; civic associations 130; constitution 131, 140; corruption 135; decline of Islamist political groups 133; economic and social problems 128–9, 134; economic reform 133–5, 139; elections 130, 131, 133, 140–3, **142**, 146n31, 167; fertility rates **17**, *17*, 18, 22–3; hydrocarbon revenues 126, 127, 128–9, 134–5, 144; illegal migration to Europe 139; infrastructure investments 135; Internet and Facebook participation **27**, *27*; Islamist insurrection 23, 130–1; mass demonstrations 4; military and security services 7, 138; need for further reforms 144–5; opinion surveys 144; peaceful protests 2011, reasons for failure 137–9; political integration of Islamists 131–3; political liberalization 129–30, 132, 133; political parties 131, 133; political reforms 139–40; population pyramid *22*; protest movement 3, 166–7; riots January 2011 136–7; riots of 1988 125, 127–9; state responsibility for economic and social development 127–8; strikes 139; structural adjustment program (SAP) 134; suicides 139; unemployment 134, 135; weak political institutionalization 143; women's political representation 140; youth-led demonstrations 23, 125
Alliance of National Forces 161
American War of Independence 9
Amin, Esam Al- 66
Ammar, General Rachid 46, 47
Anderson, Lisa 98, 99
April 6 Movement (Egypt) 60, 61, 74n14
Arab Barometer 144
Arab Gulf states 126
Arab League 76
Arab Spring revolts and demonstrations: absence of revolutionary leadership and ideology 8, 10; definition of Arab Spring 126; explanatory variables 4–8; similarities and differences with 1848 revolutions 10; social resistance movements 2011 3; spontaneity and rapidity of 11; spontaneity and rapidity of 8–9
Arendt, Hannah 8
Armed Islamist Group (GIA) 130, 132

Index 173

Association Fighting against Torture in Tunisia 43
Association of Judges of the Tunisian League for Human Rights 36
Association of Lawyers 35, 36
Association of Tunisian Judges (AMT) 44

Bahrain 1, 126
Bar Association of Tunisia 43
Belhadj, Abdelhakim 164
Ben Ali, Zine El Abidine (Tunisian president) 1, 28, 30, 32–5, 37, 46, 48, 88
Benghazi 4, 75–6, 79, 80–1
Berber language 130
blogs 66
Bouazizi, Mohamed 1, 6, 25, 31, 49, 139
Boudiaf, Mohamed (Algerian president) 132
bourgeoisie *see* middle classes
Bourguiba, Habib (Tunisian president) 37, 46
Bouteflika, Abdelaziz (Algerian president) 132, 136, 137, 141
Brinton, Crane 7

cell phones 5, 11; Libyan revolt 90; youth mobilization 26–7, *26*
censorship 45, 46
children 41, 98; *see also* fertility rates; young people
China 10, 11
citizenship 115, 123
Commission of Inquiry on Libya 96
Communist Labour Party of Tunisia 44
Congress for the Republic (CPR) 149, 150–1
Coptic Christians 148, 150, 151, 157, 159
corruption 33, 56, 88, 98, 128, 135
Cortright, David 54

Darif, Mohammed ix, 12–13, 105–24
Declaration of Fourteen Points 10
Demmelhuber, Thomas 59
democracy, transitions to 2, 129; elite consensus, effect on objectives of transition to democracy 149–51; military forces, role of 153–8; minority rights, protection of 159; sequencing of elections and constitution writing 151–3; sharia, role of 158–9, 163–4; theoretical literature 149; *see also* Morocco

Democratic Progressive Party (Tunisia) 44
demographic trends *see* population trends
deprivation 5–6; as an impetus for violence *13*
Djaballah, Abdallah 142
Djabi, Nasser 133, 143

Egypt: cell phone subscriptions *26*; corruption 56; economic grievances 55–7; economic growth **24**, 25; education system 56; elections 58–9, 150, 155–7; elite consensus, effect on objectives of transition to democracy 149–50; fertility rates **17**, *17*, 18; hybrid revolt/coup d'état 3, 4, 6; Internet and Facebook participation **27**, *27*; judiciary 163; median age of population **19**; military forces, role in democratic transition 3–4, 7, 153–8; minority rights, protection of 159; political stagnation 57–8; population growth 21; population pyramid *20*, 21; poverty 56; sequencing of elections and constitution writing 151–3; sharia, role in democratic transition 158–9
Egyptian revolution: April 6 Movement 60, 61, 74n14; Battle of the Camel 69, 71; classless nature of 54; economic grievances 55–7; emergence of reform movements 57–8; excessive violence of Mubarak's regime 69; foreign media 70; Friday of Rage 63; internet and cell phone cut off 69–70; lack of concessions to protestors 70–1; leaderless nature of 54; mass mobilization 53, 54, 64–5; military, role of 64, 70–2; Muslim Brotherhood 62–3; organization 54–5; parliamentary elections 2010 58–9; peaceful nature 54, 66–7; police 66; political stagnation 57–8; Popular Campaign for the Support of ElBaradei 61–2; prayer 55; protesters' strategy and tactics 66–8; security forces' defeat 67–8, 69; slow response of Mubarak's regime 68–9; social media 65–6; Spirit of Tahrir 12, 55, 72; tolerance and acceptance 55; trade unions 63–4; youth role 59–63, 72
ElBaradei, Mohamed 62
elections 1–2, 148; Algeria 130, 131, 133, 140–3, **142**, 146n31, 167; Egypt

58–9, 150, 155–7; Libya 161; Morocco 116, 119, 165; Tunisia 150–1
electronic technologies 5, 7, 10–11
Engels, Friedrich 9, 36
Ennahda (Tunisia) 45, 149, 150–1, 160
Equity and Reconciliation Commission (Morocco) 108–9
Essebsi, Beji Caid (Tunisian prime minister) 35–6
Ettajdid (Tunisia) 44
Ettakatol (Tunisia) 149, 150–1
European Union, response to Tunisian revolution 48

Facebook 5, 11, 15; April 6 Movement (Egypt) 61; Egyptian revolution 59, 65, 66; Morocco 110; Tunisian revolution 40, 45; youth mobilization 26, 27–8, **27**, *27*
Fanon, Frantz 38
February 20 Youth Movement (Morocco) 110, 111–12, 123, 164–5
fertility rates 6, **17**, *17*, 18
FLN (Algeria) 131, 141, **142**, 167
Forum for Democracy and Labour (Tunisia) 44
France, response to Tunisian revolution 48
Freedom and Justice Party (FJP) 150, 155

Geertz, Clifford 117
General Union of Algerian Workers 134, 138
Ghannouchi Mohamed (Tunisian prime minister) 34–5, 158
Global Trends for Youth (ILO report) 25
globalization 86
Goldstone, Jack 16
Green Alliance 167
Green Book 78, 81–2
Guibal, Michael 118
Gurr, Ted 6

Hassan II (King of Morocco) 105, 106, 107, 113, 114, 117
Heinsohn, Gunnar 16
Heydarian, Richard Javan 24
human rights 33, 43, 66, 97–8, 107, 108–9, 111
Huntington, Samuel P. 6, 143, 149

illiteracy 32
International Association Supporting Political Prisoners 43

International Labour Organization (ILO) 25
internet 45–6
Iraq 159
Islamic Movement for Change (LIMC) 164
Islamic Salvation Army 130, 132
Islamist groups 148, 150; decline 133; political integration 131–3; violence of 130–1
Ismail, Hazem Salah Abu 155
Italy 97

Jordan 1, 126
judiciary 44, 109, 123, 152, 153, 155, 163
Justice and Charity Association (Morocco) 111, 112
Justice and Construction Party (JCP) 161
Justice and Development Party (PJD) 165

Kafi, Ali (Algerian president) 132
Kawmiyyine (Tunisia) 44
Khaldoun, Ibn 117
Khemissi, Hamidi 133
Kifaya 57, 58, 60

Larémont, Ricardo René ix, 1–14, 11, 15–29, 133, 148–71
Layachi, Azzedine ix, 13, 125–47, 166
Libya: Abu Salim Prison Massacre 75, 90, 94; cell phone subscriptions *26*; corruption 88, 98; democratic transition 160–4; different characteristics to other Arab Spring countries 88–9; economic policy 83, 84; economic wealth 22; elections 161; ethnic minorities 91; fertility rates **17**, *17*, 18, 22; foreign policy 83; future of, after Qaddafi 98–100; globalization 86; independent militias 161–2; Internet and Facebook participation **27**, *27*; Islamist groups 163–4; Jamahiriya 82; Lockerbie bombing 84; military, role of 4, 7; National Economic Strategy 87; parliament 161; political and government systems 81–2; population pyramid *21*; population trends 22; public dissatisfaction with Qadafi regime 85; Qaddafi authoritarian regime 82–4, 98; Qaddafi Development Foundation

86; religious tolerance 91; repression of civil society organizations 89; sanctions 84–5; sequencing of elections and constitution writing 162–3; women 93–4; youth bulge 86; *see also* Libyan revolt

Libyan Islamic Fighting Group (LIFG) 91; *see also* Islamic Movement for Change (LIMC)

Libyan Islamic Group 164

Libyan revolt 3, 4; African migrant workers 97–8; aftermath 98–100; causes 75–6, 81–5; civil war situation 95; failure of tactics to appease and pre-empt protests 89–91; foreign intervention 94–6; foreign mercenaries 97; *Green Book* 78, 81–2; institutionalization of 79; *intifada* 80–1; lack of unified leadership and conflicting ideologies 92–3; National Transitional Council (NTC) 79, 91, 92, 93; no-fly zone 76, 79–80; Operation Odyssey Dawn 80; promises of reform 80; protests and escalating violence 76–8; salvation of Benghazi 80–1; tribalism 91–2, 96; violence 94–6; war crimes 96, 98; women's empowerment 93–4

Lockerbie bombing 84

Malthus, Thomas 16
Mannheim, Karl 7
Marx, Karl 9
mass mobilization 53, 54, 64–5
Méndez, Juan (UN special adviser) 40
Mesquida, Christian 16
Meyssane, Thierry 49
middle classes: disillusionment 5; Libyan revolt 92–3; shift of allegiance 7
military forces 3–4; Algeria 125, 138; decisions of who to support 5, 7–8; Egyptian revolution 64, 70–2; transition to democracy, Egypt 149–50, 153–8; Tunisian revolution 46–7
Mogheirby, M. Zahi 89
Mohammed VI (King of Morocco) 25, 106, 165; concept of monarchy's power and role 106–8; effectiveness rhetoric 115–16; Equity and Reconciliation Commission 108–9; New Era motto 115–16; speech of January 3 2010 120; speech of June 17 2011 134; speech of March 9 2011 110, 134; speech of October 12 1999 106; view of monarchy 113; *see also* Morocco

Möller, Herbert 16

Moroccan Human Rights Association 111

Morocco: Abbas El Fassi government 114; cell phone subscriptions *26*; citizenship 115; civic legitimacy of monarchy 117, 118; civil society 123; Closing the Years of Lead process 108–9; coalition government 2, 165–6; constitutional reform 105, 112, 121–3, 165; constitutions 113, 114, 116–18, 122–3; Consultative Council on Youth and Associative Action 123; demands for reform 111; democratic transition 164–6; economic growth **24**, 25; effectiveness rhetoric of monarchy 115–16; elections 116, 119, 165; Equity and Reconciliation Commission 108–9; extended regionalism policy 107, 119–21; February 20 Youth Movement 110, 111–12, 123; fertility rates **17**, *17*, 18, 23; Government of Consensual Alternation 115–16; human rights 107, 108–9; Internet and Facebook participation **27**, *27*; judiciary 123; Justice and Charity Association 111, 112; legitimacies, conflict of 115–16, 117–18; legitimacies, hierarchy of 116–18; legitimacy, concept of 112–14; logic of reform 105–6; mass demonstrations 4; ministries of sovereignty policy 106–7; Movement for Freedom and Democracy Now 110–11; New Political Parties Act 118, 119; political parties 118–19, 123; population pyramid *23*; population trends 23–4; power of the monarchy 106, 107–8; religious legitimacy of monarchy 106, 116–18; shift from representative to participatory democracy 105; subsidiary representivity of the monarch 113, 114; supreme representivity of the monarch 113–14; transition to democracy 116

Morsi, Mohamed 156–7

Mosca, Gaetano 7

Movement for Freedom and Democracy Now (Morocco) 110–11

Movement for National Reform (MRN) 133

Index

Movement of Society for Peace (MSP) 131, 133, 141, **142**
Mubarak, Gamal 56–7, 60, 64
Mubarak, Hosni (president of Egypt) 1, 3, 28, 53, 57, 59, 65, 68–9, 70, 149–50, 153
Mukhtar, Omar 96
Muslim Brotherhood 57, 62–3, 149–50, 151, 152, 153, 154, 155, 158, 159, 163

Nahda 131, 133
Nasserite Karama (Dignity) Party (Egypt) 57
National Association of Families of Missing Persons 137
National Commission of Consultation on Political Reforms (Algeria) 140
National Coordination for Change and Democracy (CNCD) 137, 138
National Democratic Party (Egypt) 57, 64, 69
National General People's Congress (Libya) 85
National League for the Defense of Human Rights 137
National Transition Council (Libya) 161
NATO 4, 7, 76, 94, 95, 96
newspapers 65
North Africa: economic growth 25; fertility rates **17**, *17*, 18; GDP growth rate **24**; median age of population 18, **19**, *19*; population trends 16–24; youth population **17**; youth unemployment **25**; *see also* Arab Spring revolts and demonstrations

Obama, Barack 49
Olsen, Mancur 6

Pew Center survey 2010 11
police 33, 37, 40, 46, 47–8; violence 66
Political Front for the Safeguard of Democracy (FPSD) 142–3, **142**
political nomadism 118, 119
Political Order in Changing Societies (Huntington) 143
Popular Campaign for the Support of ElBaradei (Egypt) 61–2
population trends: Algeria 22–3, *22*; Egypt *20*, 21; fertility rates **17**, *17*, 18; Libya *21*, 22; median age of population 18, **19**, *19*; Morocco 23–4, *23*; total population and youth population **17**; Tunisia 19, *20*, 21; youth bulge 16
poverty 56
prayer 55
Presidential Election Commission (Egypt) 155
public opinion polls 11

Qaddafi Development Foundation 86
Qaddafi, Muammar 1, 28, 75, 77, 79, 80–1, 160; authoritarian regime 82–4, 98; concern over security of regime 85; desire for personal glory 82; economic policy 83, 84, 86–7; execution and assassination of opponents 83–4; failure of tactics to appease and pre-empt protests 89–91; foreign policy 83; *infitah* policy 84; Lockerbie bombing 84; political systems 81–2; promises of reform to young people 88; public dissatisfaction with regime 85; sanctions 84–5
Qaddafi, Saif al-Islam 80, 81, 85–7, 90

Rahmouni, Ahmed 44
Rally for Constitutional Democracy (RCD) 33, 36, 50; militia 37–8
Rally for Democracy and Culture (RCD) 137–8, **142**
rape 38, 98
republicanism 9–10
Responsibility to Protect (R2P) principle 76
revolts 3–4
revolutions: American War of Independence 8; early 20th century 10; Europe 1848 9–10; Europe 1989 10–11; links with economic growth 24; Russian Revolution 7–8, 10, 26, 30; technology, role of 26; youth, role of 16; *see also* Arab Spring revolts and demonstrations
RND (Algeria) 141, **142**
Rothkopf, David 55
Russian Revolution 7–8, 10, 26, 30
Rustow, Dankwart 149

Saadi, Said 138
Salafist Al-Nour Party 150, 155, 159
Salafist Group for Preaching and Combat (GSPC) 130, 132
Salah, Ahmad 61

Saleh, Ali Abdullah (president of Yemen) 1
Saudi Arabia 1
Sawani, Youssef Mohammed ix, 12, 75–104
self-immolation *see* suicides
Shafiq, Ahmed 156
Shahin, Emad El-Din ix, 12, 53–74
Shalgam, Abdel Rahman 81
sharia (Islamic law) 158–9, 163–4
Shater, Khairat el- 155
Shils, Edward 7
Sidi Bouzid 1, 31, 32, 34
Skocpol, Theda 2
social media 5, 11, 60; Egyptian revolution 65–6; Libyan revolt 90; *see also* Facebook; Twitter
South Africa 149, 152–3, 159
Spain 149
strikes 61, 63–4, 139
suicides 1, 6, 25, 31, 49, 139
Suleiman, Omar 155
Supreme Constitutional Court (Egypt) 155, 156
Supreme Council of the Armed Forces (SCAF) 70–2, 153–4, 156
Syria 1, 50, 79, 126

Taj Eddine, Taybi 133
talk shows 65
Tantawi, Mohamed Hussein 153, 157
television 5, 11; Egyptian revolution 65; Tunisian revolution 45–6
Terbil, Fathi 75–6, 90
terrorism 84
texting 5
torture 66, 71, 98, 164
Trabelsi, Leila 33
trade unions 33, 35, 36, 89; Algeria 134, 138, 139; Egyptian revolution 63–4; Tunisian revolution 42–3
Tunisia: aging population 21; causes of revolution 31–4; cell phone subscriptions 26; coalition government 2, 151; corruption 33; economic growth **24**, 25; elections 150–1; elite consensus, effect on objectives of transition to democracy 149, 150–1; fertility rates **17**, *17*, 18, 21; illiteracy 32; Internet and Facebook participation 27–8, **27**, *27*; median age of population **19**; military forces, role in democratic transition 153, 157–8; military, role of 3, 7; minority rights, protection of 159; per capita government annual expenditure 31–2; population pyramid 20, *20*; secular parties 160; sequencing of elections and constitution writing 151–3; sharia, role in democratic transition 158; youth bulge 32; youth population 19; youth unemployment 32; *see also* Tunisian revolution
Tunisian General Labour Union (UGTT) 33, 35, 36, 42–3
Tunisian League for Human Rights 33, 36, 43
Tunisian revolution 3, 4, 6, 11, 88; achievements of 50; caravans of freedom 35; counterrevolutionary violence 37–8; deaths 40–1, **41**; Gafsa and Ben Gardane uprisings 31; Ghannouchi government 35; High Committee for the Achievement of the Objectives of the Revolution 36; internet and television, role of 45–6; judiciary 44; lawyers in the revolution 43–4; looting 39; military, role of 46–7; National Council for the Protection of the Revolution 36; parties and political groups 44–5; police 33, 37, 40, 46, 47–8; Revolutionary Safeguard Committees 35; stages of 34–6; technologies, use by young people 34; Tunis demonstration 34; Tunisian General Labour Union (UGTT) 33, 35, 36, 41–2; violence and nonviolence 36–7; violence of the masses 38–9; women, role of 41–2; world responses 48–50; youth, role of 39–41
Twitter 11, 15, 45; Egyptian revolution 59, 66; youth mobilization 26, 27–8

UGTT *see* Tunisian General Labour Union (UGTT)
United Nations Populations Division 18, 19, **19**, 22, 22–3
United Nations Security Council 76
United States Africa Command (AFRI-COM) 48
United States (US), response to Tunisian revolution 48–9
Urdal, Henrik 16
US Census Bureau 19

Vandewalle, Dirk 84, 85
voting: pluralities 2; universal franchise 10; *see also* elections

war crimes 96, 98
Weber, Max 117
Wikileaks 32, 45
Wilson, Woodrow (US president) 10
Wolfensohn Center for Development, Brookings Institution 25
women: Algeria 140; Egypt 159; Libya 93–4; rape 38, 98; Tunisian revolution 41–2
Wretched of the Earth, The (Fanon) 38

Yemen 1, 126
young people: access to new technologies 15; Algeria
young people: disillusionment 5; Egyptian revolution 59–63, 72; mobilization via cell phones and social networks 26–8, *26*, **27**, *27*, 40; Morocco 110, 111–12; North African youth population 2010 **17**; Tunisian revolution 34, 35, 39–41; unemployment 25, **25**, 32; youth bulge 16, 32, 86
Youssoufi, Abderrahman el- 107, 114, 115, 116
YouTube 59, 60, 66

Zéroual, Liamine (Algerian president) 132